A SOLILOQUY

OTHER BOOKS
BY FAIRFAX DOWNEY

RICHARD HARDING DAVIS: HIS DAY

BURTON, ARABIAN NIGHTS ADVENTURER

THE GRANDE TURKE: SULEYMAN THE MAGNIFICENT

YOUNG ENOUGH TO KNOW BETTER

WHEN WE WERE RATHER OLDER

FATHER'S FIRST TWO YEARS

A COMIC HISTORY OF YALE

© LIFE PUBLISHING CO.

HOME FOR THE HOLIDAYS

PORTRAIT OF AN ERA

AS DRAWN BY

C · D · GIBSON

DANGEROUS

CHARLES DANA GIBSON

From a drawing by William Oberhardt for the Division of Pictorial Publicity
during the World War

*Facsimile reproductions of this portrait and those of other members of the Division are filed in
the archives of the War Department at Washington*

PORTRAIT OF AN ERA
AS DRAWN BY
C·D·GIBSON

A BIOGRAPHY BY
FAIRFAX DOWNEY

© *Life Publishing Co.* · THE STORY OF HIS LIFE.

CHARLES·SCRIBNER'S SONS · NEW YORK
CHARLES·SCRIBNER'S SONS · LTD · LONDON

SUMMER SPORTS.

TO MY DAUGHTER

PEGGY

FOREWORD

TIME will tell, affirms one of the truer proverbs. The biographer of a living person presumes when he ventures to tell ahead of time. He lacks a distant prospect of his hero or his villain and such wisdom as he may be able to extract from the ages. Robert W. Chambers admitted the normal necessity of a detached and matured viewpoint in an appreciation of Charles Dana Gibson published in 1905.

"Great men are usually first understood when framed by the perspective of years," he wrote. "Something to give them scale is necessary. The world is far-sighted and always confused by what takes place under its nose.

"Yet there are exceptions," Chambers added, well aware that a great many people were not in the least confused but very definitely devoted to the Gibson drawings. "And while the exact measure of a man's work may not be possible when seen too closely, some achievements are too vital to await the analysis made possible after the seething sediments of the years have been precipitated. I believe Gibson is one of these men, and that the future judgment concerning his work can be properly estimated today."

Thirty years now have enhanced the perspective. That vitality, which the novelist who was also an artist praised at its height, re-animates the past as strongly as it vivified his present. And the work of Gibson's pen will endure, in excellently qualified opinions, both by virtue of its quality and its topics.

It may be agreed that other hazards and obstacles common to biographies of the living were here met at a minimum and were countered by advantages. The project originated with the author of this book and upon its suggestion received the approval without conditions of Mr. Gibson and his family. Free hands are freer still in writing of a noble character and of a man as ready as his critics to confess his mistakes and failures. This volume is autobiographical to the extent that it received the benefit of its subject's recollections, generously and unreservedly given. The estimates and interpretations, based on contemporary sources, are purely biographical.

Charles Dana Gibson's fine career is now approaching its seventh decade. May this, his unfinished story, give pleasure, especially to all who were Gibson Girls and Men, their children, and grandchildren. As for the seasoned tale of time, I am content to leave that to a later chronicler.

FAIRFAX DOWNEY.
New York City, 1936.

CONTENTS

xiv   CONTENTS

ILLUSTRATIONS

PORTRAIT OF AN ERA

AS DRAWN BY

C · D · GIBSON

LONDON: WAITING TO BE PRESENTED AT COURT

CHAPTER I

THE MAGIC OF HIS PEN

All America's a stage, one might have paraphrased in the 1890's, and all the men and women merely characters drawn by Charles Dana Gibson. Everywhere materialized living images, human copies of Gibson illustrations in books and magazines. They stepped out of *Life* into life. Fifth Avenue looked like an endless procession of Gibsons to one contemporary, who might have made the same remark of most Main Streets.

Along with the captains and the kings, he punctuated history, for he dated a decade with the lovely Gibson Girl and it is proclaimed forever hers by her grace and divine right. The edicts in black and white issued over the signature, C. D. Gibson, were more willingly obeyed than an emperor's, and they extended his vast and beneficent sway over the manners, the modes, and even the thought of a generation.

It was said of Charles Dana Gibson that he drew people as they sometimes are and were always meant to be. Not only as they might look at their best but as they might live with life at its brightest. Dreams came true, ideals were attained on his pages. With sentiment and humor he pointed a moral and adorned a drawing. Youth and beauty. Honor and decency and dignity. Love conquers all. Money isn't everything. These were his simple, universal themes. No wonder three continents and odd corners of the earth rendered him homage and loyalty.

He ruled through the power of pictures, pictures with a simple message needing no interpreter, pen strokes which seldom really required written words as captions. He could tell a whole story in a single illustration with only two figures, and the tales he told sped around the world. Gibson books were found in the palace of the last Czar of Russia after his exile and death. Gibson sketches decorated palm-leaf huts in Central America, cabins in the Klondike, Australian ranch houses, Tokio shop windows, and the cabooses of American freight trains. Society within and without "The Four Hundred" bestowed its approval on the illustrator who satirized it as often as he glorified. The girl behind the counter and the man in the street eagerly awaited magazines for which he drew, chapters in a continued romance which never lost its fascination.

He caricatured the great of the earth, gave splendid form to such heroines and villains of fiction as *Princess Aline* and *Rupert of Hentzau* and spun the graphic saga of his own immortal *Mr. Pipp.* He brought home the streets of London and the cafés of Paris, but it was his own country he loved best to chronicle and he left an enduring record of one of its most glowing periods. The small boys he sketched followed a boxing champion or listened to a veteran tell the story of his empty sleeve. His old men dreamed dreams, as in that unforgettable picture, *The Bachelor's Supper,* and his young men, too, saw visions of the radiant girls Charles Dana Gibson drew.

Only to Dame Fashion and to Mrs. Grundy had womankind pledged such allegiance as it gave Mr. Gibson. One mere man told them what to wear, how to do their hair, how to act, and they acquiesced as one woman. Myriads of pen-and-ink Galateas came alive in response to an overwhelming male demand. With the devotion of the manhood of the land dawned a second age of chivalry and a new freedom for the lively counterparts of the Gibson Girl.

Her face was his fortune. The financial reward of his handiwork rose from a few dollars per drawing to an income respected by mining magnates and railroad chieftains. And Gibson's was an art "that at once pleased the crowd and satisfied the critical." His admirable technique inspired almost all the American artists who began their careers in his heyday, and every youngster who felt the faintest stirrings of the graphic urge paid him the sincerest flattery of imitation. Hundreds of them came to him for advice and encouragement and none ever asked in vain.

Follows the story of the man and his achievement, the story of a power behind the drawing-board, the story of a sovereign whose sceptre was a pen and whose globe was an ink bottle.

LIFE PUBLISHING CO.

MR. PIPP

CHARLES DE WOLF GIBSON
Father of Charles Dana Gibson

CHAPTER II

SCISSORS AND PAPER

I

He was a sturdy, healthy boy, with blue-gray eyes, brown hair, and a large head; a child normally happy yet in a rather quiet, grave way. There was early about him an air of reliability which lessened his parents' natural anxiety in regard to the pair of blunt scissors so constantly in his grasp or hanging by a ribbon around his neck. Dana could be trusted to use them neither to cut a sister's curls nor a pillow-case but only for the purpose his father had taught him.

One day Charles De Wolf Gibson sat by the sickbed of his five-year-old son and entertained him by cutting silhouettes of animals. A paper zoo covered the counterpane, but admiring and playing with it soon ceased to be enough. Small hands reached up for the scissors and the child began to cut out figures of his own. His first attempts were crude and he seemed to realize it, for he kept trying to improve on them. Forgotten was the temporary invalid's desire to get up; all he asked now was more sheets of paper.

Beyond watching his father that day, the boy received no further instruction. Some inner, compelling impulse had been released and he obeyed it gladly and often. Holding the scissors steady with thumb in one loop and index finger lost in the other, supported by second finger hooked around the outer rim, he moved the paper as he cut. From it emerged an unending procession of paper animals which grew steadily more lifelike. He practiced incessantly and patiently, throwing away failures. When scores of crumpled balls testified to the difficulties of shaping a dromedary's lips, the young cutter explained that he had best refer to the original again. While

5

that involved another trip to the circus or the natural history museum, art that is faithful to nature should have its reward.

Scissors and never a pencil were his chosen instrument; it was years before he showed any desire to draw. Storing away images of his models in his mind, he would cut his silhouettes from memory and produce whole scenes from a single sheet, with never any pasting or other makeshifts. As he grew older, he ceased to confine himself to animals and people he actually had seen. The future illustrator of leading novels was foreshadowed in the child who came home from school to tell his mother:

"They read such a nice story in the class today. See, I will make you a picture of it."

The silhouettes in this chapter were all cut by Charles Dana Gibson when a young boy

And he would do it with the imagination and understanding which one day would make authors beg for him to delineate their

characters. He cut out the tale of the dog who guarded his master's horse, of the farmer whose mule balked. Action and humor began to appear in his work. A comical little pig carrying an umbrella tripped along beneath a tree in which birds sang his marching tune. A duck, rabbit, parrot, and dog paraded dressed in costume. A hen

led her three chicks, the nearest safe and serene, the second taking longer strides to catch up, and the last in a fluttering panic to overtake its mother. Birds desperately defended their nest from a serpent crawling along the limb; the delicacy and intricacy of the cutting of the foliage, the beaks, and the snake's forked tongue were remarkable. A boy holding a cockatoo on his wrist displayed a most natural mixture of pride and alarm. Dana's father challenged him with a difficult assignment, a terrier crouched with a rat in his mouth and one under each forepaw, and the child executed it admirably. A silhouette of a pretty little maiden in bonnet and bustle about to dig in the sand records the first appearance of the Gibson Girl.

Dana's parents could not help but be impressed with this precocious talent. They pinned up some of his dogs and elephants on the walls of the parlor where relatives, of their own accord, admired them. Although they were careful to avoid spoiling him or making him self-conscious, his mother and father were unable to resist occasionally displaying his ability. The boy playing in the yard would hear a tap on the window, a "come in, Dana," and he would answer a summons to cut silhouettes for guests. Without any sense of showing off (he believed what he did was easy and that anyone could do it who tried), he would quietly comply and leave hastily. He had been made sensitive by an uncle whose distorted idea of fun was to focus attention on the boy until he cried with embarrassment, so he preferred to dodge whatever compliments might be forthcoming.

Once, however, he caught the comment of a stout lady and it set him thinking. After observing the child's extraordinary accomplishment, she fatuously remarked that her husband, a captain in a Boston militia regiment, had a man in his company who could cut silhouettes every bit as well. Perhaps the man actually earned his living that way, the boy reasoned, since soldiering must be its own reward. Then why couldn't he, too, make money out of a skill which he had thought of only as an amusement?

He broached the idea to his older brother Langdon, who was strongly for it. They decided that if a certain little girl up the street approved, they would launch the new business without delay. She was enthusiastic and the three children met by appointment on her doorstep shortly after sunrise next morning. While the other two supervised anxiously, the working member of the firm commenced cutting out a large stock of his very best figures until the steps, their show window, were covered with horses, dogs, goats, cows, and an assortment of wild beasts.

"My two partners," Dana Gibson remembered, "were wondering why the streets were so deserted and the little girl, whose curls were somewhat awry, and who still had a little sleepy look in her eyes, was beginning to look disappointed, when there was a rattle of wheels over the pavement and the milkman drove up to the door. This suggested to us for the first time that we had commenced business rather too early in the morning. I shall never forget that milkman. He was a young man with a pleasant face, and when he jumped from his cart with a shrill whistle and took the pail from the side door, he looked so good-naturedly at us that by the time he had dipped his ladle into the big cans and filled the pail with fresh milk that the little girl was to drink later, we had almost

CHARLES DANA GIBSON

Cutting silhouettes at eight years of age

gathered enough courage to ask him if he did not wish to buy some of our paper figures. His attention was attracted by our anxious looks, and in reply to his look of inquiry we pointed to the steps and explained our business. He had a sense of humor and took in the situation at a glance."

True to his professional interests, the milkman favored the silhouettes of the cow and the horse, but he insisted on bargaining. He would buy one of each if they were cut out while he waited. The order was quickly and competently executed, and the milkman paid the agreed price of three cents so cheerfully that the partners wondered why they had not asked more. After the cutter had given full measure by autographing each product, the purchaser drove away, wishing them good luck.

The milkman was their only customer that morning. Neither the baker's man nor the butcher's boy was in the market. Since the firm was getting hungry, shortly before breakfast partnership was dissolved with the declaration of a dividend of one cent each.

Art for its own or amusement's sake is seldom discouraged by a sale. Twice the lad was paid five dollars for selections of his silhouettes. Yet it was more the urge within him that kept him cutting figures so continually, figures of children and animals still. Before he was twelve he had the first professional showing of his work, his parents venturing to send his silhouettes to a regular art exhibition. Few artists ever have enjoyed a happier first critique.

"Perhaps the most remarkable thing in the whole exhibition," wrote a critic, Clarence C. Cook, "are the frames that contain the silhouettes on white paper cut by Master Dana Gibson, a boy now of eleven or twelve years old, but who cut many of these figures—and many of the best of them—when he was but eight years old. In almost every case they are cut from the idea in his own mind, not copied from other pictures, and they are done without any aid whatever from teaching; the work is the product of instinct without training. The subjects are all of life in action. Whatever is done is done with a perfection that we never saw surpassed."

Here was a talent, mysteriously inherent and too strikingly manifest to be any mere parlor trick. As to whence it came, one may trace back the multiple threads in the fabric of heredity and, if the search be far and wide enough, discover the source of almost any skill. The ancestry of Charles Dana Gibson offered a broad choice —statesmen, ministers, soldiers, sea captains and privateersmen, merchants, and artists. Most of them gave something, some clearly marked bent or trait, to the boy who was born at Roxbury, Massachusetts, on September 14, 1867. Since the artistic contribution was the dominant one, it is fitting that we first summon the shade of his maternal great-grandfather, William Lovett, of Boston, painter of miniatures.

The first "Gibson Girl"

II

Art offered only a precarious livelihood in the Colonies and its
prospects were little improved after the Revolution, although that
conflict, like all wars, furnished a supply of generals in full uniform
to be painted. William Lovett's chosen calling was hampered by a
handicap which few native artists besides his elder contemporaries
and fellow New Englanders, John Trumbull and John Singleton
Copley, were able to combat. Their countrymen were generally
convinced that art flourished only in the Old World; and only in
Dana Gibson's day would American artists begin to overcome that
stubborn dogma. Lovett sent abroad for his colors, but, unhappily,
possible clients went abroad for their sittings or patronized visiting
foreign artists. It was this hard fact which induced him to insert
in a Boston newspaper a delightfully Gallicized advertisement, here-
inafter quoted just as it appeared in print:

GIULLAUME LOVETT

*Peintre en Mignature a l'honneur de prevénir meme les
Citoyens Francais qu'il Exécute tout ce qu'il a rapport á son
art avec la plus grande célerité et precision, ceux qui vaudront
l'honneur de leur confiance et lui transmettre quelques-ordres
particuliers, il espere qu'il feront satisfaits il demeure rue de
Tremont.*
Boston, Decembre 1.

Portraits executed with utmost speed and fidelity by a resident
of the *"rue de Tremont"*—French or native-born Bostonians could
hardly ask more. Perhaps William Lovett might have conquered
the foreign art complex of his compatriots had his career not been
cut short by death at the age of 28. At least he passed on the torch
of his talent to his descendants. Charles Dana Gibson's mother possessed a trace of it and for him it was augmented by an artistic
strain from somewhere in the male line, since a flair for drawing

MRS. CHARLES DE WOLF GIBSON

With her two sons, Langdon and Charles Dana. Dana is on the right

was marked in Gibson's father, and his first cousin, William Hamilton Gibson, was an artist of note, particularly for his studies from nature.

Dana Gibson's deep-seated love for the sea and sailing came from several forebears, among them Mark Antony De Wolf, doughty New England privateersman of the early 1700's. One of his sons, James De Wolf, was Dana Gibson's mother's grandfather, and another son, William De Wolf, was Gibson's father's great-grand-father, giving his parents a degree of consanguinity.

It was James De Wolf who became the family patriarch and founder of its fortunes. This altogether remarkable man was, like his father before him, a successful privateersman and an importer of slaves when dealings in black ivory were still considered respect-able. Leaving the sea to settle down, he built up his fortune to several millions of dollars and was rated as the third richest man in the United States. At one time he owned most of the site of Louisville, Kentucky. He sat in the legislature of Rhode Island, and his State later sent him to the U. S. Senate. His home, "The Mount," a shrine of Dana Gibson's youth, was long a landmark of Bristol. Many were the benefactions he conferred on the community, one of them being the Bristol poorhouse, surrounded by a spacious farm. When told there was no local need of so much ground, the old gentleman drily remarked: "Oh, my grandchildren will be coming to live on that farm yet, and they are accustomed to plenty of room." The prophecy came uncomfortably close to truth, for descendants frittered away the De Wolf fortune. While none of them resorted to the poor farm, some were forced to exert "mighty efforts lest they should."

The direct and collateral lines of Danas, Cottons, Bradfords, and Marstons bequeathed a heritage of good blood, health, and strength to Charles Dana Gibson. He would develop the sturdiness of his uncle, James De Wolf Lovett, one of the outstanding athletes of his time, a great baseball player and a member of the original Oneida football team, memorialized by a monument on the Boston Common as the first organized football club in America. Some of the eloquence of his preacher ancestors he would also have to make him a leading toastmaster. From a beloved grandmother, Josephine De Wolf Lovett, who used to furnish him some of the first jokes he illustrated for *Life,* he would acquire the highly useful gift of a sense of humor.

III

New England on both sides of the family for generations. New England little adulterated by other strains since John Gibson came from old England about 1634 and settled in Cambridge, Massachusetts. Such was the descent of Charles Dana Gibson, and it is not surprising that the section least soluble in the great American melting pot should have bequeathed him some of its inbred traits. Its stern and rockbound conscience, for one, and its enterprise, and more of its Yankee shrewdness than is usually the lot of the artistic temperament.

Years of transplantation in New York would never make him any less the New Englander. He must have smiled when he was illustrating *Life* jokes on the prim and bookish maidens of Boston, not at the jokes but because he knew them for stock humor. His mother was a Bostonian, and Josephine Elizabeth Lovett was a merry, lively girl, more than a bit of a tomboy. Even when she had attained the dignified age of sixteen and a fashionable gray gown with fur pelisse, she had not been able to resist coasting down the snowy slopes of Boston Common in the midst of a sled-full of boys. It happened to be a last fling, for as the sled whirled under a pond bridge, Miss Lovett glanced up with dismay into the disapproving countenance of her father.

Because of their descent from the De Wolf brothers, Josephine
Lovett and Charles De Wolf Gibson were distant cousins, and
cousinship, however distant, is always readily acknowledged when
it lies between an attractive girl and a handsome lad. These two
were soon eager to claim that and more. Charles, attending the
Boston School of Technology, went courting often to the Lovett
home. When the talk of elders on the impatience of youth, the demands of education, and the cost of living grew too pointed, the
lovers kept trysts in the gallery of temperance society meetings.

Then the Civil War conveniently roughened the course of true
love. Though Charles was only seventeen in '61, he answered the
call to the colors and sought a commission from Rhode Island. Refused on account of his age, he went to Washington to ask an appointment to West Point from Lincoln himself. Three days the
young fellow waited in an anteroom tracked by muddy boots and
the miry wheels of Tad Lincoln's goat cart. At last he was ushered
in, and a gaunt figure standing with his back to the fire stretched
out a long arm and gripped his visitor's hand without a glance
until he had finished his talk with a delegation. Then the kind,
homely face, lined with weariness, turned and young Gibson made
his speech and presented his thick packet of letters of recommenda-
tion. The President gently handed them back. He knew, he said,
what was in them and he was sure the applicant was the good lad
the letters called him. But the West Point places were going to
sons of officers killed in battle and wasn't that right? His caller
left without his appointment but with a precious memory.

But Charles Gibson had not long to wait for his shoulder straps
after all. Union losses let down the age bars, and he obtained a
lieutenancy in the Fourteenth Rhode Island Heavy Artillery, U. S.
Volunteers. After serving gallantly through several campaigns, he
came home on furlough to Bristol in '64 and there on the spacious

porch of "The Mount" found his charming and vivacious cousin opportunely down from Boston for a visit.

The tall, good-looking young officer apologized in embarrassment for the appearance of his blue flannel shirt and war-worn uniform; he had not, he explained, had opportunity to make himself presentable. He may have seen in the girl's eyes that nothing could have made him quite so presentable. With a rustle of billowing hoopskirts and a martial clank of sabre and jingle of spurs, they sat down close together on the steps and told each other many things until some tactless member of the family called them.

Wartime is a romantic and compelling setting which sweeps away both lovers' hesitations and parental opposition. The soldier and his sweetheart were married later that year and went, inevitably, on their honeymoon to Niagara Falls.

It was marriage on a shoestring, but the bridegroom's father, the first Charles Dana Gibson, as a firm member of the successful National Car Spring Company, had been able to promise help. When the post-war depression destroyed his ability to keep that promise, the young couple faced a struggle that was never to be altogether relaxed during their life together. It diminished neither their love, their courage, nor their desire for children. Their eldest child, Langdon, was born in Boston in 1866. They were newly established in the first home of their own, a little cottage in Roxbury, Massachusetts, when their second son was born twenty months later, September 14, 1867. Charles Gibson was absent because of the death of his father, and his wife was alone when she knew her child was about to be born. She managed to call a doctor and during the delivery administered the ether to herself. The boy was christened Charles Dana Gibson for his paternal grandfather.

After a third boy, Le Baron, who died at the age of two, three daughters were born: Elizabeth Langdon, Annie De Wolf, and

Josephine. Mr. Gibson's job as a salesman for his late father's firm took him and his family west, first to Chicago, then to St. Louis, young Dana amusing himself and other passengers during the journeys by cutting silhouettes. Finally the Gibsons were able to settle permanently in Flushing, New York.

It was a happy household in which they brought up their five. The children would never forget their parents' devotion to each other and to them. "Our home," Dana Gibson remembered, "was free from all personal strife, and harsh words between our parents were unthinkable." Yet the financial cloud which never left the horizon could not be entirely hidden from the youngster. He would observe the grave faces of his father and mother as they sat at a desk each month before a pile of papers and he knew they were worried by things called bills which were hard to pay. The boy watched them with an aching distress which left a deep impression. Perhaps he could grow up soon and help them.

He was beginning to turn from scissors now, laying them aside as childish things for a pencil. Already he could draw a dog with proper foreshortening. He would illustrate his history examinations at school, and his panoramic pictures of the Pequot War, with stirring combats between redskins and settlers, told the story far better than the verbal efforts he mustered. Teachers seemed to think chalk and blackboards were for writing and figuring. Dana felt them as an almost irresistible invitation to draw.

At home the boy was invariably encouraged. Charles Gibson, who often illustrated the letters to his family written during business trips, continued to draw for and with his second son. The image of an idolized father survived in the handsome men Dana Gibson later drew, most of them smooth-shaven, since Mr. Gibson wore only rather dashing sideburns, believing that no man with hair on his face should be allowed to kiss a child. In emulation of the

From a drawing done by Dana's father to amuse his young son

Gibson Man, bushels of American beards and mustaches would be sacrificed in the '90's.

Josephine Lovett Gibson was equally encouraging to the boy's artistic efforts, always managing to spare money from household

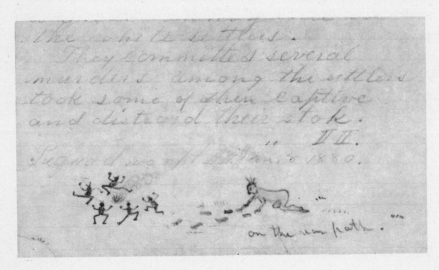

Part of a composition on history by C. D. Gibson in 1880—"The Pequot War"

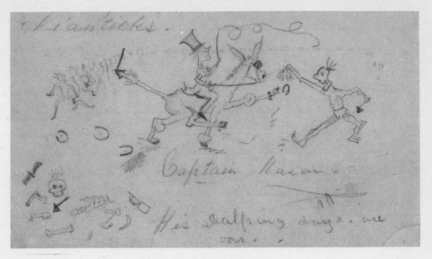

More of "The Pequot War"

expenses to buy him drawing materials. She lived to know that the fond hopes a mother cherishes for her son sometimes are realized. After her death in 1923, there was found among her papers the following character sketch of Dana, left ready to the hand of some future biographer who would be grateful for such a glimpse of a mother's insight and a mother's love.

IV

"Very few people would give credence that there could be, in a child's life, between the ages of five and twelve years, any marked qualities of character whereby one could place any assurance as to what kind of a man he was going to make.

"Yet Charles Dana Gibson (as a child) was the exemplification of that one great fundamental truth—'The Boy is Father of the Man.' The same temperament, the same inborn noble traits of character so noticeable in his childhood, have followed him into middle life.

"To my mind the child and man are so wonderfully blended, that the intervening years have not diminished one iota of his personality.

"He was a strong, healthy child, always happy, free from all taints of morbid moods, always finding amusement with his scissors, paint box and pencils.

"He was a child of keen perception—great thoughtfulness, sensitive, shrinking from praise of any kind—rather than courting it.

"He loved birds and animals. They generally predominated in the little cuttings that fell from his scissors. The purity of thought of a subject was always dominant in everything he did.

"His power of comprehension in reasoning was considered 'remarkable for a child' and this childish philosophy he practiced in cases of disappointment of any kind was enough to disarm all rules to the contrary.

"His boyhood and school days were attended with no less interest. He was a lover of home and always found time to play with his little sister Beth in the nursery.

"He would tell her story upon story of the long journeys they were going to take together through the wilds of Africa to hunt lions and tigers and then he would describe the thrilling situations in the most blood-curdling terms. And just at that point when it seemed impossible for him to escape the claws of a lion, he would take his pencil and sketch (in a minute) an illustration of how wonderfully he was saved by his little sister, placing himself in the most ridiculous and helpless situation so as to give her all the pleasure and praise.

"At another time a neighbor's cat had been making off with some of his young chickens and the means he took by way of assuring his little sister that his mind would be at rest in the future regarding the safety of his chickens was a little illustration showing her skill in handling the situation to his great satisfaction and admiration.

"He never posed as the rescuer. His unselfishness in making others pleased with themselves was perfectly natural to him.

"But little did I think in those early days that the time was coming when his name would resound from shore to shore.

"And that the world would laugh and weep by the power of his mind.

"A little incident of his school days is worthy of notice.

"It was just before Christmas and his first year at the high school in Flushing, L. I. His mind was very much alive with the spirit of the season, and he longed no doubt to express in some way what his mind's eye pictured to him.

"Finding himself alone in the 'auditorium' surrounded by a long line of black-boards and plenty of colored chalk lying about, was a temptation too great to be resisted.

"He seized the opportunity and with bold and rapid strokes brought out the most colorful, vivid picture of Santa Claus and his Christmas ride over hills and valleys and through ice and snow, and never were deer pictured with more life and frolic than the ones that drew that sleigh—everything seemed in motion.

"As he was making the last few strokes he looked up and saw the principal of the school, Mr. Williams, standing in the doorway.

"The feeling that came over him was that without leave he had been doing something worthy of censure.

"I, knowing nothing of this little episode, was surprised by receiving a note from Mr. Williams saying he had something to show me at the school. It is needless to say my curiosity was aroused. Mr. Williams, taking a key from his pocket, opened the auditorium door saying, 'I keep this door locked, Mrs. Gibson, for fear something will happen to these pictures your son has put upon the board. And I wanted you to see them. I come in and look at them every day. It's a pity ever to erase them.'

"Dana was very ingenious and clever with tools. When he was quite a lad, he built a canoe without a chart or any other help.

From *The New York World*

"It never saw water until finished and was carried down to Flushing Creek on the shoulders of himself and another boy. The sails were made of unbleached cotton.

"And one Wednesday morning he and his brother set sail—
(after packing the stern with enough food to last for several days).
And the following Saturday found them at Narragansett Pier after
a most perilous journey in a violent storm.

"And, to this day the name of 'Judith' fills my heart with thank-
fulness—for mothering my two boys around that Point in a 15-foot
canoe.

"So with these few sketches of the child life (of one who has
filled volumes) I must close—as they were only the forerunner of
greater things to come.

"And it is a mother's pride I feel in bringing to light these little
incidents in proof that the 'child was father of the man.'"

© Life Publishing Co.

HIS FIRST LOVE

CHAPTER III

APPRENTICE TO ARTS

I

Flushing in the 1870's and '80's was a pleasant and peaceful Long Island community whose shade trees, grass borders, and neighborliness were safe for some years still from the engulfing tide of New York City. Its trees were its particular pride and no town in the United States could boast arbors of greater variety and beauty, for Flushing lay in the midst of three tree nurseries, the oldest dating from the seventeenth century Huguenot settlement. It was an ideal environment for growing boys. Every lad's backyard was the gateway to real countryside, the beginning of a trail to woods and rivers, a corridor down to the sea.

Those paths to adventure were most alluring to Langdon and Dana Gibson when they followed the leadership of a friend, some years older than they but infinitely companionable and entertaining with his woodcraft and nature lore and his fascinating way of imparting them to boyhood. He was destined to make quite a reputation for it, and the Gibson boys whom Daniel Carter Beard then initiated into the mysteries of scouting were the forerunners of a long and loyal line.

The three of them would take long winter hikes through driving snowstorms, studying the habits of animals and birds. Summers they would jog-trot for miles through the woodland, holding to a compass bearing and never turning aside for streams or swamps. The youngsters climbed trees for young hawks and church steeples for owls which Dan Beard raised. Under such exploits the fine physiques the brothers had inherited developed rugged strength and stamina. The knowledge of birds Langdon acquired would win him the post of ornithologist on one of Peary's Arctic expeditions. Dan Beard also taught how things were made and there Dana was an apt pupil. Any Flushing resident who needed a dog house or a chicken coop knew where to go for a competent job, done for the fun of it. Stone masons and a potter's wheel held the boy spellbound; and whenever ground was broken for a new home, a volunteer helper arrived who only moved out when the tenants moved in.

But Dana Gibson had shown too much skill with scissors to be allowed to concentrate on carpentry tools. Ever since the triumphant exhibition of his silhouettes, his parents had been mindful of the critic's admonition that the training of a child with such a gift was a matter of no small importance and that he might, if put amid the right surroundings, develop into an exceedingly clever sculptor. A family council, called to consider the question, delegated Mrs. Robert L. Cutting, who knew the right people to know the right surroundings. Mrs. Cutting obligingly took her thirteen-year-old cousin into New York City and urged his reluctant footsteps into the office of George B. Post.

That noted architect received his beautiful caller and her charge with old-school courtesy and gave his attention to the errand. Having explained it, Mrs. Cutting departed, leaving her problem for solution. While the problem waited uncomfortably, Mr. Post considered the available arts. Several of them were lavishly represented in the Cornelius Vanderbilt mansion, built on his designs and then receiving its finishing touches. Murals by John La Farge and carved columns and caryatids by Augustus Saint-Gaudens in a handsome setting provided by Post's own profession graced the imposing French chateau at Fifth Avenue and Fifty-seventh Street. Since sculpture had been mentioned as the lad's most likely bent, painting and architecture were quickly discarded and Mr. Post called for his brougham.

In the carriage, the young aspirant to the arts nervously surveyed his mentor from formidable waxed mustache to white waistcoat and white spats in the height of the mode. It seemed presumption then to interrupt the dignified silence of the awe-inspiring personage whose grandson would one day marry the daughter of this youth he had in tow. Up to a former stable on West Thirty-sixth Street rolled the brougham and its occupants alighted to enter the studio of the celebrated Saint-Gaudens.

The boy stood dazed on the threshold, gazing at Art in the making. Scaffolding, ladders, pedestals, and all the other mud-stained properties of sculpture cluttered the barnlike room. White plaster casts of hands and feet and medallions of heads hung from walls and beams, lending a Bluebeardlike air to the place. Several apprentices stared curiously at the stranger. A model in Colonial jacket, knee breeches, and striped stockings relaxed near a mass of clay from which his image was emerging to become *The Puritan*. Engaged in conversation with Post stood the studio's presiding genius, a tall, gaunt man whose flaring red hair, beard, bushy brows, and piercing eyes gave him the awesome aspect of Michael Angelo's Moses. The waiting boy was beckoned over.

"He cuts things out of paper," remarked the architect noncommittally, producing evidence provided by Mrs. Cutting.

Saint-Gaudens looked from the silhouettes to their author and demanded: "Did you do these?"

"Yes, sir."

A long finger pointed at the model for *The Puritan*. "Cut that man out."

Scissors and paper were brought and the boy hesitatingly made the attempt. The striped stockings seemed to hypnotize him. Never before had he cut from a model, only from a picture in his mind, and he achieved a figure which was recognizably a man in knee

Photograph by Brown Bros.

AUGUSTUS SAINT-GAUDENS, IN HIS FORTIETH YEAR,
AT WORK IN HIS STUDIO

From a painting by Kenyon Cox in 1887

breeches but no better than that. However, the sculptor, less sceptically, ordered him to do something else. Swiftly the scissors snipped
out a charming little study of a lad sitting on a log fishing. Saint-
Gaudens commanded a boy on a donkey; before it was complete
he called for a second boy riding behind the first, and the addition
was promptly made.

The apprentices, attracted by the interest their master was showing, joined the group. One of them, a yellow-haired youth of sixteen, watched the extraordinary performance of the younger boy
with a growing feeling of insignificance. Here, he thought, was a
newcomer who would enter the studio and be its star. But Frederick MacMonnies, before long to be Saint-Gaudens' assistant and
later to achieve fame in his own right, had mistaken his own destiny
for another's.

"All right. Go to work," the sculptor gruffly told the boy when the last silhouette was finished.

If sculpture was to be his art, the new apprentice was now "amid the right surroundings." But this art cast no spell on him. His silhouettes were outline, a single profile; sculpture demanded many

THE GROWTH OF GREATNESS.
LITTLE DANA.
TAKEN WHEN FOUR DAYS OLD.

Published in
Life in 1895

profiles. His mind, quick to see a picture in one dimension, was not inclined to move around a subject and visualize it from all angles. Modeling in clay from the cast of a hand ignited no creative spark in him, and the studio errands which were the lot of the youngest apprentice were just so many chores. At thirteen, statues seemed cold and dull affairs, while the woods and waters of Flushing and Bristol were warm and inviting.

The boy's thoughts were in the country as he trudged the city streets one day on an errand to a photographer's shop. There they gave him a small piece of ruled tissue paper, marked with faint pencillings, for delivery to his master. As he sauntered dreamily back to the studio, the scrap of tissue was crumpled in a moist palm. Gradually, automatically, it was rolled into a tiny, sodden ball, still clutched but forgotten.

Visions slowly fading, the messenger stood before a busy, hurried master whose kindly nature became high explosive under the pressure of work.

"Did you go to the photographer's?" Saint-Gaudens barked.

"Yes, sir."

"Well, where is the drawing?"

"Oh." A hand meekly extended the soiled wad of paper.

The red beard bristled and the eagle eyes flashed. Then poured forth a stream of those "oaths, curses, and objurgations" in which the master was fluent, and the brief apprenticeship of Charles Dana Gibson to Augustus Saint-Gaudens was abruptly terminated.

II

The sculptor's spatula was abandoned as an unappealing tool and scissors and silhouettes outgrown. But when, after a summer of seafaring and camping, Flushing High School reopened, Dana Gibson again found in his hands pencil, pen, and chalk. His use of them as instruments of education betrayed no scholarly brilliance, nor did he evince any special proficiency in drawing class. Nevertheless the artistic urge in him was reawakened and when it was unguided and untrammelled it gave promise of power. The Christmas decorations in colored chalk on a classroom blackboard, which Mrs. Gibson remembered so proudly, were her son's outstanding school achievement. His ambition was stirred by the praise he received, particularly that of the schoolboard member who was the local butcher and whose comments on the anatomical correctness of the Gibson reindeer were regarded as coming from one who spoke with authority.

It began to be conceivable that one might care to work seriously at art, even to adopt it as a career. Dan Beard said it meant hard work and he, as a hard-working artist making a success, could be credited. He was always ready to help his younger friend with criticism, and the boy lost no opportunity for practice. He became a scene painter when the community staged a play for the benefit of Flushing Hospital. Commissions came in occasionally from relatives. An uncle ordered a large scale copy of an ancestor's portrait. Pictures from the French magazine, *L'Illustration,* impressed the lad to the point of copying them regularly; the arrival of a new issue set him to work on it at once, though it involved giving up such good sport as a rowing race or a skating rink party in New York.

Certainly he was willing to toil away at art and to make sacrifices. But they must be his own, since they might so easily be in vain. Adolescence mistrusts its own glowing, ambitious visions which may turn out to be only mirages. You never knew till you reached them, and growing up to the point where you could find out seemed an interminable business. Might there be, the boy wondered, a pot of gold at the end of art's rainbow? Would people actually pay you for drawings you would gladly do for nothing? Unless they did, art was an impossible luxury for Charles Dana Gibson.

Out of the besetting perplexities and torturing uncertainties of the age which is even more awkward mentally than it is physically, the boy grasped one conviction, one he held all his life although he was to overcome the handicap in his own case—the conviction that an artist starting his career should have some outside means of support to tide him over the first lean years. Short rations and a garret could be contemplated, but even they cost something. They cost more than a boy who was getting old enough to help his family felt he had any right to ask. The sight of his parents figuring silently and seriously on bills every month was not to be forgotten by a sensitive youngster.

Art was long and money was fleeting. If only he could learn how to make enough of the latter to justify the former. He told his troubles to his father and that understanding gentleman, listening gravely to the soul-struggles of fourteen, went to see his neighbor, William Elliman. So there was a job that summer for Dana Gibson in Wall Street where, nobody doubted in the year 1881, one might study to best advantage that important, if not preeminent art, the art of making money.

III

Boys who carried messages in Wall Street dared not loiter like boys who ran errands for sculptors. The tempo of finance was fast and the threat of telephones, though still few and undependable, spurred young Mercuries. Dana Gibson crumpled no order slips in his hand while he revolved rapidly on his orbit between the office of Buttrick and Elliman, at 16 Wall Street, and the New York Stock Exchange nearby. He learned to take his post in the noisy corridor of the Exchange building and cock an ear for the shout of "Buttrick" by one of his company's brokers from the floor. Running and taking the scribbled token of an order executed, the messenger would rush it back to the office. There was a dash-and-go of excitement about it and no chance for dreaming, even of fortunes to be made.

But in the slack period after the market closed, office-mates saw that the boy was busy with pencil and paper. A look over his shoulder disclosed that he was inscribing neither the dollar signs nor the graphs which are the favorite art of the Street, but frivolously foreign subjects. It boded ill for his future as a financier.

And yet unfinancial pictures may win acclaim even in Wall Street.

That rare phenomenon transpired as a result of an event of national importance.

Since the shooting of President Garfield on July 2, 1881, the attention of the country had been fastened on his gallant fight to recover from the wounds inflicted by an assassin's bullets. When he succumbed after two months, memorials of all sorts were arranged. Among these was the idea of Charley Deacon, Wall Street doorman and character, of a fitting tribute from the boys of the financial district. He proposed a competition between the messengers for the best sketch of the late President, the prize to be financed in the most approved local manner by a pool contributed to by the competitors themselves.

Charles Dana Gibson handily won the one-dollar award with a drawing made from a photograph.

How much more grandly loomed that prize than the fifteen dollars of his monthly wage which vanished so swiftly for lunches and commuting. For it was not the amount but the manner of its earning. The Garfield sketch gave him priceless assurance, the first he could really believe in his heart, that he was an artist. Perhaps, after all, he could serve art without first serving Mammon—could make his way unsubsidized in the career that beckoned him so imperiously.

In the fall he was glad to shake the reputed golden dust of Wall Street from his feet and return to Flushing to finish his education.

IV

His family could afford to keep him in high school three years longer, but college was out of the question. It seemed no great deprivation to him. Few of the other Flushing boys went, since most of the community's families were in as modest circumstances as the Gibsons. Many residents were formerly well-to-do New

Yorkers, who, as a society gossip sheet put it, moved to Morristown, N. J., the Oranges, N. J., or Flushing, depending on whether they had lost some, more, or most of their money. Life in Flushing was all the more pleasant for no need to keep up with the Joneses.

Since Flushing would not go to college, college came to Flushing. Teams from the campuses could count on plenty of redoubtable opposition from the Flushing Athletic Club and the Nereus Boat Club. One of the star athletes of those organizations was Dana Gibson. Outdoor life had developed his inherited sturdiness, and growing into manhood he shot up to a height of six feet one and one-half inches, with the symmetrical, well-knit and muscled build of an ideal crew man. He became a first-rate oarsman, a strong swimmer and weight-thrower.

When the Columbia track team came to Long Island for a meet with the Flushing A. C., the visitor's champion shot-putter found no opposing entry in his event. Knowing that he could not collect the gold medal without a contest, he asked someone to compete. Gibson entered simply to be obliging and to his dismay won.

Rowing was also a favorite local sport. The Gibson boys and Dan Beard were members of the crew of the Nereus Boat Club, strong rival to the New York Rowing Club in many a race on the Harlem River. The latter club, selecting a four-oar crew to take part in a college regatta at Philadelphia, leaned heavily on the Nereus strength. Its boat, as finally seated, had John Livingston at stroke, William Harper as Number 2, Langdon Gibson at 3, and Dana bow. This crew won its heat but lost the final to Cornell, Pennsylvania rowing third.

There was many a good time at these sports clubs, the centers of Flushing's social life. Dances at the boathouse where the trim shells swung overhead from the rafters. Saturday afternoon barge parties, with a score of long sweeps manned by stout oarsmen and inboard

Frank Northrop   B. Gillam   V. Gillam
Fred A. Guild   C. D. Gibson   Grant Hamilton
Arthur H. Scribner   Daniel C. Beard

NEREUS BOAT CLUB DAYS

beside each rower a seat where his lady fair reclined at ease, admiring her partner's watermanship and offering some of her parasol's shade. Landings, the ladies elaborately assisted, and picnics on the rocky shore of Flushing Bay. Songs and flirtations by moonlight.

Such were the playing-fields and promenades of Flushing and they seemed compensation enough for the loss of college to youths not particularly studious. Dana Gibson, leaving high school, was content to finish his education at an institution which he was sure would benefit him more than any university course—the Art Students' League of New York. The cost of tuition was only $5 a month and that could be afforded. At Dan Beard's studio, he took his League entrance examination, which consisted in making a drawing of a mask of Voltaire. On its submission, the candidate's talents were adjudged sufficient to justify training and he was admitted to day classes in 1884.

SOME RARE BIRDS.

The Dan Beard influence expressed in later years

CHAPTER IV

LIFE AND HOPE

I

"The occupation of necessity of the upper floors, and no elevators in the building, prevents some of the ablest women students and members from attending." Thus an apologetic section of a report of the Art Students' League of New York, referring to its otherwise well-equipped building at 38 West Fourteenth Street. That institution was all unaware that the pen of one of its new scholars named Gibson would in a few years help make American girls athletic enough to manage stairways, not to mention bicycles, billows, and tennis balls. Yet enough of the weaker sex, capable of climbing and enamored of art, were enrolled to require three "life" classes, modestly separate from the two for men.

While the League regretted its lack of lifts, it pointed with pride to its student body of 400 and to its corps of instructors, the best in the country, including Kenyon Cox, William Sartain, Walter Shirlaw, William Merritt Chase, J. Alden Weir, J. Caroll Beckwith, Thomas Eakins, Edwin H. Blashfield, Frank E. Scott, and Frederick Dielman. It boasted a guild spirit, being co-operatively run and managed by its students, and a growing atmosphere, now noticeable only a decade after its founding. What if all the embryo Rembrandts and Da Vincis who could afford it deserted to sail and enter the *Atelier Julien* and the *Beaux Arts*? Paris was the undisputed capital of Art, and *la vie Bohême* flourished not in Manhattan. Nevertheless the League could and did specify numbers of its graduates who were making good at home, among the younger men and women achieving prominence being: F. S. Church, C. Y. Turner, Howard Pyle, W. H. Shelton, C. S. Reinhart, C. A. Platt, W. St. John

Harper, G. R. Donoho, Fred Juengling, George Inness, Jr., D. M. Bunker, J. E. Kelly, R. F. Zogbaum, A. C. Redwood, C. D. Weldon, Thoré de Thulstrup, Miss Dora Wheeler, and Mrs. M. R. Dixon.

With such shining examples, art was real and earnest to Dana

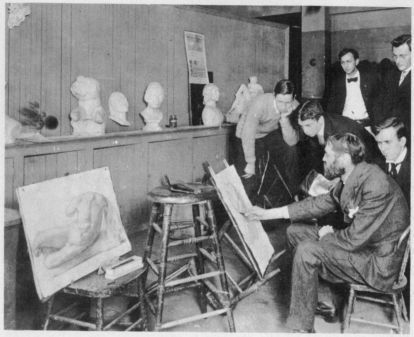

Photograph by Brown Bros.

KENYON COX DEMONSTRATING TO A CLASS AT THE
ART STUDENTS' LEAGUE

Gibson and the other young draftsmen and painters, as well as to the older artists, the designers, and the engravers who gave their evenings to night classes while they spent their days in the practice of their profession. Therefore dilettantes were rare at the League where, warned its prospectus, "only serious workers were allowed to join classes."

Gibson toiled away at his drawing board in "antique" and "life" sessions, working in charcoal, wash, and in pen-and-ink, the medium he liked best. At a board in front of him sat Robert W. Chambers, who ultimately would relinquish art to write novels about artists. Natty garments and a broad expanse of collar and cuffs, magnificently reflecting highlights, proclaimed Chambers the best-dressed man in the class. Beside the student from Flushing sat a fuzzy-haired Kansas Citian who let it be known that in his home town he had already sold crayon portraits made with what he called an "ostrich egg finish," a strange glaze he attained by putting his eyes out of focus as he drew. He was the envy of the class until its teacher, George de Forest Brush, condemned the technique as frightful. In the back row bulked the husky Frederic Remington, former Yale football star and the class's strong man champion, having won the title from Gibson in a forearm-bending contest. As if that were not sufficient to clinch a reputation, Remington, fresh from the West, could be induced to display a tintype of himself in full cowboy regalia standing beside a real Indian. The League and its prosaic models could not hold him long. After a few weeks he departed in search of Sioux, cavalrymen, and bucking bronchos.

Like most of the other students, Gibson could not wait until he finished school to test the practical value of the art he was learning. After classes, he went searching for commissions and, finding none, attempted to drum up some. Hearing of a man who wrote poems for children, he called on him and arranged a collaboration. The result of the venture was nil, since the poems were bad and the pictures worse.

"Dear Papa," he wrote, when his father doubted the value of that enterprise in illustration at its outset, "I received your letter this morning full of good advice and will try to profit by it. It is very true about having a higher aim of art than illustrating children's books and I want to get there if I possibly can, but everyone who has ever reached the goal has had to start way down and if I expect to come out of school a polished artist or keep in school till I make one, I will get sadly left. You see, if I commence now to build up some sort of a trade, by the time I have to make a living I will have some kind of reputation worked up. Even in that line, anything to make money with, and if it is in me to make a great artist, it will surely come out."

For two years, Gibson studied at the League, absorbing the groundwork, the ABC's, the artisan's part of his profession. The impatience of youth and his sense of the economic pressure on him would endure no more. If he were to go on, he felt, he must drag the rest out of himself, and it was high time he was about the business of making a living which, as Chambers remarked, the majority of us have to do long before we know how.

Gibson struck out for himself in the summer of 1885. He had come out of school a far more eager than polished artist. How few signs his work then showed of being gifted! No wonder it was invariably refused. Again and again he made the weary rounds of the magazines, and in after years, interviews with art editors would be a favorite, wistfully-drawn theme of his. He learned the trick of departing by the back door of Harper & Brothers on Franklin Square; if you descended by the famous iron circular stairway with a bundle of rejected drawings under your arm, you met other artists going up and they were embarrassingly aware of your debacle. More than a few times he completely abandoned unsigned sketches submitted to magazines because he had done better ones since and was ashamed of the prior efforts. Also it was policy to prevent editors from becoming habituated to saying no.

Once he labored for days on a pictorial series for a varnish manufacturing firm—a use for varnish each month in the year. The firm refused it, asked its resubmission and then rejected it finally. Vainly he haunted the new photo-engraving plants springing up in downtown New York on the theory that they might be a market for the pictures they could reproduce so easily and cheaply. But the photo-engravers had no more use for this struggling artist than the exacting wood-engravers, now being outmoded, who took such pride in their fine line-cuts.

No fledgling ever tried harder. He lost many of his boyhood

THE FUNNY ARTIST

A favorite wistfully drawn theme of Gibson's

friends by being too busy to see them. Through the father of one loyal one, however, he obtained a commission to illustrate the catalogue of the New York Trades School. Although Gibson earned $50 from this, it did little to lessen his increasing discouragement. After all, it was work that had come to him through influence, not merit, work he would not have been given otherwise.

"When you get out in the stream," his father would encourage him, "the current will be going your way." And his mother would open a magazine and challenge him: "See this picture. Somebody got money for it. I'd be ashamed of you if you couldn't do better than that."

There seemed little justification for his parents' belief in his future. Against a long series of failures stood only the trades school catalogue. Apparently there was more money in dealing in nature direct than holding a mirror up to it. When Gibson walked in from Flushing to the Long Island City ferry, he carried a pair of telegraph pole spike-irons with which he climbed trees to capture owls, bought by taxidermists at fifty cents each. Or he trapped squirrels in demand by florists who put them in cage-wheels to serve as lively window displays.

So it was a depressed and disheartened young artist who one winter's day in 1886 carried a slim portfolio of drawings to the office of *Life*. Diffidently, almost hopelessly, he left them for inspection by the editor, John Ames Mitchell.

II

The magazine which was Mitchell's brain-child was then barely three years old. Since it had lasted that long, its staff, ever fond of punning on its title, had reason to hope for more than a short *Life* and a gay one. Along with *Puck* and *Judge,* born in 1877 and 1881 respectively, it had survived the high infant mortality among American humorous periodicals of which some twenty-five previously had perished prematurely and more or less expensively. Before these three new wearers of cap and bells stretched long, successful spans. Keppler of *Puck,* Ike Gregory of *Judge,* and Mitchell had chosen the psychological period when a nation which had taken itself soberly and seriously for a hundred years was proudly discovering and vaunting its sense of humor.

For seven years Mitchell had studied painting and architecture in Paris and won some successes in both. Then he illustrated two books of light verse, enjoyed it tremendously and was doomed to his fate. Friends vainly attempted to dissuade him from that venture which ranks as one of the wildest of games of chance—launching a magazine, especially a humorous one. Mitchell was determined, convinced that there was an opportunity to exploit his own and others' talents in that field. Similar magazines long had flourished abroad; *Puck* and *Judge* were straws in the wind; and newly-developed photo-engraving offered splendid opportunity to black-and-white art. These were favorable elements of a bet the short end of which Mitchell took, risking a legacy of ten thousand dollars against heavy odds. The die cast, he converted his studio at 1155 Broadway, New York City, into an office and set about recruiting a staff.

Edward S. Martin, who as a founder of *The Harvard Lampoon* had been "afflicted with identical delusions," was enlisted as literary editor, and, except for intermissions due to ill-health, was a prop of *Life* for many years. He in turn brought in another young Harvard man, Andrew Miller, who became the magazine's exceedingly able business manager. Mitchell, Martin, Miller and later Masson and Metcalfe. It was not surprising the legend arose that a position on the staff of *Life* depended upon one's name beginning with M or an education at Harvard.

The original trio bestowed on their enterprise a title which seemed to cover everything and plunged into the appalling task of bringing out a sheet which would be funny or at least entertaining every week for fifty-two weeks a year.

Fat bundles of returns—unsold copies dumped back on the office by dealers—brought dismay for month after month. The editors were almost ready to believe an overheard remark to the effect that their paper was poorly named and the antonym would have been a better choice. That it turned the corner before one year had elapsed and before its capital had vanished testified to Mitchell's editorial genius, and the tribute was the more extraordinary for his having conjured most of his material out of thin air. While he knew the type of art and text he wanted, they were virtually non-existent. Possessing the ability to produce both himself (a clever illustrator and satirist were lost when Mitchell finally concentrated entirely on editing), he also owned the rarer gift of inspiring and directing the creative urge in others.

Thus it happened that a goodly company of pen-draftsmen gradually were rallied to *Life's* black-and-white banner. Early members of the corps were W. H. Hyde and Harry McVickar, who tilted at the foibles of the world of Society to which they both belonged; the latter drew patent-leather shoes with a sheen which was the despair of polish manufacturers. F. G. Atwood graphically chronicled events, current and past. Palmer Cox paraded his brownies and E. W. Kemble his comical darkies. Oliver Herford looked at cats and kings, drew them and put witty verses in their mouths. "Paris" under the signature of Albert Sterner placed the *cachet* on the costumes of his modish ladies. Gray-Parker's pictures spurred Anglomaniacs to fury and horsey folk to admiration.

Mitchell filled the space between drawings with pithy text. His and Martin's editorials were good sense, lightly and concisely presented. Early numbers were graced with poems by James Whitcomb Riley, Henry Guy Carleton, and G. T. Lanigan, threnodist of the Ahkoond of Swat. Brander Matthews provided dramatic criticism. Condensed novels were contributed by Henry A. Beers, a Yale voice crying out in a Harvard wilderness. The versatile and fertile John Kendrick Bangs furnished anything and everything from jokes to travesties.

Individual and unique in drawing and writing—such was *Life*.

Mitchell made it so. The magazine did not merely amuse. It anticipated trends and wittily took them off. Swiftly it became a power, wielding the sharp weapons of satire and ridicule. One of its mastheads, drawn by Mitchell, represented a hard-riding knight with pen-lance couched and levelled at the posterior of a devil who fled like the social and political smugness, meanness, and hyprocrisy he symbolized. Never was *Life's* courage dampened by such evidences of disapproval as the bomb once placed on its doorstep or by libel suits, not one of which it lost. It dared attack whomever or whatever it thought deserved attack, and readers and even advertisers, who chanced to be irritated, turned friends again when they had their laughs at others whose toes were stepped on. Independence proved to be both good business and good fun.

Life was the modern equivalent of the medieval jester whispering, between quips, words of wisdom and sentiment in the ear of a sovereign people. Its influence was tremendously augmented by features with no normal place in a humorous magazine. There was, for one, its battle against injuries caused by Fourth of July fireworks. (Can any one who saw it ever forget the cartoon, "The Glorious Fourth," of a family gathered around a blinded boy while rockets, seen through a window, soar against the night?) Another benefaction to which the magazine rallied subscribers was its fresh air fund which sent so many poor children from the slums on country vacations. These campaigns stimulated circulation and advertising "at a time when people of quality and purchasing power considered joke papers a little undignified," and they delivered *Life* from the usual confinement of its kind in clubs and barber shops, admitting it to homes. Yet they were neither the logical moves nor the carefully-conceived strategy they have been called. Without ulterior motives, they sprang from Mitchell's heart.

Not least in the factors in *Life's* success was its devotion to the cosmic impulse. Love made both the world and Mr. Mitchell's magazine go 'round. The editor "had a vast sympathy for lovers and that was one of the things that kept *Life* young and commended it to youth." One of those books he had illustrated, *The Summer School of Philosophy at Mount Desert,* overflowed with cupids and courtship, with beaux and banjos, with demure maidens who inquired of chaperons if canoeing were dangerous and were told that it was not as long as you stayed in the canoe. Most appropriately a cupid became *Life's* graphic mascot and the familiar spirit presiding over its pages. On Mitchell's original cover, boy and girl cherubs danced to Father Time's fiddling, and the medallion of a bride stood as a sort of summary of much of its table of contents.

III

A future expert delineator of love themes, that young artist who had left a batch of drawings at *Life,* plucked up nerve enough to return a few days later. This time there would be no addition to collections of unsigned, unhonored and unclaimed Gibsons cluttering up and annoying art departments around the town. He would simply pick these up, take them home and throw them away. Slowly, reluctantly he climbed the stairs. The memory of a towering six-footer and his dragging footsteps lingered with the descending Oliver Herford, slight and sprightly from having just sold a drawing for a cover.

Those hundreds of rejections had drained the novice's confidence. He could not know that *Life* was receptive and hospitable to newcomers. So far as he was concerned, the magazine might already have made its subsequent threat that its next office would be surrounded by dank moats as receptacles for artists expecting the staff to teach them how to draw; that it would maintain deep dungeons where miscreants who submitted jokes from *Punch* of 1849

Designed and drawn by J. A. Mitchell

would be punished by a sentence to read the *New York Tribune*. The threat of such terrors would not have strained his imagination, as he was led, almost thrust, into the presence of John Ames Mitchell.

Gibson saw a pair of kindly eyes twinkling at him through glasses, a warming, reassuring smile above a trim, Parisian beard, a slightly rotund, compact figure. Mitchell's welcome was courtesy itself, although he was about to go out to lunch and that is never the best moment to confront an editor. He glanced over the sketches submitted.

The scales of fate hung balanced. Much of *Life's* prosperity was weighed with Gibson's future that day, the pointer swinging between an acceptance or rejection.

Rejected   J. A. M.   Accepted

As seen by a contributor

W. H. Walker once drew a cartoon of Mitchell as he appeared to an artist after an editorial decision: a beaming saint in a halo if he had accepted the drawing; Satan himself if he had turned it down. The latter aspect was a spoofing slander, for no editor, unless it were Richard Watson Gilder of *The Century,* was better versed in the gentle art of rejecting gently.

The awful suspense increased, as Mitchell separated one small sketch from the others. Privately he thought it "reasonably bad" as a drawing, yet it showed promise and this was the type of young artist he wished to encourage. The timely humor of the idea was strong in its favor. All New York was captivated by the lovely song that Geraldine Ulmar as *Yum-Yum* was singing in *The Mikado*:

"THE MOON AND I."

Gibson's first contribution to *Life*

Ah, pray make no mistake,
    We are not shy;
We're very wide awake,
    The moon and I.

The words and music must have been running through the head of the editor, as he looked at this picture of a comical little dog straining at his kennel chain to bay at a big moon, and read the caption, "The Moon and I."

Mitchell smiled that warm smile of his. It was the saintly smile. He tapped his lips with the gesture of reproof he used when he feared he was going to stutter. Then he said: "We're taking this one, Mr. Gibson."

Charles Dana Gibson, with a bow to Gilbert and Sullivan, was a successful contributor to *Life* by virtue of a drawing accepted and paid for on the spot at the rate of four dollars.

He walked on air as he left the office. Without any influence brought to bear, without any circumstances favoring him, he had sold a drawing to a stranger, to the editor of a real magazine. It *could* be done. Sighting a restaurant across the street, he realized that the walk in from Flushing that morning, plus the excitement of his triumph, had made him ravenously hungry. By way of celebration the elated young artist blew in seventy-five cents of his four almighty dollars on a large chicken pie.

AT CONEY ISLAND.

Count Perrigretto (from Naples): Excusa; but zoze people, what do they?
Stranger: Why, they're bathing.
Count P.: A-a-ah! and what time ze Lunatic Asylum Directore come alonga to putta zem back?

One of Gibson's drawings in *Tid-Bits* in the early Eighties

CHAPTER V

HERO OUT OF ALGER

I

That night *Life's* latest contributor bent over the center table in the sitting room at home. His jubilant pen dashed off drawings until the oil lamp burned low. Next morning when he rushed in with his output of six to Mr. Mitchell, the verdict was against him.

"Not so good as your first, my lad," said the editor. "I'm afraid we can't use these."

The same fate befell the next four drawings submitted. But it was "my lad" now—no longer the formal "Mr. Gibson," and each refusal was softened by Mitchell's cordial encouragement and sympathetic understanding. *"Life* regrets that it cannot accept your contribution. Rejection implies no lack of merit" . . . thus were phrased the slips which many an unsuccessful artist and scribe received, slips which they suspected of being wringing wet with crocodile tears. It was evident to Gibson, though, that Mitchell was really sorry at having to decline his drawings; that merit *was* implied and was recognized. All that was needed was a little more of it.

Mitchell revealed his reasons for rallying those early Gibson endeavors in a confession made five years later. The occasion was the 1,000th number of *Life,* for which Gibson, who was already in the I-knew-him-when stage, had drawn the cover.

"Having myself, as a professional, done some climbing up the slippery hill of Art," the editor wrote, "I detected beneath the outer badness of these drawings peculiarities rarely discovered in the efforts of a beginner. For the beginner, as a rule, shows far more admiration for technical cleverness than for the more serious qualities of drawing and composition; and he endeavors to conceal his shortcomings by elaborate and misdirected labors.

"But this beginner had started out on fresher lines. His faults were good, able-bodied faults that held their heads up and looked you in the eye. No dodgings of the difficult points, no tricks, no uncertainty, no slurring of outlines. To be sure his ladies, in consequence, were often clad in boiler iron and although he and the Almighty, at that time, were holding different views as to the effects of light and shade, there was always courage and honesty in whatever he undertook."

Such was the discerning attitude of "The General," as *Life's* staff began to call him, toward this new recruit of his. Gibson, sensing that Mitchell wished heartily that he would succeed, never sank back into the slough of despond. He had come through once; he could do it again. Reverses steadied him, making him turn out more careful work. Its reward was revived acceptances by *Life*—of more dog drawings, travesties illustrating titles or lines from Shakespeare, sketches of comic Irishmen or darkies, the latter no match for Kemble's or A. B. Frost's, not even the one blushingly lifted from a figure by the latter artist. *Puck* took a few drawings at $10 and $15 apiece. It later offered a contract, but Mitchell was keeping him close by that time. The tireless artist adorned a theatre program with scenes and portraits of the cast of Belasco's and H. C. DeMille's play, *The Wife*. For a medical supplies catalog he ground out forty comic spots at $2 each.

It was quantity production certainly and the curse of quantity was on it, yet he strove always for improvement and progress. Wasn't it, he reflected, like taking down a mountain to reach the ore—a sort of mining operation where you dig out so much dirt and get so much gold to the ton? Or a variety of natural-artistic selection with an ultimate survival of the fittest. There would always be a gap between his aspirations and his achievements. If somebody would buy your stuff while you were experimenting and you did need the money, that was all right, providing your purpose was honest all along.

In the month of Gibson's first triumph, four- and five-dollar checks added up to $33. His income slowly rose and fell through October's $49 to November's glorious total of $184.50, payment for no less than fifty drawings. Nevertheless he had a right to be delighted with earnings of that amount. The golden age of American illustration had dawned, but few illustrators were yet converting it into much cash, not even Edwin Austin Abbey. Frost's annual income of $5,000 was widely envied.

The Moon and I had appeared in *Life* of March 25, 1886, inconspicuously to some but memorably and magnificently to its author. It was unsigned. Thereafter his pictures were proudly claimed with a heavy, black signature, "C. D. Gibson," until that was replaced by the familiar, fine script by-line, more or less illegible but really unneeded on drawings so distinctive in style they could have been no one else's.

Mr. Mitchell's magazine proved to be more than the source of a small but regular stipend to the young man who was still only one of its minor artists. For his contributions there attracted the attention of another editor, Charles Wolcott Balestier, novelist, literary entrepreneur, and future brother-in-law of Rudyard Kipling and collaborator with him on *The Naulahka.*

II

Files of the now forgotten magazine, *Tid-Bits,* contain numerous early Gibsons, none of them remarkable for drawing, but many interesting because of their subjects and their flavor of the period. From 1886 to 1888 it was a providential outlet for the busy artist who was turning out more pictures than *Life* was yet ready to print or persuaded to pay for handsomely. *Tid-Bits* was poor pay, too.

NEW YORK, DECEMBER 11, 1886.　　　　　　　　PRICE FIVE CENTS.

WARNED IN TIME.

Leader (to first bass) : Look 'r heah, 'Rastus ! Dey yaint no charnch ob gittin 'vited in de house ef de ole man hez reason ter 'spect dey's a nearthquake comin'.

The *Tid-Bits* cover

However, when it was bombarded with all the prodigality of the Gibson pen, its cashier was forced to disgorge weekly checks which totalled up to gratifying sums.

When Balestier had been called to edit *Tid-Bits* in 1885, he changed it from a hybrid almanac and clippings sheet into a humor magazine, a competitor in the *Life-Puck-Judge* field, and he attracted to it artists and writers of note. Gibson used to fill in gaps between more distinguished contributors, his task the inglorious odd jobs of art which crop up in every editorial shop—such trivia as tail-pieces and vignettes. He welcomed that opening and widened it. If other artists refused to illustrate skits in which they saw no humor, Gibson obliged though the humor escaped him also. When the dilatory Mr. Balestier would demand at noon a drawing which must be ready, cut made, to go to press at 2:45, his henchman could be depended upon to provide it promptly.

For the first time Gibson experienced the joyous sensation of knowing that his work really was wanted. It was, he thought, like a run of fish when you've waited two years without a nibble. Of course he fished as hard and fast as he could. Balestier came to depend upon him increasingly, and soon, to have Gibson handy, induced him to move his workroom in from Flushing and become the proud tenant of a studio all his own in the Alpine Building at Thirty-third Street and Broadway.

In his studio, the rent of which had to be justified, Gibson drew more furiously than ever. Once he feared he was going blind, but opportunity was knocking too hard for him to rest long. By now he was a general utility man for *Tid-Bits,* risen from "spots" to pages and double-pages. Cartoons of National Guard troops at summer camp gallantly making a corkscrew charge on champagne-bottle cannons; of the New York Giants, shrunk to a collection of midgets after that baseball team had suffered a disastrous season.

"MY elder brother!!"

"It is our duty to see that our successors commit their crimes in a conscientious and workmanlike fashion.

Gilbert

A FRAGMENT of the original Ms. of "Ruddygore"

© Tid-Bits

"R·U·D·D·Y

THE NEW GILBERT & SULLIVAN OPERETTA, PRESENTED FOR THE FEBRUARY

"G·O·R·E,"

FIRST TIME IN AMERICA, AT THE FIFTH AVENUE THEATRE,

11, 1887.

At Balestier's call day and night, Gibson was liable to receive orders to attend his chief at the theatre. Arriving ahead of time, he would wait patiently in the lobby. At last Mr. Balestier, effectively late, would appear, slight, intense and elegant in opera hat and Inverness, and followed by his one-man retinue make an imposing entrance and progress to seats. There under the lordly direction of his employer Gibson sketched dramatis personae in action, while few of the audience remained unaware that a double-page of scenes from *Ruddigore* or some other hit of the day might be expected in the forthcoming issue of *Tid-Bits*. Next morning Gibson was at work on his drawings by eight o'clock and the layout was ready at eleven.

He half realized that facility might be a dangerous thing. But money was coming in and it never occurred to him to refuse a commission or an editor's whim. Readily and ingenuously he drew whatever Balestier told him to draw. New York weather which the editor disliked was safe, enough to attack. It was when Gibson's pen was led into personalities that he learned a lesson he never forgot.

Balestier, in spite of or perhaps because of the fact that he had been a contributor to the *Atlantic Monthly* under the editorship of William Dean Howells, joined the group delighting in poking fun at the stories and novels of the man who was at that time rising to the commanding position in American letters he would hold for so long. Howells, *Tid-Bits* sniffed, was writing a novel, surprisingly with the scene laid in Boston, and dealing largely with psychological pork and beans. Howells had found it impossible to live in the country—there would be a plot around his house. Howells, as cartooned by Gibson on Balestier's orders, carried about a bottle labelled "Plot Detector," indispensable to his readers.

And then, not long after the appearance of that unkind allegation, its perpetrator was invited to dine with William Dean Howells.

The scene at the dinner table that night might well have furnished a theme for that popular future Gibson series with the caption:

THAT DELICIOUS MOMENT

When You Find Yourself the Dinner Guest of a Famous Author
Whose Stories You Have Publicly Proclaimed Plotless

Neither Mr. Howells nor any one else mentioned the unfortunate cartoon. Gibson was saved from confessing he had drawn it thoughtlessly and from making the equally embarrassing admission that he never had read any of his host's works. Nevertheless he spent a most uncomfortable evening.

One more pointed incident was required to bring home the lesson. It occurred during Balestier's attempts to develop his reliable staff artist into a political cartoonist. That training was not altogether successful, for Gibson was little interested in politics. It would take him most of an afternoon to work up the emotion necessary to produce a convincing cartoon. Ashamedly he acknowledged to himself that he could not see any particular difference between the Republican and the Democratic parties, a difficulty common, then and later, to many more politically-minded than he.

However *Tid-Bits* never doubted it was staunchly Republican, and Gibson was commanded to draw accordingly. Make handsome portraits of those sterling candidates, Benjamin Harrison and Levi P. Morton, Balestier decreed, and his trusty artist obeyed. Lampoon that dangerous Democrat, President Grover Cleveland, and his pernicious ideas on free trade, came the next edict, and again the faithful slave of the pen bowed to the will of his master.

Gibson launched many cartoon attacks on Cleveland. The one that came back to haunt him was entitled "The First Case of Free Trade Fever." It depicted an extremely sick-looking Cleveland lying in bed, a sheet over his ample middle and half his body black with the ravages of the disease loathsome to all true and high tariff Republi-

"Time," formerly "Tid-Bits"

TIME

THE FIRST CASE OF FREE TRADE FEVER.

Consulting Physician Dana: I see: A case of Black, or June Fever. Half the body gone already. At this rate there won't be a white spot on him by November.

Doctor Randall: Yes, yes; I warned him of it! But do ye really think it's all up with him, Doctor?

Consulting Physician Dana: Oh, yes; hopeless you know—ye can't stop a thing like this. And once let it get among the poor working people, and it will kill them off like sheep.

cans. In grave·consultation at the bedside stood Senator Samuel Randall and Editor Charles A. Dana in the character of doctors, both of them distantly kin to the artist here rudely caricaturing them. Beneath the picture ran this dialogue:

CONSULTING PHYSICIAN DANA: I see a case of Black, or Jungle Fever. Half the body gone already. At this rate there won't be a white spot on him by November.

DR. RANDALL: Yes, yes, I warned him of it! But do you really think it's all up with him, Doctor?

CONSULTING PHYSICIAN DANA: Oh, yes, it's hopeless, you know. You can't stop a thing like this. And once let it get among poor working people and it will kill them off like sheep.

Not long after the cartoon was printed, Gibson was invited to a party in Marion, Massachusetts, and there found himself confronted by the victim he had blackened with so much ink and "free trade fever." Cleveland apparently had not seen the picture. At any rate he did not refer to it and another awkward occasion passed.

That was enough. Gibson seldom drew acidly personal cartoons again until the days when Kaiser Wilhelm II indulged in a yearning for martial glory.

Although politics was a favorite target, *Tid-Bits* by no means neglected the fair sex toward whom it was little inclined to be sentimental or romantic. It offered to supply bustle-wearers with bolsters so they could lean back in a chair and be comfortable. It advised its feminine readers that the beauty given the figure by a full chest could be increased from four to six inches by exercise, a method preferable to approximating the same effect by contrast with a tightly-corseted waist; better a Diana or a Venus than a wasp, opined the magazine. Again, it impudently wondered how fashionable females with veils rigged fore and aft and reefed tight could possibly blow their noses in case of sudden need. And how it scolded the lady shoppers who succumbed to the current custom of taking nips in the stores to recuperate from the fatigue of the bargain counter, the charges appearing on their dress bills as "small trimmings."

TENNIS IS SUCH A REFINED AND PRETTY GAME, ESPECIALLY WHEN PLAYED THESE EARLY SPRING DAYS!

Less gallant pens than Gibson's handled such subjects. He would not have enjoyed them. Besides, the Gibson Girl was not yet born, and he was still only on the threshold of his career as a social satirist. The first of his pictures of that type to appear in *Tid-Bits* was a drawing of a mixed doubles match of tennis—the men in tight knickers and the girls in straw hats and long skirts with bustles, and all of them mired in the mud of the court. "Tennis," read the caption, "is such a pretty game, especially when played these early spring days." It was still generally conceded that tennis was violent exercise, not to be recommended for women unless practiced with a great deal of caution.

There will always be an opening for the New York Giants. The Dime Museums would Jump for Them.

© Tid-Bits

Gibson, his work now in demand by better markets, ceased drawing for *Tid-Bits,* newly rechristened *Time,* in 1888. Its sands were almost run. Two years later it was combined with *Munsey's Weekly* where, it was announced, would be retained "all its best elements," a clarion often sounded down the years by the much-merging Mr. Munsey.

III

The pages of the Gibson account books (carefully kept by the New Englander, not the artist) are like chapters in a novel by Horatio Alger, Jr., *Bound to Rise* or perhaps *Sink or Swim,* with plenty of swimming these days and little sinking. May, 1888—$358. June—$408. October—$600. *Life* was regularly paying him $250 a month that year. Advertising, "that jovial bishop who wed commercialism to art," bestowed several blessings on him. For promotion pictures in their behalf, the Ivers & Pond Piano Company paid him $20, and the Methodist Book Concern the same.

Pictorial adornment of advertising was still drab, but the attractions of artistic regalia began to be realized when Frank Doubleday of *Scribner's Magazine* drew attention to the "back of the book" by sandwiching Frost's inimitable animal comic strips in between the ads.

Gibson's drawings for Chicago, Burlington & Quincy Railroad advertisements were pioneering in the art-advertising field; novel also was such an effort by a railroad to sell its service to the public on any but a take-it-or-leave it basis. These drawings, for which the line bought space in *Life* and elsewhere, were pleasing and alluring. One recommended that tourists scale the peaks of the West. Another hymned the joys of summer resorts in the open spaces to be reached via the Burlington. Picnic or piazza courtships. Burro rides for

· LIFE ·

A SCENE IN THE MORAL FUTURE.

WHEN THE SUGGESTIVE REFORMER SHALL HAVE "PURIFIED" AMERICA AND · LIFE · ALONE REFUSES TO BE COMSTOCKIANIZED.

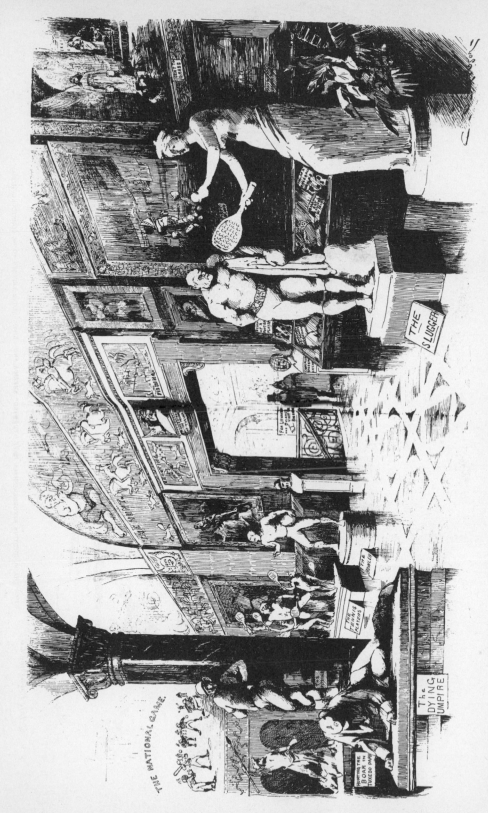

THE ART MUSEUM OF THE FUTURE.

the same purpose, conducted by charming little Indian cupids. Fishing and bear hunts and, for old bucks not equal to such sports, invigorating drafts of spring water.

Life, like *Tid-Bits,* still insisted on political cartoons from Gibson and he, though he was more than ready to yield the palm in that line to Nast and Rogers, obliged. Anyway that assignment possessed one saving grace: it gave him a chance to draw animals, a favorite subject of his since silhouette days. Elephants, providentially picked as the symbol of the Grand Old Party, always had a special appeal for him. Just as he used to visit circuses and natural history museums to make certain of his details, Gibson now obtained a permit to station himself in the aisles back of Central Park Zoo cages for a close study of his models. The cartoon, "Time!" in *Life* of 1888, a boxing bout between the G. O. P. pachyderm and the Tammany tiger, was a corking good job. It marks Gibson's high point as a political cartoonist.

In *Life* the artist found an opportunity to make an *amende honorable* for all his *Tid-Bits* digs at Cleveland by representing the great Democratic leader as a victorious gladiator leaving the arena after one of his conflicts with Congress. Yet Gibson was unwilling to be confined to politics nor did Mitchell demand it. The two formed the habit of lunching weekly together to think up subjects, and in the concoction of ideas the editor declared Gibson took his share. What a variety of topics fertile minds and ready pen spread across the pages of *Life!*

When the Suggestive Reformer Shall Have Purified America and only Life Refuses to Be Comstockianized. Horses in trousers, birds in bloomers, and all Nature muffled up as voluminously as mankind, with only rebellious *Life* cupids flitting about *au naturel.*

Disrupting the War Clouds by Personal Combat. John L. Sullivan, seconded by Bismarck, knocking out Czar Alexander into the

· LIFE ·

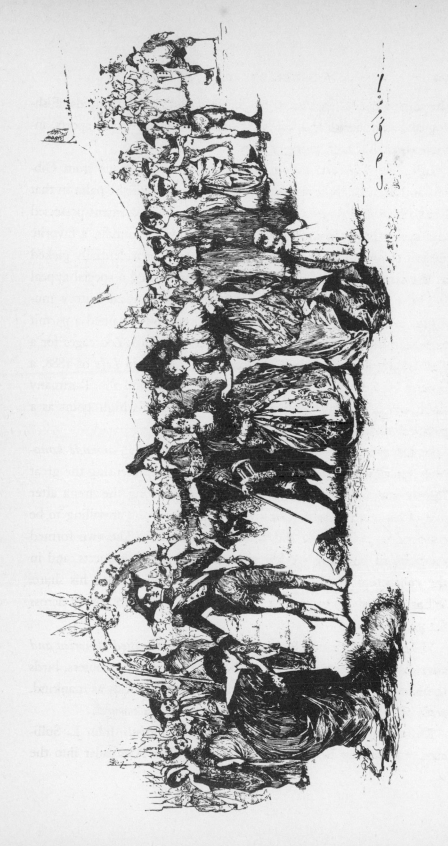

THE BATTLE OF BUNKER HILL

AS IT MIGHT HAVE BEEN IF OUR ANCESTORS HAD TASTED THE DELIGHTS OF ANGLOMANIA.

© *Life Publishing Co.*

arms of the Russian Bear, while Franz Josef and Queen Victoria, with son Edward held by the hand, watched from the ringside. Another Gibson-Mitchell solution of war threats of 1887 showed European monarchs bound to the mouths of their own cannon. *Who opens the ball now?* asked *Life*. As for our Indian wars of the day, Gibson saw them less glamorously than Remington. To the former, U. S. cavalrymen were hunters tally-hoing after a poor, exhausted redman-fox.

The Art Museum of the Future. Gibson, all for up-to-date sports, had given the Venus de Milo arms and a tennis racquet, put boxing gloves on men-at-arms and changed the Dying Gladiator into a ditto baseball umpire.

As always, *Life* enjoyed gently spoofing the British, and a splendid chance offered itself when Buffalo Bill took his Wild West show to England in 1887, confirming a rather general British impression that life throughout the United States was like that. There was first-rate satire in Gibson's cartoon showing New York ladies shopping on bucking bronchos and an Indian attack on a covered wagon crossing Fourteenth Street. "Her Majesty's desire to see untutored savages in their natural lair," added the caption, "may lead to a New York visit, probably under the management of D'Oyly Carte."

Tease the British in a friendly way, but smite Anglomaniacs hip and thigh. No mercy on Americans silly and unpatriotic enough to ape every fad and fashion from across the pond. Such was *Life's* motto and Gibson illustrated it enthusiastically. He drew a dude standing over the fallen bust of George Washington to propose the health of the Prince of Wales whom a throng of Americans knelt to worship (as indeed they virtually did when he visited this country). For the Fourth of July *Life*, Gibson drew both the cover and the center page which pictured the Battle of Bunker Hill as it might have been if our ancestors had been afflicted with Anglomania.

· LIFE ·

© Life Publishing Co.

THE MILLENIUM FOR AMERICAN AUTHORS.

WHEN THE NOXIOUS PUBLISHER SHALL BE DONE AWAY WITH AND THE AUTHOR SHALL DEAL DIRECTLY WITH HIS PUBLIC.

A BIRTHD

AS "LIFE" IS SIX YEARS OLD THIS MONTH, WHAT BETTER WAY OF CELEBRATING

UR PROSPERITY THAN BY REMEMBERING SOME LESS FORTUNATE CONTEMPORARIES?

VE VICTIS

THRILLING EVENT AT A SUMMER RESORT.

A MAN!

About this time Gibson's social cartoons began to appear more frequently. Girls in the ballroom, on the seashore, and on the ballet stage whence they consoled gentlemen forced to spend the hot weather in the city. A full page lamented that Niagara Falls, that paradise of honeymooners, abounded in swarms of annoying hack drivers and guides, drawn as insect pests. The Hearts versus Dollars theme already was absorbing the romantic young artist, who was gradually edging out McVickar, S. W. Van Schaick, and other draftsmen of love and society topics.

Once more Gibson ventured on personalities, but this time prudently. He drew a pretty lady driving a donkey cart laden with wardrobe trunks down the steep incline from the Temple of Fame. In spite of the quacking geese in dress suits escorting her, *Life's* cupid barred her path with the warning: "Excuse me, madam, but your 'social influence' is taking you in the wrong direction." The lady, as a trunk marking indicated, was Mrs. James Brown Potter, wife of the nephew of the popular Bishop Henry Codman Potter, and a society belle and amateur actress.

As Cora Urquhart, a New Orleans beauty, Mrs. Potter had stormed social citadels in New York and other cities with her looks and her dramatic recitations, then the rage as a parlor trick. *Curfew Shall Not Ring Tonight, The Charge of the Light Brigade, Paul Revere's Ride,* and *Jim Bludso* were among the ringing selections which she collected in a book, *My Recitations,* having a wide sale. But the prize number of them all was *'Ostler Joe* by George R. Sims.

'Ostler Joe shocked auditors to the core. They gasped, blushed, applauded and wept over it. When Mrs. Potter rendered it tellingly in Washington at a Cabinet member's party, it outraged the modesty of Miss Cleveland, sister of the President, so severely that the host found himself in difficulties at the White House. Of course the news created a vast demand for copies of the poem.

The winsome wife of *'Ostler Joe,* narrate the verses, bore him a baby son who one day beckoned into the cottage a handsome villain passing by. "And the baby Joe had prayed for brought about the mother's sin."

> Aimie listened and was tempted—she was tempted and she fell,
> As the angels fell from heaven to the blackest depths of hell,
> She was promised wealth and splendor, and a life of guilty sloth,
> Yellow gold for child and husband—(*slow and tragic here*)—and
> [the woman left them both.

Far away in mighty London, Aimie, it seems, rose to fame.

> Quick from lord to lord she flitted. Higher still each prize she
> [won. . . .
> Next she trod the stage half naked, and she dragged a temple
> [down
> To the level of a market for the women of the town.
> And the kisses she had given to poor 'Ostler Joe for naught,
> With their gold and precious jewels rich and titled roués bought.

Anyway, *Joe* forgave all, came to comfort her dying moments, and the poem ended on a moral note.

The celebrity of Mrs. Potter's recitations won her a place as an early indorser of cold cream and an offer from an astute manager to go on the stage professionally. There she appeared in such gorgeous and modish gowns that unkind critics were moved to remark that her thespian triumphs should be credited to Worth (the Parisian dressmaker, not the quality). In adopting acting as a career—as *Life* advised—Mrs. Potter was courageous, for the *élite* still looked down upon the stage as a low and immoral calling and thus the lady sacrificed her social position and the good graces of the socially prominent clan into which she had married. Oliver Herford signalized the choice with one of his most noted *bon mots*: "Actresses will happen in the best-regulated families."

Thus timely topics, transitory or momentous, flowed through the

LIFE.

WHITHER?

A Well Wisher: EXCUSE ME, MADAM, BUT YOUR "SOCIAL INFLUENCE" IS TAKING YOU IN THE WRONG DIRECTION.

TIME

Gibson pen and the presses of *Life*. Though his style was still unformed, his cartoons were pointed and his caricatures exceedingly clever. Moderate but unquestionable success was crowning his efforts.

How he had worked for it! The amount he accomplished would have worn out half a dozen ordinary illustrators. Arthur Brisbane and other friends who called at his studio during working hours were apologetically but firmly turned away with the word that he was drawing a model, paid to pose, and he could not afford to stop. The day after the great blizzard of '88, Gibson was eager to reach his New York studio to complete several unfinished drawings. At the Flushing station he learned there would be no trains for two or three days. Without snowshoes, the husky artist, the only man from his home town to venture on the journey that day, ploughed through six miles of drifts to Long Island City where he caught a ferry which managed to push through ice floes to Manhattan. He struggled across the snowbound city through streets where almost all traffic was paralyzed and he saw only the horses of Barnum's circus being exercised in the deep snow in front of the original Madison Square Garden. Having finished the drawings, he stayed at his studio overnight. He had accomplished a considerable feat, but he always remembered it with one regret. That evening the theatres had been free to all who could reach them and he had not discovered it until too late.

Gibson was earning enough money now to support himself and to help out at home. There was even some to spare—enough to finance a longed-for trip abroad. A pilgrimage to those glorious and fabulous metropolises of Art, the London of Ruskin, the Paris of Murger. The Meccas of every American neophyte in art who could swing, beg or borrow the price of the adventure. There was some mystery over there, surmised young Mr. Gibson, and now he was bound to find out what it was.

CHAPTER VI

ART PILGRIM'S PROGRESS

I

Great grandfather *"Guillaume"* Lovett, painter of miniatures, also had been aware of the mystery over there, and although he could approach it no closer than the *"rue de Tremont,"* Boston, had reverenced it from afar. His more fortunate descendant, Paris-bound, refused to pour his name and address into a French mold. Nor, like many of his fellow-pilgrims from America, would he consent to dress the part. Beret, velveteen jacket, and baggy corduroy trousers? Never on Charles Dana Gibson, not even in a day when artists looked like artists. On him such apparel would have seemed like pink ribbon tied around Plymouth Rock. The only concession to the unusual in attire he ever would make was the stand-up collar rising to his strong-hewn jaw and that, far from conveying Bohemianism, lent him in later life the aspect of a bald and benign bishop about to pronounce an apostolic blessing.

When as a handsome chap of twenty-one he stopped over in London, costume was uppermost in his mind, for his good looks attracted too much feminine attention for him to be careless of what he wore. Since it also seemed advisable for a penman who portrayed well-dressed men to be one, the first English artist he visited was a tailor.

It was a trifle ironical in view of the cartoon he had drawn for *Tid-Bits* about a year before: a picture of a man on a sinking ship thrusting back a woman from the last place in a lifeboat, meanwhile explaining that she had only her life to save while he was in charge of a precious consignment, the Prince of Wales' old coats being imported to New York as fall fashion models. Without a qualm, the satirist was outfitted with suits inspired by the royal wardrobe.

The tailor was an affable and genial soul. Realizing that he had to do with a Yankee greenhorn, a stranger and friendless, he invited Gibson for a dogcart spin in Rotten Row. It was out of season, nobility and society were absent from the city, and their favorite drive might in the meanwhile be enjoyed by a tradesman without violation of Victorian proprieties. Thus the artist was given his first glimpse of the city which in a few years would sing the praises of his drawings: *London As Seen by Charles Dana Gibson.*

Clothed fashionably and shown the sights, the pilgrim remembered his pilgrimage. It came upon him suddenly that he was at last in Europe on soil sacred to Art and its masters, quick or dead, the work of whose hands had inspired him since first he grasped a pen. Across the Channel lay the Spain of Fortuny and Vierge, the Germany of Dürer and Wolf, the Russia of Karan D'Ache, the France of Daumier. Here was the England of Hogarth, Cruikshank, Leech, and Keene. This was the very city of *Punch* the peerless, paid homage by draftsmen and humorists everywhere. And nearby lived one of its brightest stars, George Du Maurier, long the object of Gibson's youthful adulation.

A lengthy hansom cab drive to Du Maurier's home in Hampstead seemed the simplest solution of London's maze. Bolstering up his courage, Gibson called on the kindly, bearded Englishman and introduced himself with these words:

"I'm Charles Dana Gibson. I'm an American. I draw and you have been my master for years."

It was just such worship as Du Maurier in his turn had given Leech and it began a long friendship. Nor did Gibson exaggerate his debt. His early fine-line technique stemmed from Du Maurier, whose series, such as *Social Agonies,* were translated into the American scene by Gibson's *That Delicious Moment* and others. Just as the girls Du Maurier delineated were called the tall granddaughters of Leech's

GEORGE DU MAURIER.

plump little ladies, so might the Gibson Girl (now on the verge of making her *début*) have claimed relationship as an American cousin. The family likeness was plain when she was young and she and her British contemporary by Du Maurier were appearing together in the American quality magazines. *Life* printed several composites in which girls by the two artists met in the same picture. There and thereafter for American devotees the Gibson Girl demonstrated her superior loveliness over her elder, slightly taller relative from the Old World.

The Du Maurier maiden was statuesque and her noble proportions sometimes reminded one of her creator's admiration for "that mighty, beautiful but most uncertain quadruped, the thoroughbred horse." The Gibson Girl was stately, too, but more animated and graceful because, among other reasons, she wore a few less than the eight petticoats encompassing her British cousin. Du Maurier regarded the girls he drew with "love tinged with awe." The young man who portrayed the Gibson Girl lost his awe in his ardor. There lay the essential difference. Only *Trilby* would rival the Gibson Girl in her own country, and *Trilby* was a creature of glowing words as well as lines.

Comparing the two artists' work, *Encyclopædia Britannica* in its eleventh edition remarked that Gibson "in his admitted devotion to Du Maurier, in reverence for beautiful women beautifully attired, has led some critics to set him down as a mere disciple, while his powerful individuality has led others to accuse him of monotony; but a serious examination of his work has seemed to reveal that he has gone beyond the genius of Du Maurier in sophistication, if not in variety, of subjects and treatment. As much as any other artist, Mr. Gibson has studiously tried new experiments in the new fields opened by modernized processes of photo-engraving, and has been an important influence in both English and American line-illustration."

INTRODUCING *a new mechanical process by which the familar creations of two widely different schools of illustration are forced to meet and exchange views.*

' THE RANK IS BUT THE GUINEA'S STAMP."

Lady Leonora of the house of Du Maurier: HOW VERY INTERESTING! BOTH OF YOU AMERICANS AND BOTH ENGLISH COUNTESSES! THE NOBLE FAMILIES INTO WHICH YOU HAVE MARRIED HAVE NEVER KNOWN A *mesalliance*—SO—MAY I INQUIRE WHAT WAS YOUR TITLE IN AMERICA?

One of the Gibson Girls. FEE SIMPLE.

A composite: Du Maurier and Gibson Girls

Rivalry between dreams of fair women was still in the future, nor would it ever be other than friendly. It was as master and disciple that Du Maurier and Gibson met on that day in Hampstead, talking of art and of France. None could dwell on either topic more delightfully than the author of *Trilby, Peter Ibbetson,* and *The Martian.* His enthusiasm sped the parting guest across the Channel.

II

Behind a mustachioed, patent-leather-hatted coachman, Gibson drove through Paris, capital of Art, City of the Mystery. What backgrounds it offered an artist! Glimpses through grilled gates of quaint courts with fountains and flowers. The glorious sweep of the boulevards. Terraced restaurants and sidewalk cafés. And, more fascinating, the types and the crowds against those backgrounds, for Gibson never would be content with a scene for its own sake but must people it. Strollers and groups around the tables. Passengers thronging the imperial, top deck of the buses majestically drawn by teams of three monumental white Percherons. Now and again an open victoria enthroning and displaying to perfection a resplendent lady of the *haut* or *demi monde*. So onward to the *Atelier Julien* to enroll as a student.

The nose of the tall American wrinkled as he turned from the *Rue du Faubourg St. Denis* into the Gallic redolence of a courtyard. He climbed the stairs of the building at its rear, mounting past a workshop where the plumage of birds was being odorously treated with chemicals to supply the vast demands of millinery. His feet stirred the dust of months of palette scrapings when he entered the *atelier* and registered proudly as a pupil of Boulanger, Lefebvre, and Bouguereau, though all three failed to appear during the weeks of Gibson's course.

According to immemorial custom, the students marched the *nouveau* out to set up the drinks, and Gibson, feeling like a plutocrat with most of his $500 still intact, thought he got off cheaply. The merry crew swaggered back, touching up vegetables on stalls en route with their paint brushes. There were other initiation stunts but none of the rough horse-play to which the Frenchmen were inclined because the English and Americans were allied to protect

THE OPERATIC CRISIS.

their novices. Besides, Gibson began winning strength tests and was obviously too formidable to be tackled.

He stuck industriously to his drawing board despite discomforts and distractions. Traditional Gallic dislike of open windows rendered the rooms distressingly stuffy, and whenever a big Frenchman indulged his habit of belching sonorously it roused a sturdy Anglo-Saxon chorus of, "Thank God for a breath of fresh air!" Through the studios constantly wandered peddlers, offering for a few sous apiece prints and photographs of masterpieces, tokens of what might be achieved by these toilers. Yet the pursuit and capture of beauty on paper or canvas was little encouraged by the men and women who lined up stark naked Monday mornings for hire as models. The student from New York, who would specialize in the comeliest of mortals, drew these ill-favored specimens of humanity no less zealously. And he and his confreres gave the professor's bi-weekly critiques close and deferential attention.

Nights brought the reward of relaxation after hard work. It was Exhibition year, the Eiffel Tower had been opened and Paris was gay. Gibson enjoyed the festivities, New England conscience tempering youthful spirits. He attended the Bal Bulier and saw the wicked *can-can* danced with a bounteous and daring display of petticoats and black stockings. Again he encountered his fellow-apprentice to Saint-Gaudens, Frederick MacMonnies, who flatteringly asked him if he were the Gibson drawing for *Life*. MacMonnies, costumed for the ball as a diver, had removed his helmet. Whereupon revelers fell upon him and filled his rubber suit up to the neck with wine and beer.

Even after roistering Saturday nights, Art dragged her sleepy slaves into composition class on Sunday mornings when Biblical subjects usually were chosen as appropriate to the day. The Prodigal Son was a favorite selection, particularly with young painters

THE CIRCUS IS HERE!

whose failing remittances from fond aunts or other financial sup-
porters forced them to consider going home and the reception they
would meet. Gibson need not picture himself in that rôle. He spent
no more of his substance in a foreign land than he had planned, and
when funds dwindled down to steamship fare, he left the *Atelier
Julien* after a course of two months and sailed for New York.

So that was Paris and that was the Mystery over there he had
sought to divine. Was it so much of a mystery after all? He hardly
realized then that he had performed its rites and entered the fane.
Yet in fact he had. He had worshipped at the shrine of Art in Paris
in the springtime of life. And with all the other neophytes he had
shared the dream those sparkling days bestowed—the dream that
some day, somehow, against all the heavy odds, he would be a great
artist.

A VERY COMMON CASE.
ALL HE NEEDS IS A CHANGE OF DIET.

CHAPTER VII

"ILLUSTRATED BY C. D. GIBSON"

On those precious dreams brought home from Paris, many a young artist might have been willing to pay duty. The Customs would have passed most of them as valueless delusions.

But Gibson's swiftly took on the semblance of reality. He grasped his pen with a new mastery and his style developed unsuspected vigor, sloughing off its earlier indecision and vagaries. Such was the almost magical effect of Paris, a consequence out of all proportion to the brevity of his stay and the inconsiderable instruction given him.

He had only been back in New York a short time when the most important magazines began to open their pages to his drawings. *Life,* as his show window, had displayed his wares to advantage. John Ames Mitchell, generously ready to share talents he had discovered, bestowed high praise upon Gibson's work in an article which carried the weight of authority.

Americans like an idea in their pictures, wrote the editor in an article in *Scribner's Magazine* (December, 1889), and if they can have it well told, graphic, technically good, and with a touch of human nature, they like it all the better. The faces an artist draws, he continued, must own an interest in themselves, and then he added:

"Perhaps no American artist in black and white now before the public is the happy possessor of so many of the desired qualities, and in such happy proportions, as Mr. Charles Dana Gibson. And of these qualities the rarest and not the least important is the ability to draw a lady. It seems to be a faculty in itself, apart from others, independent of all artistic feeling, and one which no amount of education can create."

Other editors had use for an illustrator who could offer his pen to a lady and escort her gallantly through the pages of their magazines. Gibson was summoned by arbiters of editorial elegance for the Big Three: Richard Watson Gilder of *The Century,* Charles Dudley Warner of *Harper's,* and E. L. Burlingame of *Scribner's.* Such particular art editors as Alexander Drake of *The Century,* Charles Parsons of *Harper's,* and later Joseph Hawley Chapin of *Scribner's* blessed an artist whose work reproduced so well and was always ready on time.

Readers began to look for the legend, "Illustrated by C. D. Gibson," printed in small type, as conservative as the signature beneath the drawings themselves. Those drawings enhanced stories, novels, and essays and promoted the sale of magazines and of books in which they reappeared.

Not only *Harper's Monthly* but its *Weekly,* along with its *Bazaar* and *Young People* sought the services of the artist back from Paris. The book department of the honored house on Franklin Square commissioned him to create in ink the image of the debonair *Mr. Van Bibber* whose adventures the equally debonair Richard Harding Davis had related serially in the *New York Evening Sun.* For *Scribner's* Gibson illustrated Sarah Orne Jewett's story, *The Luck of the Bogans,* first and last of his pictures of any note to be reproduced by the vanishing art of the wood-engravers. His nautical drawings for Frank R. Stockton's humorous novel, *The "Merry-Chanter,"* appeared in *The Century.* A barroom scene in another story for that periodical was objected to as drawn with too great fidelity. For Mr. Gilder, filled with solicitude for readers' morals, carefully curbed drinking, slang, and other vulgar and uncouth habits in which characters in his magazine might attempt to indulge. Deferentially Gib-

"As the old men looked young Dan Bogan came stumbling into the shop"

From *Scribner's Magazine*, January, 1889. Illustrating *The Luck of the Bogans* by Sarah Orne Jewett

THE LADY AND THE TIGER.

Bishop Gullem: YES, IT IS A GOOD WORK   .D I TRUST YOU BELIEVE IN MAINTAIN-
ING FOREIGN MISSIONS.

"INDEED I DO. WHY, PAPA SEES MR. CLEVELAND EVERY DAY ABOUT ONE!"

© *Life, 1893*

son tidied up his barroom and was rewarded with a coveted invitation to one of the Gilder Sunday night salons. The guest mistook the time and arrived at 8 for an 11 o'clock party. Caught in his bath, the gracious and intuitive editor sensed the consternation of the early arrival and forthwith called him in to sit on the edge of the tub where Gibson enjoyed an exclusive interview that was the envy of every other aspiring artist and author in New York.

The new luminary in illustration was welcomed into a brilliant constellation which had seemed infinitely distant such a short time before. That inner circle of artists, the Salmagundi Club, hung several of Gibson's drawings in its black-and-white exhibition. No less than Edwin Austin Abbey and John Sargent praised the expression of his *Bishop Gullem,* social prelate, for whom Gibson posed himself, looking into a mirror, pursing his lips and assuming a righteous and episcopal air.

Abbey took an instant liking to the younger man and asked him to drop in at his studio. Gibson found his host absorbed in drawing an old silver tea set, a minor detail of a picture, with the attention to correctness and period so characteristic of him. Congeniality deepened and Abbey, soon to be married, invited his highly pleased caller to attend his bachelor dinner and serve as an usher at his wedding.

Ceremonial dinners by the hundred lay ahead of Gibson, with himself in the toastmaster's chair at many of them, but none would remain more memorable than this party of Abbey's in his studio in the Judge Building, at Fifth Avenue and Seventeenth Street. Here he sat down in a group of the foremost in the American fine arts, seeing them for the first time at close range, treated by them as their peer. Sargent, who had just finished his portrait of the restless and temperamental dancer Carmencita, having persuaded her to pose by gifts of jewelry and kept her amused by eating entire cigars. Saint-Gaudens, whose cordial treatment of his former apprentice let it be inferred that illustration's gain was sculpture's loss. The talented painter, John Twachtman. Charles F. McKim, of the celebrated firm of architects, McKim, Mead & White, who would one day design a house for Gibson. McKim's brilliant partner, Stanford White, about to build Madison Square Garden. A. B. Frost, to whom Gibson uncomfortably confessed the appropriation of one of his figures and was absolved.

What a jolly party it was! Time and again Frost rose to tell a story which he never finished, being invariably interrupted by a Negro quartet who sang as well as he might have drawn them. The versatile White commandeered all the fruit on the table to erect a model of the Garden which, he explained, would pay for itself with admission fees for its roof and tower. When the banquet of bear steaks and other substantial viands had been cleared away and toasts drunk, the assembled artists decorated each other's dress-shirt fronts. Gibson went home with an unique memento: an original Frost, Sargent, Abbey, Saint-Gaudens, Twachtman, White, and McKim on one canvas.

Next morning Gibson's mother called him hurriedly to Flushing to the bedside of his father, suddenly and mortally stricken with pneumonia. Langdon Gibson, then on Stanton's perilous exploration of the Grand Canyon of the Colorado, could not be reached.

Charles De Wolf Gibson was justly proud of his two sons. He had looked forward to every number of *Life* for Dana's drawings, and now his last hours were cheered by his younger son's story of his new, celebrated friends.

Dana Gibson lost in his father an idol and a counsellor whose gentleness and wisdom he remembered from early boyhood. "What," Mr. Gibson used to ask his boys, "is your favorite way of washing ears?" And later when they were grown: "It is up to you boys to provide the children you will have with a good mother. I did it for you." He would not see the grandchildren he had hoped to see, but when they came his artist son would write of him for them: "By repeating to you children some of the things he told us, I have tried to make up to you what you lost by not knowing him."

Mr. Gibson died with the comforting assurance that his two capable sons would take devoted care of their mother and three sisters. Langdon, entering the manufacturing field, would rise to become production manager of the General Electric Company. For Dana, art was now tipping her golden cornucopia more bountifully than ever.

II

In 1890, Charles Dana Gibson was earning from six to eight hundred dollars a month, $300 of it from *Life*. Its editor often used this right-hand man of his to illustrate his (Mitchell's) own short stories, light, dexterously-done vignettes of fiction comparable to the *Short Sixes* H. C. Bunner wrote for *Puck*. For *That First Affair* Gibson drew a comical mastodon lumbering through the forest, trunk clutching a bouquet to be presented in a prehistoric courtship—a splendid bit of animal caricature. Another Mitchell story occasioned *The Bachelor's Supper,* which for many always would remain their favorite Gibson. It pictures a distinguished, white-haired gentleman who stands at the head of his deserted dinner table, eyes closed, glass raised in a toast to the wraiths of sweethearts of his past from the little girl of his school days to the last lovely might-have-been. Far more than an illustration, it poignantly tells a story in itself. Every elderly bachelor in the land, not to mention numerous benedicts, sighed sentimentally over that picture and cherished it.

Other authors privileged to choose their illustrators began to nominate Gibson. The majority, compelled to defer to editors' selections, were grateful when their manuscripts were given an artist whose remarkable insight enabled him to depict characters as imagined by their creators. Most thankful of all were the scribes who had cudgeled their brains to make mere words convey the grace, beauty, and endearing young charms of the divinity who was their heroine. In

© *Life Publishing Co.*

A BACHELOR'S SUPPER

support of their text, Gibson's pen materialized their dream girl and brought her to warm life on the opposite page.

So, as the answer to the author's prayer, the Gibson Girl at last made her *début* in the pages of the best magazines.

She had been some time making her formal entrance into society, this débutante of 1890 who would claim a whole decade and more for her season. There had been several years of sub-debdom when she was undeveloped and a trifle awkward while the pen that launched her acquired finesse. Now a technique of fine lines, fastidious cross-hatching and subtle shading limned a tall, radiant being, her gaze clear, fearless and direct, her nose slightly and piquantly uptilted. Her lips fine-modelled and alluring. Her soft hair crowning a serene brow and caught up into a dainty *chignon*. The graceful column of her neck rising from the decolletage that barely concealed her delicately-rounded bosom. Her slim waist emphasized by the bodice cut of her gowns, gowns still with the vestige of a bustle and with full, smoothly-fluent skirts—such, in inadequate phrases, was the Gibson Girl in the year when she came out and swept into vast popularity.

She was American womanhood idealized. She was, as has been pointed out, the American Girl glorified, long before the era of Ziegfeldian showmanship. She might, in those days before bathing beauty contests had sordidly commercialized the term, have been called Miss America. In *Life,* where she was thus far known only as the pretty girl C. D. Gibson drew or sometimes as "Penelope Peachblow" (so christened for the popular, delicately-colored peach-blow vase), she was increasing the circulation of that magazine and its male subscribers.

It is a curious fact that in the first specific acknowledgment of her charms the Gibson Girl was forced to appear under an assumed name.

It happened in the guarded pages of *The Century*. Nathalie Harris (Mrs. John Hays Hammond), desiring to describe her heroine in the most glowing terms possible, declared that "she looked like a Gibson Girl." An eagle, proof-reading eye spotted it. Immediately a council of editors convened. The Gibson Girl was not well enough known, they decided, and did not *The Century* stand like the Rock of Gibraltar against all innovations? Blue pencils swung into action. Let the reference be to some imaginary delineator of beauty.

An amazed author, along with other confused readers, learned that the heroine of the story was so beautiful that "she looked like a Goodrich Girl."

III

The Gibson Girl graced the pleasant essays which Charles Dudley Warner wrote for "The Editor's Drawer" of *Harper's*. She retired for a moment when *Scribner's* assigned her artistic sire to illustrate Richard Harding Davis's *Gallegher: A Newspaper Story,* for there were no women in that grand yarn. However, it was *Gallegher* that inaugurated the famous Gibson-Davis collaborations and they filled a striking but more or less unnoticed gap in the Gibson Girl's life.

The Gibson Eden had been peopled in reverse order. It was a paradise enshrining an utterly desirable Eve and lacking an Adam. Nobody seemed to miss him much. If there were a vague male or two on the outskirts, few paid any heed. Men feasting their eyes on the solitary Gibson Girl projected themselves into the picture and in their own opinion filled the vacancy very satisfactorily indeed.

But the Davis stories described heroes who *were* heroes. You could not disregard nor ignore them any more than you could Davis himself. They were the handsome Dick Davis, spun out of the heroic, dramatic stuff that was the essence of that incurable romantic, only slightly touched up by the bright colors which fiction permits, though actuality may dull.

That was the entrance cue for the Gibson Man, greeted by a welcoming chorus from feminine beholders. Gibson haled the not unwilling Davis into his studio and made him pose for his own paladins. At times for the spice of variety, Gibson substituted as a model the dashing James De Kay who was allowed to retain his blond mustache despite the artist's prejudice. Gibson, were it not for his modesty and shyness, might have drawn himself.

They sauntered through *Life,* did these Gibson Men, chivalrous

"Why, it's Gallegher," said the night editor.—Page 170.

From *Scribner's Magazine*

suitors and squires of dames. They performed exploits and achieved adventures through most of the Davis stories, happy in the charming vicinity of *Princess Aline, Miss Catherwaight, Hope* and *Alice Langham* of *Soldiers of Fortune,* and other appealing Davis heroines who were Gibson Girls.

These belles and beaux won vast popularity for the two comrades-in-arts who created them. Gibson was always delighted to illustrate a Davis story and the latter acknowledged his debt in his open-hearted way. "Personally I owe Dana a great deal apart from what I've got out of his friendship," R. H. D. declared. "The aid he has

103

given me in selling my books by means of his illustrations has been incalculable. And this is no idle compliment but purely a' business fact. Where a book of mine without illustrations would sell ten copies, if Dana put a few pictures of long-legged men in it, it would sell twenty."

Gibson and Davis, their ships coming in together, landed to convert their countrymen from medieval fancies; to modernize their castles in the air; to garrison them with knights and ladies of today—with, in fact, the selfsame folk who scanned the Gibson drawings and the Davis stories. Here, in these two gallant young fellows, were Burne-Jones and Tennyson in modern dress. Re-discoverers of an ancient truth—that romance can live more vividly in a prosaic present than a glamorous past—they deserved well of the Republic.

"When Gibson arrived on the scene," wrote H. I. Brock, "romance was yearningly retrospective and fatally haunted with pale seductive echoes from Tennyson's *Idylls of the King.* . . . Richard Harding Davis had also arrived and was finding something just as good as the old romance, not in Gothic tales of knighthood in flower (faded and pressed dry between the leaves of dusty old books), but in the living present.

"That present might be represented by the Man-About-Town in tails and topper (garments with a rare magic spell for the rustic majority then) with, to match his splendor, the girl ivory-shouldered and arrayed in swirling flounces. Or it might be in the outdoors of adventure, associated with riding boots of the latest English cut which the promoters of mines in South America and such places were supposed to wear, and which mightily intrigued a back country as yet unacquainted with pink coats in the hunting field, or any of the fancy toggery that went with them.

"Davis might go where he would. He began as reporter. Gibson also began as reporter. He drew what was right under his eyes.

Mrs. Gibson posed for both girls

And among the things right under his eyes and shouting for attention was the American girl. As in a different garb and other attitudes she has been under the eye of every artist since."

IV

"He drew what was right under his eyes." Gibson, in choosing to picture the contemporary scene, followed the tradition of great draftsmen before him, of Dürer, Daumier, and Hogarth, of Keene, Leech, and Du Maurier. It was not the easier course. The past was safer. As applicable to artists as to writers was *Mr. Dooley's* classic warning: "Th' further ye get away from any peeryod, th' bether ye can write about it. Ye are not subject to interruptions be people that were there."

Risking interruptions, Gibson inscribed true social annals of a vivid epoch seen with a keen and understanding eye and set down by a gifted hand. His pages reveal Americans of the end of the nineteenth and the first of the twentieth century as they lived and moved and had their being. How faithfully he recorded is testified to by the fact that artists today use his drawings as unquestioned reference for authentic details of the period.

Thus with pen devoted to his own day Gibson took prominent place among talented illustrators, ranked as the most brilliant group in the history of American art—a first-rate man among first-rate men. In this golden age of American illustration, his characters played leading parts in a pageant in black-and-white splendidly staged in magazines and books. Out from wings of type, before backgrounds of streets by Pennell, countryside by William Hamilton Gibson, or panoramas by De Thulstrup, trooped a varied and memorable company. Gibson Girls and Men. Abbey's Shakespeareans. Pyle's knights and pirates and Colonials. Remington's Indians and cowboys. Frost's hunters and comical cats. Kemble's coons. Soldiers by Zogbaum and dainty Japanese women by Blum. Dan Beard's *Connecticut Yankee at King Arthur's Court* and Birch's *Little Lord Fauntleroy*. Woolf's waifs, politicians by W. A. Rogers, and fiction-folk by Brennan, Smedley, Sterner, and Reinhart. Such were some of the members of an all-star cast who still stage spirited revivals when bound volumes are opened.

Fine craftsmanship characterized the work of these illustrators. Turn the pages of the best magazines of the period and you tour art galleries in miniature. Look back of the art that conceals art and you may discern that genius which Carlyle defined as an infinite capacity for taking pains. The pen, accurately and exquisitely wielded, was in its prime. Where wash, charcoal, crayon, and oils were used, sloppy, slapdash techniques, as a means of glossing over

AMERICA'S TRIBUTE.

poor draftsmanship, were not tolerated. This was the heyday of black-and-white, with color printing (in more than one or two separate shades) still in the future.

And fine craftsmanship manifest in originals extended through the various mechanical processes of reproduction: plate cutting and engraving and printing. The invention of zinc-cuts and photo-engraving, ending the era of wood blocks, had made cheap and rapid reproduction possible. To the fact that his star had begun to rise just at that moment, Charles Dana Gibson was immeasurably indebted for his widespread popularity. For him, art and science were in fortunate conjunction. Pen—camera—printing press. Not until the coming of motion pictures and radio would there exist comparable media for reaching masses.

V

Pen couched like a lance, in the manner of the knight on *Life's* masthead, Gibson tilted against a foreign foe in 1890, a pennon of red, white, and blue streaming as he charged with patriotic fervor.

The Century sounded the charge by giving him for illustration an anonymous novel entitled *The Anglomaniacs*. For some time only Editor Gilder's sister, through whom it had been confidentially submitted, knew the identity of the author. She was Mrs. Burton Harrison, who as a young matron had come North after the Civil War with her lawyer husband, members of a small army of aristocratic Southerners who added a welcome leaven to New York society. Mrs. Harrison, taking pen in hand for another purpose than polite correspondence, adopted the precaution of anonymity as befitted such a radical step. A remnant of an old taboo lingered. It still was not quite ladylike to write for publication and for money. Furthermore society might resent one of its own writing so unsparingly of its foibles and follies.

NOT ALL IN THE MARKET.

But, as Edith Wharton likewise discovered, society dotes on being paraded in print. Multitudes in the outer darkness were just as eager to read of the whims and extravagances of the elect. Persuaded by popular acclaim for her opus, Mrs. Harrison confessed authorship. She already had privately acknowledged unqualified approval of its illustration with this entry in her diary:

"Have just seen the drawings for the AM's. They are done by Charles Dana Gibson, a new young artist for whom *The Century* people and others predict a brilliant future. I am simply delighted with them. I hear Mr. Gibson says drawing these social types has opened up a new vein to him which he enjoys greatly."

Society was indeed a rich lode. Gibson dug into it with the expertness of one who knew his way around the mine. He was then striding familiarly beneath many striped canopies into candle- and gas-lit ballrooms and treading a measure on polished floors. That ability of his to draw a lady, which Mitchell mentioned, derived from study of fair originals. The personable young Mr. Gibson had been facing them gallantly in *vis-à-vis* chairs and entertaining them in Turkish corners. Society girls, duly chaperoned, were fluttering up to his studio to pose. No wonder the damoiselles in shimmering ballgowns, fancy dress costumes, and billowing skirts and yachting caps he drew for *The Anglomaniacs* looked to the manner born. As for the clothes in which he attired the men characters, those habiliments seemed to have been made in London by a tailor with "special appointment to his Highness, the Prince of Wales."

Gibson's enjoyment of society balked at its Anglomania. That frenzy for anything and everything English was grafting strange embellishments on our native stock. Pink coats and cricket pads. Broad a's and high teas. Canes and the trouser cuffs whose pioneer wearers were taunted with: "Must be raining today in London!" Such innovations might be condoned and some of them even adopted

"TAKE MY ARM, THEN. I 'LL STEADY YOU."

From *The Anglomaniacs*

in due course, but not the Anglomaniacs' burning urge to deck their
family trees with a British or Continental title. That un-American
craze aroused the Gibson ire and scorn. The eagle perched on his
pen and screamed.

History was repeating the yearning which George Washington

TWO BLIND WOMEN

had sternly repulsed when a body of undemocratic fellow-country-men sought to crown him and create an American nobility. Though the Constitution cramped that craving, there was a way around it and the dollar sign showed it. In from the mines and railroads of the West rolled the great fortunes, snowballing through Wall Street, pyramided on New York real estate. Given American heiresses and impoverished peers, the ancient law of demand and supply operated as inevitably as ever. Mothers and daughters went shopping abroad, first for gowns and hats, then for crests and coronets. Plutocratic fathers supplied the sinews vaingloriously or under duress like the one in *The Anglomaniacs* who roared indignantly: "What man wants to work his head off to lay up money and then see a fool and a profligate walk away with it and his daughter into the bargain, so that his grandchildren may have handles to their names and learn to despise America?"

One newspaper published a list of American women deserving, in its profound opinion, a place in the peerage. A confidential agency of San Francisco ran advertisements in German papers offering twenty-million-dollar, home-grown wives to titled foreigners. With fanfares and flourishes, with columns on columns of print, sketches, and photographs, the press chronicled every international wedding. It was futile to protest that the publicity given them was over-lavish, snobbish and un-American. Not only Society but all walks of life devoured every word about them with avidity.

Many a pretty head was turned by the hullabaloo over the triumphs of the ennobled sisterhood. American girls were fascinated by "romances" reminiscent of their childhood's fairy tales of princely heroes. They ignored the fact that many of these modern versions required a commercial twist to make them come true. That the Prince, before he wakened Sleeping Beauty with a kiss, had arranged with her sire for a hefty dowery. That Cinderella's royal lover was

THAT DELICIOUS MOMENT.

WHEN YOU MEET THE NOBLEMAN YOUR DAUGHTER HAS CAPTURED IN EUROPE.

not interested in the fit of her tiny slippers but in her fairy god-mother's ability to foot the bills.

Editorials vainly thundered against these international mesalliances, castigating them for taking money out of the country and branding them as human sacrifices with the bride in the title rôle, as some of them undoubtedly were. But it was the satirists, more than the viewers with alarm, who did yeoman service. Hordes of them rushed into the fray when it was thickest—in 1895, year of magnificent Paget-Whitney, Castellane-Gould, and Marlborough-Vanderbilt nuptials. It was the third which, in its preliminary and final stages, roused the wits to headlong and hilarious charges. The new game at Newport, ran one quip, is "Here we go 'round the Marlborough bush." F. F. Richards in *Life* drew the Duke as a ragged Columbus landing on our shores while the Vanderbilt family as a wealthy Indian tribe offered him their daughter's hand. "The Jook iv Marlburrow," affirmed the inimitable *Mr. Dooley,* "is a young lad an' poor . . . I dunno how he done it, whether th' Ganderbilks asked him 'r he asked thim. Anyhow, it was arranged. 'Twas horse an' horse between thim. The Ganderbilks had th' money, an' he was a jook."

Gibson's pen transfixed title- and heiress-hunters in issue after issue of *Life*. Mitchell did not need to stir him up for that campaign. The artist was bellicose, fired by the Spirit of '76. This pursuit of American girls by dukes, belted earls, and such looked to him like a belated but sinister British revenge for the Revolution. As a patriot, he was bound to fight it. It wasn't the money annexed by the fortune-hunters that he minded. But when a dissipated, decadent, calculating nobleman wed an American girl for her fortune and treated her like a slave after he had it—that was more than could be contemplated by Charles Dana Gibson. American girls (especially pretty ones) for Americans. Marriage for love, not for love of money. That was

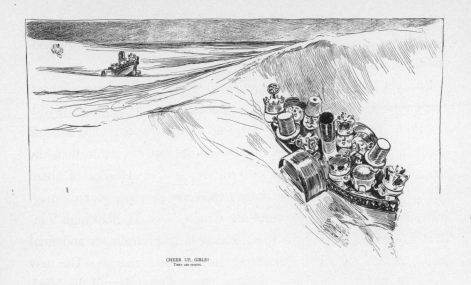

CHEER UP, GIRLS!
They are coming.

part and parcel of the Gibson philosophy and the heart and soul of the Gibson graphic saga.

He was resolved to defend his countrywomen to the last drop of ink against all comers from *Burke's Peerage* or the *Almanack de Gotha*, and the satiric eloquence of the scores of drawings he produced reveal the strength of his feeling. *America's Tribute* depicted the British lion, diadem perched on his lordly mane, entering an arena where knelt, half in appeal, half in terror, a group of beautiful girl victims. *Two Blind Women* showed an American bride leaving the church with her titled husband, while a sightless beggar woman sat forlorn at the portal. In *Cheer up, Girls! They Are Coming*, boatloads of grotesquely comic counts and baronets were seen steaming across the Atlantic to the American gold fields. Another drawing pictured Gibson Girls pitching rings for canes in a carnival booth, each cane top the head of a leering, monocled scion of the nobility. Gibson's genius for expressions was never better exemplified than by the starkly tragic look on the face of the fine old American in *When You Meet the Nobleman Your Daughter Has Captured in Europe:* a father confronted by a beaming wife and queenly daugh-

THIS CAN HAPPEN.

THE AMERICAN FATHER MAY BE AMAZED AT FINDING HIS ENGLISH SON-IN-LAW NOT AN UNDESIRABLE ARTICLE.

ter with a miserably puny trophy brought down in the House of Lords. Not a few counterparts of the protagonist in that picture must have groaned over it in apprehension or retrospection.

The keen-edged weapon of ridicule, as wielded by Gibson and others of the home guard, was never completely victorious, for it clashed against the mighty instincts of vanity and acquisitiveness. Yet those motives had been thoroughly unmasked, hysteria quelled, and much ground gained.

When Gibson visited London a few years later, he fraternized with the foe. He liked the English and they liked him and his London and American drawings. Coals of fire were heaped on his head by one English critic who remarked that a nobleman to Mr. Gibson was a bully, idiot, monkey, roué, and not much of a gentleman, but the defamer was, nevertheless, an artist of great talent. The Gibson Girl's creator could hardly resent it when members of the British peerage professed a lively admiration for her.

Few men can help but be mollified by kind words. Yet the concessions Gibson made cannot be laid to blandishments nor construed as abandonment of a cause. It was simply that one whose sense of fair play was always strong came to see another side of the picture.

Great Britain, it dawned upon him, preferred that her title-holders marry within the realm. Fortune-seeking was not the motive for every westward march of the peers, and numbers of them were undamaged by purple and ermine. Gibson, who once had employed a line from *The Mikado* to advantage, might have illustrated a stanza from *Iolanthe* after his London sojourn, for he had learned to

> Spurn not the nobly born
> With love affected,
> Nor treat with virtuous scorn
> The well-connected.

High rank invites no shame—
We boast an equal claim
With him of humble name
To be respected!

In a spirit of *noblesse oblige,* an enlightened artist began sketching such pictures as: *This Can Happen. The American Father May Be*

THE LATEST NOBLEMAN.
"Girls, girls, don't press his Grace! He can only take one of you, and with him it is purely a matter of business."

Amazed at Finding his English Son-in-law not an Undesirable Article, wherein a rugged old gentleman collapses into the butler's arms as his child presents a handsome Briton, as upstanding as any Gibson Man. Later one of *Mr. Pipp's* fair daughters was permitted to marry happily into the British aristocracy.

Be it said, to lull base suspicions, that the Anglo-Gibson entente was cemented years before a sister-in-law of the party of the second part became Lady Astor.

LIFE'S SUNDAY VISIT TO THE METROPOLITAN MUSEUM.
SUGGESTED AS A GOOD DESIGN FOR A TAPESTRY TO BE HUNG IN THAT PROGRESSIVE INSTITUTION.

VI

While he was launching his attack against bargains in blue-blood, Gibson was also hotly engaged in battle against a blue law.

The Metropolitan Museum of Art, New York City, was closed Sundays tightly and traditionally and every effort to open this oyster with its pearls of art had failed signally for more than twenty years. In 1871 two subscriptions were made on a written pledge that the institution would never unlock its doors on the Sabbath "as a place of amusement." Even the telling arguments of Joseph H. Choate proved futile at a board meeting in 1880. Adamant trustees tabled his resolution. Backed by many clergymen and Sabbath unions and prudently fearing the withdrawal of support, the trustees sternly resisted pressure by the public and the press. It was in vain for the irreverent to point out that the museum soothed the spirit as no dull sermon could, or for the realists to observe that patronage of art on Sundays was preferable to patronage of saloons.

Although a concession of opening the museum evenings was wrung from its authorities finally, that did not suffice. Sunday was the only possible day for many potential visitors.

The press continued its campaign, with Mitchell's *Life* in the van and Gibson its standard-bearer. He drew a double-page, *Life's Museum of Humbugs*. Therein were exhibited Howells' novels (to the artist's later regret); Ben Harrison and Republican elephant; Henry M. Stanley (not, of course, on the score of his gallant rescue of Livingstone but because of the advertising testimonials he signed); Ward McAllister, society's major domo; Mrs. Potter, relegated to the Chamber of Horrors for shocking people with *'Ostler Joe;* the Kendalls, an English stage couple, depicted as marionettes for acting love scenes with such stiff propriety that Queen Victoria was pleased, —and a set of highly unflattering busts of the trustees of the Metropolitan Museum.

THE METROPOLITAN MUSEUM STILL CLOSES ITS DOORS SUNDAYS AGAINST THE WORKING PEOPLE.

BUT IT IS TO BE HOPED THAT CHARITY AND PROGRESS, ASSISTED BY *LIFE* MAY IN TIME HAVE SOME INFLUENCE OVER THE SPIRIT THAT SEEMS TO GOVERN THAT INSTITUTION.

· L I F E ·

SUNDAY AT THE METROPOLITAN MUSEUM.

Chorus of Trustees: Very narrow minded old cranks are we,
Just as pious as pious can be;
For the laboring man we don't care a D,
And he SHAN'T get in to his own Musee!

Again Gibson pilloried those unhappy gentlemen, representing them as a gloomy and sanctimonious glee club chanting this chorus:

Very narrow-minded old cranks are we,
Just as pious as we can be.
For the laboring men we don't care a D,
And he shan't get in to his own musee!

Hammer and tongs, Gibson kept at it and at last the assault of the allies succeeded. The governing board yielded and the museum swung wide its gates in 1891. One trustee wrathfully resigned. A bequest for $50,000 and other financial support was cancelled. However, a legislative grant was made for expenses, and Sunday became the day of largest attendance.

A descendant of the Cottons and other Puritans had played a prominent part in breaking the old-time Sabbath.

CHAPTER VIII

SOCIAL REGISTRAR

I

It was in these early years of his social cartooning that Gibson performed the feat of changing critics into models. While it was a trick any artist might envy, Gibson was inspired to it more by gallantry than guile. A pretty young thing, looking up saucily into his eyes at a party one evening, told him she had not liked a picture of his—the one of a girl foreswearing the world, the flesh, and the devil for Lent. That girl, declared the fair critic, was not at all stylish-looking, and one should be, Lent or not.

Young Mr. Gibson, who was inclined to agree with all pretty young things, admitted his fault, but hastened to tell this one how she could help him avoid it in the future. If only she would come up to his studio and pose for a drawing, the girl in *that* picture would be so attractive and *à la mode* that nobody could complain.

Of course she was delighted to come. Somehow the word got around. Another daring maiden pointed out that Mr. Gibson had gravely erred in a matter which might be forgiven a mere man but not a delineator of well-dressed women. He had actually drawn an overskirt longer in front than in back. This mistake also was corrected by means of a study of a properly draped overskirt and its wearer. In the same mutually enjoyable manner was disarmed another critic who justly objected that the Gibson Girls in last week's *Life* seemed to have patronized a tinsmith, not a modiste, for their gowns.

So it went. New York society girls and girls from out of town gathered each her chaperon and repaired to the studio in the Alpine Building, there to pose their prettiest before the Gibson drawing

HIGH CHURCH OBSERVANCES
THE NIGHT BEFORE LENT

board. Helen Benedict and Rita Hone of New York, Lizzie Lynch of Flushing, Maude Bennett and Lucy Beamis of Boston, Netta Pinchot and Betty and Helen Campbell of Philadelphia were among the volunteer models who appeared incognito in Gibson drawings. Sometimes a girl who had caused the artist a heart throb might be pictured carrying a bag with her initials on it. However, likenesses were unmistakable, and a young lady could leave a copy of *Life,* open at the important page, on her library table and not fail to be pleasingly identified by callers. To be drawn, even anonymously, as a Gibson Girl was as thrilling as to be chosen one of the favored débutantes whose miniatures were commissioned painted by that perennial old beau, Peter Marié, for his private collection of American beauties.

Equally obliging models were the young lawyers, literary and business men who dropped in at the studio of their friend Dana Gibson. Albert La Montaigne, Tompkins McIlvaine, Eugene O'Sullivan, Jim DeKay, Dick Davis, and the rest were ordered to march up to the stand and strike an attitude in their best man-about-town or cotillion leader manner. Now and then one of them arrived with his lady love and posed with her to illustrate a sentimental he-and-she joke for *Life* such as:

> Will you share my lot, Penelope?
> Yes, if there is a brownstone front on it.

or

> HE: I have three thousand a year. You could certainly live on that.
> SHE: Yes: but I should hate to see *you* starve.

To the volunteer models it was all a great lark—a combination charade, *tableau vivant,* and the taking of a sort of glorified tintype. Although the chaperons had cause to feel neglected, the young artist who had suffered from their omnipresence felt justified in

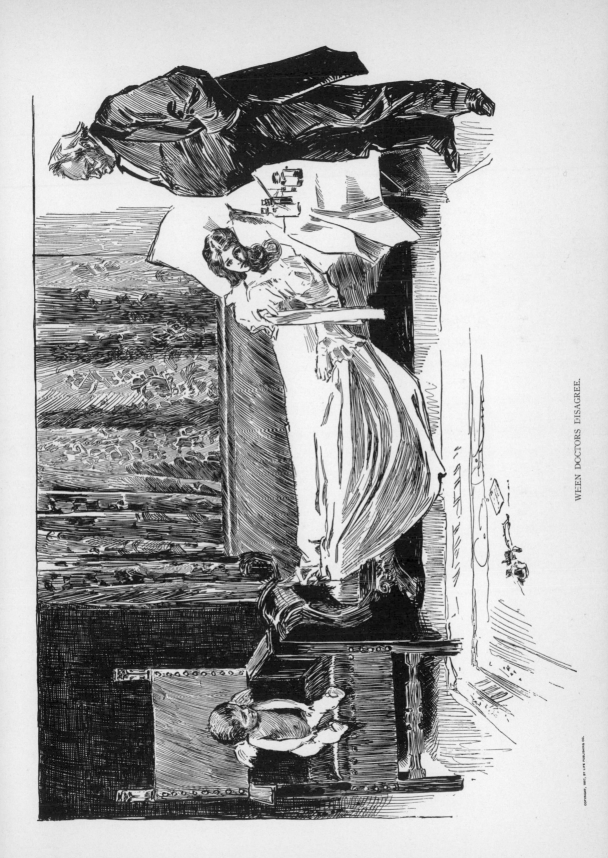

WHEN DOCTORS DISAGREE.

letting lovers escape from them in his pictures. Gibson's pretty youngest sister, Josephine, entered both into his drawings and the spirit of the occasion, posing whenever a little girl was needed as in *The Bachelor's Supper* and the *Van Bibber* story, *Her First Appearance*. Only babies were unavailable as models for this bachelor artist. His attempts to "fake" them—*Life's* cupid, for instance— were sketchy until Dan Beard paternally instructed him that babies are long-waisted and short-legged, not vice versa.

As a result of first aid from the social register, the young ladies and gentlemen who paraded through Gibson's cartoons and illustrations were undeniably authentic. Which fact was duly acknowledged as follows in an 1892 review of his work.

"Mr. Gibson," it ran, "is a young man with a clever pencil and a large number of friends—men and women who own very smart clothes and know how to wear them. Exactly how much of his success he owes to the latter would be difficult to say—probably a great deal. While it is a very easy thing to procure a model for Venus in the costume or lack of costume in which she is usually shown, or a man who looks a Hercules, it is a most difficult thing to find professional models who will carry themselves or wear their clothes like members of Mr. McAllister's One Hundred and Fifty. Mr. Gibson's friends have solved this difficulty by frequently posing for the characters in his sketches."

That was true as far as it went. Gibson was indeed fortunate in having his source material walk in and present itself; in having his costume references animated before his eyes. What the reviewer had failed to note was the fact that the volunteer system is as undependable in art as it is in war. Gibson's society friends were blessings as models but not unmixed ones. He soon learned that it was the part of folly to pose a young lady, used to considerable attention, and forget her for an hour while he concentrated on his drawing. Too many of his amateur sitters held the stage conception of a studio as a pleasant club, an annex to Bohemia where the artist, rarely afflicted by labor,

gave most of his talents to providing atmosphere and entertainment. That idea must be discouraged if he were to accomplish anything.

With their patrician good looks, their air of being to the manner born, Gibson's friends did him an invaluable service in giving him, as he expressed it, his latitude and longitude. Once he had his bearings, he was forced to keep on his course with less distinguished but more amenable help.

So most of the characters in the Gibson society drawings were professional models. Although ballrooms, formal dinner parties, and opera boxes were outside their orbits, in the Gibson drawings they graced every occasion with distinction. They played their parts, as good models can, and Gibson's pen transformed them with magical strokes into a fashionable aristocracy. Some of the girl models needed little more than faithful portraiture to represent them as belles of the ball, especially the Irish-American beauty, Minnie Clark, also a model for Saint-Gaudens and William Merritt Chase, and the loveliest Gibson Girl of the early '90's.

At times Gibson provided gowns from the wardrobe of cast-offs given him by friends. More often the models, dressed with the smartness of the average American girl, required no borrowed plumage, since Gibson was able to embellish and adapt. Gibson Girls were attired in the most becoming fashions their creator observed, plus little innovating touches in the tilt of a hat, the set of a sleeve or the hang of a skirt, which actually set new styles. In a day when published reports of the Parisian modes were still only rudimentary, Gibson drawings were favorite fashion plates, and they were accused of competing with Butterick patterns. Clothes, while they did not make the Gibson Girl, always enhanced her charms. A search of his work reveals only two nudes: one a statue in a street scene, the other an Eve modestly masked by foliage.

Models liked to work for C. D. Gibson. He was one of the first artists to pay a model, once engaged, whether the light was good or not; to pay for a half-day though the drawing might have been finished in less. Though exacting, he was invariably considerate. That, he believed, was only self-interest, since an artist's accomplishment could not help but be influenced by his model's mood. Whether or not an artist and his model were, as Gibson phrased it, "on the

SOCIAL NUISANCES.

THE MOTHER WHO ALLOWS YOU TO ADMIRE THE BABY.

same wire," accounted in his opinion for most of the good pictures in the world and most of the bad ones.

To many people, a studio, like the stage, was fraught with sinful glamor. Prurient imaginations pictured the privacy of the atelier as a cloak for clandestine lovemaking and assorted high jinks. The business man (seldom assisted in the '90's by attractive secretaries and stenographers) was both suspicious and envious of the lot of the artist for whom pretty models posed nude in line of duty.

In an attempt to base such popular innuendoes on fact, the *New York World* once sent a girl reporter to various studios to masquerade as a model. Canny Dan Beard gave her a difficult pose no amateur could hold and dismissed her when she failed. The cause of yellow journalism was no more successful at Gibson's studio. When the girl after making various advances provocatively asked his help in fastening her dress and it was gently and impersonally given, she tearfully confessed the trick she had been assigned to play for the sake of sensationalism.

II

"Don't you find New York society empty and unsatisfactory?" one Gibson character on the cover of *Life* asked another.

"Not necessarily," came the answer. "You can take your choice in that respect. There is the Bohemian set, all brains and no style; society proper with a fair amount of each, and 'The Four Hundred,' all style and no brains."

However endowed mentally or modishly, society in all its phases was the source of inspiration for hundreds of drawings by Charles Dana Gibson, drawings which uniquely record the American social scene from 1890 on into the second decade of the twentieth century. A panorama in black and white, they passed from drawing-board through printing press into the pages of magazines and books to become the valuable artistic archives of a period.

They are more than accurate annals, more than pretty pictures, more than fashion plates. Most of them, appearing singly as cartoons in magazines, had to be pointed; had to convey a satiric, romantic, or amusing idea. Consequently each tells a tale and might be termed the art equivalent of a chapter in an historical novel. In

A LITTLE STORY.
BY A SLEEVE.

them you see modes and manner in action. *A Little Story by a Sleeve,* for instance, does more than inform that leg-of-mutton sleeves were fashionable in the '90's; it reveals that for a couple caught in a conservatory just after an embrace, leg-of-mutton sleeves could be a crushing betrayal.

These society cartoons are drawn of course from one man's viewpoint but it is a singularly comprehensive one. Gibson contemplated his subject with the detached and amused tolerance of *Life's* cupid or *Puck's* Ariel exclaiming, "What fools these mortals be!" as well as from the vantage point of the insider. His birth and breeding gave him the entrée to society, yet he never was made dizzy by the social whirl. He was as bitterly aware of its snobbery and artificiality as he was keenly appreciative of its admirable elements: the charm of gracious living, of courtesy and dignity, the cultured heritage of wealth and leisure.

It was Gibson's good fortune that for the first decade or so of his experience the social stage was never more picturesquely set. Gorgeous backdrops were never lacking: Fifth Avenue chateaus, palazzos, and brownstone mansions for dinner parties and receptions; Trinity, Grace Church, St. George's, St. Thomas's, and St. Bartholomew's for fashionable weddings; Delmonico's, Sherry's, and the Waldorf-Astoria for balls and cotillions; the Metropolitan Opera and Madison Square Garden; those favored watering places of the *haut monde*—Newport, Saratoga, Bar Harbor, Lenox, Tuxedo, White Sulphur, Narragansett, Old Point Comfort. Amid the grandeur of such scenery were performed the pageants, comedies, farces, and extravaganzas of society, which were reproduced by Gibson with such infinite zest.

Further to his advantage was the spotlight of national attention. A vast and heterogeneous audience was intently absorbed in the performances of society, at this period a good show due for a long New York run and not yet split up into many, mediocre vaudeville acts. Not only was society pleasantly preoccupied with dramatizations of its own activities but the provincial balconies and the plebeian galleries were equally entranced. It was a phenomenon of American democracy then at its height, due to decline but not to disappear.

The New York families of Dutch descent, New York's oldest aristocracy, never figured by name in Gibson's social comedies. His cast was anonymous with a single exception. He could not escape billing one star—Ward McAllister, society's capable master of ceremonies and guardian of the gates. "Dude" McAllister, Lord High Separator of the Sheep from the Goats, whose estimate of the capac-

· LIFE ·

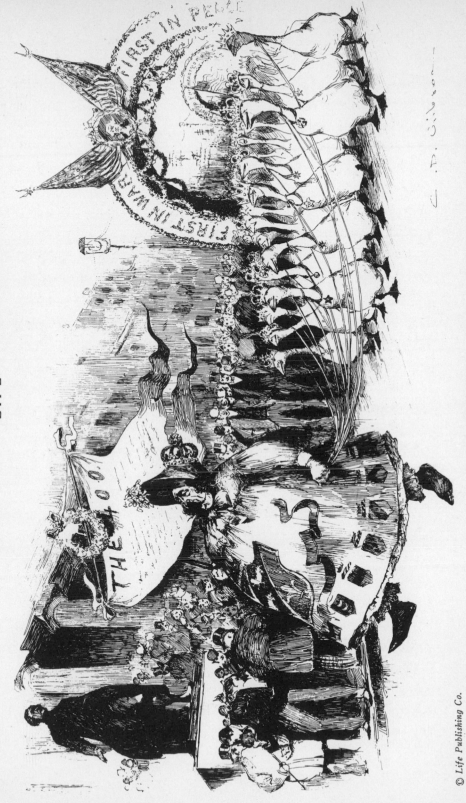

FOR THE CENTENNIAL PARADE.

SINCE THE UNFORTUNATE MR. WARD McALLISTER HAS NOTHING ELSE TO DO, WHY NOT ALLOW HIM TO EMBELLISH THE PROCESSION?

© Life Publishing Co.

ity of Mrs. Astor's ballroom created "The Four Hundred," later reduced by him to a super-select One Hundred and Fifty.

Pompous, arrogant and toplofty, called "the greatest snob that ever lived," McAllister was an ideal butt for the slings and arrows of outrageous satire from all sides. With what was either sublime indifference or sly appreciation of the publicity, he stood the fire and constantly exposed himself to more. He submitted fondly to the photographer and inevitably to the caricaturist. Proud of his fancied resemblance to the Prince of Wales, he could not have been greatly annoyed when *Life* proposed to run Ward McAllister and Albert E. Wettin of Wales on a society ticket for President and Vice-President of the United States. Whoops of joy from the humorists greeted the appearance of his naïvely self-revealing book, *Society As I Have Found It. Life,* beneath a sketch of a patrolman dragging two inebriates in evening togs before a police captain, jested:

CAPTAIN: What's that you've got, O'Hara?
ROUNDSMAN O'HARA: Society as Oi have found it, sorr.

Gibson gleefully opened fire on the symbolic Mr. McAllister, picturing him (drawn behind a magnifying glass to insure his being seen at all) as riding on a hobby horse at the head of a parade of "The Four Hundred." Each marcher appeared with tabards and banners emblazoned with his escutcheon. Fur pelts, lumber, groceries, and money bags were among the designs on these coats-of-arms of American aristocracy. Again, McAllister was depicted as an old woman ladling out "society slush" to pedigreed poultry, and once more Gibson drew him as goose girl herding a flock of the élite. Reprinting the latter cartoon with a big goose substituted for the goose girl, *Life* remarked that perhaps the first version had been slanderous. Whether it was slanderous to the "Autocrat of Drawing-Rooms" or to goose girls, the impudent magazine did not state. At any rate, there was no doubt whom the big goose represented.

THE MERRY-GO-ROUND.

But a few years later the cartoonist was willing to draw his victim as a bird of a different feather and award him the proverbial wisdom of the owl. As a judge of feminine beauty, McAllister's taste was excellent. Gibson never questioned it nor ceased to be grateful for it when its possessor invited a certain lovely young girl from Virginia to lead the grand march in the Patriarch's Ball.

III

The cover drawing of Gibson's book, *The Social Ladder,* depicts a comely maiden most becomingly gowned who smiles at the object she holds in one dainty hand. It is a tiny ladder up which a silk-hatted donkey is laboriously and zealously climbing.

Money, which makes the mare go, made the ass climb. The Gold Rush on society was at its height in the '90's. Fortunes were spent, every wire pulled, no stratagem left untried by frenzied aspirants to the charmed circle. One powerful, new-rich Wall Street operator, after futile attempts to be placed on a jealously-guarded invitation list to an annual ball, threatened its board of governors with financial reprisals unless he were included. Perforce they yielded, but when the financier attended the function, he found only a few guests present; society had boycotted him and the ball. With such stubborn tenacity on both sides was the battle fought, the exclusive old guard slowly but inevitably retreating. As early as 1890, *Life* chuckled that "The Four Hundred" had risen to "The Fifteen Hundred" because Wall Street got control and watered the stock.

Gibson hated snobs, and the most insufferable snobs of all were social climbers who had "arrived." He would not mourn for the fate of "The Four Hundred," yet successful efforts to make wealth synonymous with social position offended his sense of the fitness of things. Therefore he pictured the climber's progress as pitilessly as Hogarth did the rake's, with the former lots less fun *en route.*

MRS. STEELE POOLE'S HOUSEWARMING.

Gibson's socially ambitious dowagers were purse-proud, be-jewelled, obnoxious creatures, plump or scrawny, who lorded it over wisps of husbands. These downtrodden consorts, providers of the pelf to buy a way into the company of the elect, were captains of industry, but they were led by the nose. Meekly and wearily they followed their dominant halves up mountains of money bags and skulls or helped pick-axe a passage into the homes of offish aristocrats. Climbers met shattering rebuffs as depicted in that caustic cartoon, *Mrs. Steele-Poole's Housewarming,* wherein an ugly, over-dressed hostess is seated in a great ornate hall, alone save for yawning flunkeys, and waiting for guests who would never come. Nor was the goal, as Gibson perceived it, worth the costly, heart-breaking struggle. In *The Merry-go-round,* successful climbers plod dismally and eternally around a coin-strewn ring. And then there is that cartoon which shows the shallow triumph of a wasted old dame reclining in a magnificent bed and gloating over the society column notices of her gowns and gems read to her by—in cruel contrast— a freshly pretty young maid servant.

Sham and venality as rungs of the social ladder were abhorrent enough to Gibson. But he wielded his pen most savagely when youth and love were sacrificed in a "suitable" marriage to social ambition and wealth. The intensity of his feeling is clear in all his drawings on this favorite theme of his.

A calculating dowager proudly watches her beautiful daughter wed to a dissipated scion of the aristocracy, the bride's hands bound, the minister's eyes blindfolded. An heiress, perched on a heap of gold, forlornly awaits bidders. A young wife, seated by her garrulous, doddering spouse, is far away in her thoughts, and the caption warns her: "These young girls who marry oldish millionaires should not be wandering over the plains with impecunious cowboys when their husbands are trying to entertain them." In that memorable

HIS EVER-LASTING EXPERIMENTS—WITH ILL-MATED PAIRS.

drawing, *His Everlasting Experiments with Ill-mated Pairs,* one cupid drives a coach through the snow while others tumble despairingly from its top. Dragging it in harness are joined unhappy men and women, some struggling on, some reeling or fallen—youth linked with age, grief with drunkenness, lovers yoked apart yearning for each other. Into these drawings, straight from the artist's

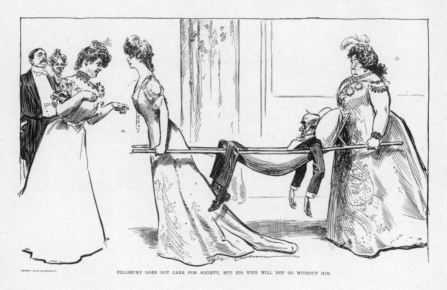

PILLSBURY DOES NOT CARE FOR SOCIETY, BUT HIS WIFE WILL NOT GO WITHOUT HIM.

heart went pity and scorn and burning indignation that such things should be.

Most of the Gibson social chronicles are in a lighter vein. Still in one of the most amusing groups of these a strong undercurrent of sympathy is evident. Never a butterfly in his younger days and somewhat of a hermit later on, Gibson was convinced that society and its obligations might bear down rather too heavily on husbands and fathers and he said so humorously in black and white. He drew the husband who wants to go home early from a party and the wife who doesn't. He sighed graphically for the socially exhausted

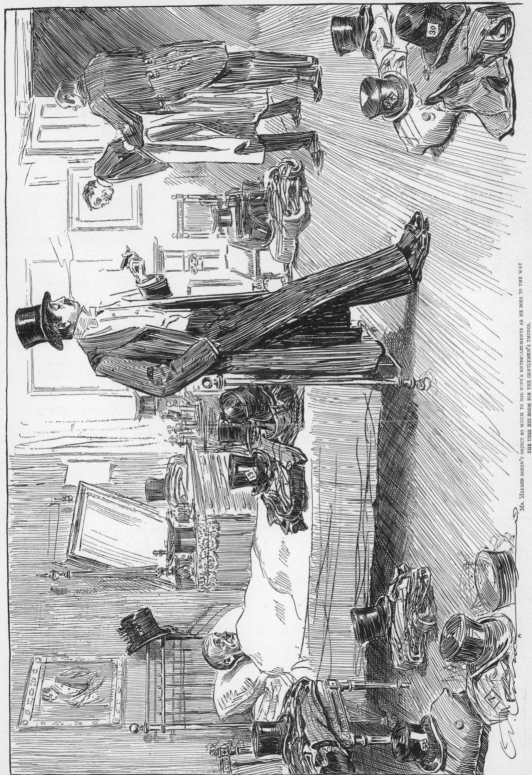

MR. MEEKER DOESN'T OBJECT SO MUCH TO HIS WIFE'S ENTERTAINMENTS AS HE DOES TO THE WAY
SHE USES HIS ROOM FOR THE GENTLEMEN'S THINGS.

gentleman borne willy-nilly to the ball on a stretcher, with his determined wife and daughter as the stretcher-bearers. He deplored the lot of conscripts marched to musicales where they were only a bird in a gilded chair. He proclaimed the joy of the average female adorning herself for a fancy-dress party and the stubborn but futile resistance of the average male. What, he suggested feelingly, was the financial damage of finery for the ladies of one's household compared to the acute embarrassment a man suffered when dragged into the terrifying haunts of dressmakers and forced to witness the mysteries? That even a plea of fatigue might not save a host was demonstrated both hilariously and pathetically in the picture of the poor old chap who has retired, only to have his bedroom made the gentleman's cloakroom and his very bed—and he in it—used as a hat and coat rack by grinning guests.

It was a crusade which culminated in the sore trials of *Mr. Pipp* in society abroad. Everywhere multitudes of socially involved husbands and fathers gave it their heartfelt, though guarded, approval.

Nor did Gibson forget backstairs. His social gallery, without a competent domestic staff, would have been as inadequate as society itself. So solemn butlers and trim maids staffed his pictures and, as in *An Imitation of the Lady of the House,* relaxed in the absence of their employers. How strongly Gibson's drawings appealed to the servants' hall is illustrated by Wallace Irwin's story of a party at the home of Everett Shinn at which Gibson was the guest of honor. During a musical program, Shinn led Irwin into the hall and ordered, "Look at that." The servants, all Swedes, were gazing rapturously through a crack in the door, their blue eyes focused on the honored guest. The oldest one, the cook, whispered, "Meester Shinn, please before de party is over could ve shake hands vit Meester Gibson? Ve could write back to Sveden and say ve haf met de greatest man in America."

STUDIES IN EXPRESSION.

AN IMITATION OF THE LADY OF THE HOUSE.

IV

But gentlemen-in-waiting, designing dowagers, snobs, callow youths, foreign noblemen, long-haired social lions, and the rest were only minor characters. To Gibson, ladies fair were the glory of society —or of any institution, for that matter—and society's real *raison d'être* was to supply a brilliant setting for beauty and romance.

So pretty girls played the leading rôle in the Gibson social cartoons, as pretty girls so often do in art, letters, and life. They gathered armsful of favors at the cotillions. Flanking a young man at a dinner party, they made his head spin like a top in an effort to talk to them both. They queened it in an opera box, thoughtfully enclosed by the artist with plate glass, since the dear things *would* talk during the music. Before Lent they were gay, during it they were fashionably penitential and afterwards gayer than ever. As rival beauties, they greeted each other with cordial handshakes, while free hands held axes behind their backs. With charming hesitancy, they took the arms of dinner partners, embarrassed swains whose proposals of marriage they had refused the night before. During Leap Year, they turned the tables on the other sex, usurping its prerogatives. They were demurely aware that they were the chief exhibit at the Horse Show and that the quadrupeds in the ring went unnoticed except by a few horsey folk.

"Are you exhibiting in the Horse Show this year?" one gentleman asked another in a *Life* joke.

"Yes," the second answered. "I'm sending my daughter."

The assemblage gave heed when Alfred Gwynne Vanderbilt, president of the Horse Show Association, resplendent in gray topper and box coat, high-enthroned on the box of his coach, sceptre-whip in hand, tooled his four famous grays around the ring, with the guard blowing flourishes on his long trumpet. That was a

THE HORSE SHOW.
How the animals appear from the boxes.

1893

WILD ENTHUSIASM AT THE HORSE SHOW.
During a critical event in the ring.

1897

spectacle worth the watching. But let the Duchess of Marlborough enter the Garden and no horseman or horse had a chance; Her Grace's box was almost mobbed. The crowd streaming around the promenade turned eyes outward toward the boxes, not inward toward the arena.

Ladies fair and their cavaliers sometimes tried to suit their conversation to the occasion. They commented carelessly on the turnout of phaetons, rockaways, surreys, spiders, *dos-a-dos* and *vis-à-vis* carts. Their talk sounded knowingly horsey. "That brood mare girths awfully well. . . . That chestnut stands over a lot of ground, don't you think. . . . Just the sort to pop a sixteen-stone man over a five-bar gate and not feel it. . . . Ah, there's what I call a rare stamp of a cob. . . . There's the makings of a grand mare in that youngster" . . . and so on and on. Anyway, it was a good bluff and only the listening grooms grinned discreetly behind their hands. Soon enough the subject veered to frocks, the funny people from out of town at Del's last night, and the Waldorf's Horse Show ball, with its mass of fascinatingly appropriate favors.

Gibson social butterflies as partners or opponents ruined the bridge game of hopelessly enamored and distracted young men. Their pre-announced appearance as Juliet at a fancy dress party recruited regiments of Romeos. If sometimes they proved heartless, they repented swiftly and rushed out into a winter night in their ball gowns to rescue poor, abandoned cupids, prone in the snow. Or their blushes furnished the answer in *Puzzle: Find the Girl Who Has Just Been Kissed.*

V

An artist laureate, equally with a poet, is entitled to his perquisites. Society appreciatively conferred them on Charles Dana Gibson by making a social event of his first exhibition.

When friends with difficulty persuaded Gibson to this venture, the small gallery of Sanchez & Miller on West Twenty-third Street accepted the show. The artist's hopes were not high. The two young men who recently had opened the gallery would, he thought, have exhibited anything for a starter.

From the outset the showing was a great success. Society flocked to it. The girls and men who had posed for Gibson arrived in force,

© *Life Publishing Co.*

PUZZLE

A funny story. Find the Englishman

brought their friends and made it the talk of the town. Subscribers to *Life* and other magazines for which Gibson drew and authors and readers of books he had illustrated swelled the attendance. Sixty of the twenty- by eighteen-inch originals sold at prices ranging from $20 to $200. Stanford White paid $1,000 for a group of drawings to decorate a hotel he was building at Garden City, Long Island. Prestige and sales were augmented by later showings in Boston, Philadelphia, and Chicago.

Critics called some of his figures out of drawing and Gibson took note for remedy. Others quarrelled with his choice of subject. He was entirely on the wrong track, one complainant declared, in "wasting himself on a debauch of summer girls, nicely-modelled, suitably-frocked creatures for whom one has a tolerable admiration. But it is rather sad. Gibson is the greatest of American cartoonists. This is his *métier* and he has no business fooling about with the petticoated prettiness of the summer girl."

THE UNAPPRECIATIVE AUDIENCE

An old gentleman describes his grandchildren

Gibson, the objector continued, was a funny dog in the old days when he drew for Wolcott Balestier of *Tid-Bits*. It was a pity that an artist who could put more expression into the little, leering eyes of the G. O. P. elephant than most artists could get into a human face should decline to the portrayal of the society girl.

The lady or the elephant, the lady or the tiger? Beauty or the beast? The choice had been easy for Gibson. In the spring a young man's fancy does not lightly turn to thoughts of politics. The critic's asseveration went unheeded, and campaigns and national issues were for the most part ignored until woman suffrage gave the Gibson Girl the vote.

In devoting so much of the work of his pen to the social scene and its loveliest ornaments, Gibson followed the path of Du Maurier and other great social satirists. The further he followed it, the broader he found it. Only part of it was marked "Fifth Avenue." Most of the signs read "Main Street."

RIVAL BEAUTIES

CHAPTER IX

DISCOVERY AT A FAIR

I

A Gibson Uncle Sam—one of the best conceptions of that revered figure—stood hesitant in a *Life* center page. Would he offer his World's Fair bouquet to the beauteous Miss New York or to the ugly, parvenu Miss Chicago?

An acrimonious contest was waged over Uncle Sam's favor. Slurs flew west and east. New York partisans, sniffing that uncouth Chicago was no place for an exposition showing the advance of civilization, quoted a sentence from the *Arabian Nights* against their Illinois rival: "Nor are there in this city any who understand science or writing or aught save money-getting."

Speaking of money-getting, Chicagoans retorted, once let Tammany Hall get its clutches on so vast an enterprise as the Fair and enough wampum would flow into the war chest to swamp the whole G. O. P.

That telling argument registered strongly with Republican legislators. Anti-Tammany *Life* could not ignore it nor could it sanction the proposal of Central Park as the site for the Fair in New York City. Another Gibson cartoon pictured Miss New York forbidding the Fair her cherished park which would not have recovered for years from the devastation. Therefore when Congress awarded the prize to the middlewestern metropolis, the Fair was gracefully relinquished in a third Gibson drawing wherein Miss Chicago (how the lady's looks had improved!) was crowned with laurel by *Life's* cherub.

No wonder the exhibition was victoriously called the Chicago World's Fair, though its proper title was The World's Columbian

TO THE CITY OF CHICAGO.

WITH *Life's* HEARTY CONGRATULATIONS ON THE ARTISTIC CONSUMMATION OF A GREAT WORK.

Exposition in honor of the great sailor from Genoa who four centuries before had sighted a land named for another man. However, it was considered that a Scandinavian artist went too far when he sent to the Fair his painting entitled, "Leif Eriksson Discovers America."

In spite of slights to the shade of Columbus, the spirit of discovery still was rampant at the Fair. There the Old World rediscovered the New, and the New was startled out of its isolation into international consciousness. Americans came to a sudden, awed, and stimulating realization of their own national capacities and achievements. Most amazing of all was overwhelming evidence that the fine arts, so long deemed peculiar to the Old World, were flourishing on our soil. Columbus, learning it was not India he had reached after all, could not have been more surprised than the average American citizen when his eyes beheld the native art triumphs of the Fair.

Gibson returned from a second trip abroad to join the mighty migration converging on Chicago. Saint-Gaudens' former apprentice and Post's one-time protégé may have felt some momentary qualms on his choice of the pen when he gazed upon the spectacular statuary and imposing buildings which had risen as if by enchantment on the shores of Lake Michigan. Here was the dream city of sculptors and architects come true. Their brightest visions had materialized, and it did not matter greatly that the spell would break and all this splendor vanish like a mirage in a year and a day. Marshalled by D. H. Burnham, C. B. Atwood, and J. W. Root, architects had raised palaces, pleasure domes, and pavilions in dazzling white and sumptuous color. They had revelled in vistas and prospects and had the time of their lives. For once sculptors forgot to be envious of the glory that was Greece and the grandeur that was Rome. Gibson's friend, Frederick MacMonnies, let genius

SKETCHES AT THE FAIR
SOME ELECTRIC EFFECTS.

soar on a colossal group: Father Time steering a galley; eight maidens, symbolizing the arts and sciences, bending to the oars; Fame conning a course in the bow, and Columbia bearing a torch enthroned above all. Daniel Chester French reared a statue of the Republic. Approaches were decorated with elks by A. P. Proctor and such a concourse of other American fauna—buffalos, bears, and mountain lions, that visitors to the exposition might well have gone away chanting, "I went to the animals' fair."

There were few art atrocities. Everywhere were the allegorical and emblematic figures beloved of the artist. In sculpture or on canvas, Truth, Beauty, Civilization, the Spirit of America, and the rest displayed their nude or revealingly draped forms with impunity. Descendants of the Puritans gasped, tried the novel experience of being broadminded and liked it. Why be shocked by such chaste personifications after the Midway where the hoochie-koochie dancers wiggled to the Fair's most popular tune, "The Streets of Cairo"?

For the first time, American mural painters came into their spacious own. In the galleries of the Palace of Art, oils by Americans vied for favor with contemporary paintings in the European exhibits. On all sides were heard complaints that American artists, yielding to the ancient prejudice, had depicted mostly foreign scenes; and public admiration for such appealing native subjects as Thomas Hovenden's *Breaking Home Ties* signalized an hitherto unheard-of art-patriotism.

Gibson, magnetically attracted by his own work as any artist is, haunted the Liberal Arts Building, where the great American publishing houses glorified themselves and their contributors. Ten leading monthly magazines boasted that their combined circulation had reached the stupendous total of half a million copies; that each woodcut cost from $200 to $300 and each process cut $100.

The Century particularized that for every issue it paid out $10,000 to writers and artists, and that rates had doubled in twenty years. Along with the book publishers, the magazines displayed original manuscripts—Lew Wallace's *Ben-Hur* drew crowds—and original illustrations by Pyle, Frost, Kemble, Remington, De Thulstrup,

AT THE FAIR

The European idea of it

Reinhart, and Gibson, with Abbey's splendid Shakespearean drawings in the place of honor. Gibson risked standing near his own exhibit of thirty-six pen-and-inks and three wash drawings to eavesdrop on comments and escaped with few ear-burnings.

Some of Gibson's current Leap Year cartoons might have been ideally shown in that edifice which was one of the Fair's most striking signs of the times—the Women's Building. But the work of man was banned there and Leap Year principles ruled. The building was designed by the woman winner of a national architectural competition limited to women. It was crammed with evidence that in many fields of endeavor the female of the species was as capable as or superior to the male. All the decorations and exhibits were the work of women. The Gibson Girl had a rival in the delicately charming statuettes of maidens of the day by a young Chicagoan, Miss Bessie Potter (later Mrs. Vonnoh). Women sculptors executed the statuary ornamenting the building's roof: a group representing typical feminine characteristics and virtues, with the central figure a sprightly damsel, at her feet a pelican, emblem of love and sacrifice—for its offspring. In opening the building, Mrs. Potter Palmer, speaking on the spheres, rights, and duties of women, avowed: "Thus it is hoped in a measure to dispel the prejudices and misconceptions, to remove the vexatious restrictions and limitations which for centuries have enthralled the Sex."

That hope was destined for an earlier realization than those who entertained it dared expect, and the artist from New York who drew women so well would have not a little to do with it. Thenceforth his drawings offered proof that the Gibson Girl, a high-spirited and independent creature to begin with, had seen the Women's Building at the World's Fair and learned something to her advantage.

Man or woman, there was not an artist who was represented at or visited the Fair but sensed that a new epoch had dawned for the fine arts. Then and there American art entered into its Renaissance.

II

Twice Gibson journeyed to the Fair, for him as for thousands of others, an ever-memorable occasion. He wined and dined in fellowship with the renowned artists who created its glories. He scanned its artistic and scientific exhibits, proud that he was an American.

· LIFE ·

Wiener Cafe

SKETCHES AT THE FAIR.

AT THE AUSTRIAN CAFÉ 'WEEN THE BAND PLAYS.

© Life Publishing Co.

Strive as he might to keep personally in the background, he and his work were too widely known. People pointed out the tall, good-looking chap who strode through the grounds, and they saw a metaphorical Gibson Girl on his arm. Her duplicates in the flesh fluttered up, eager to meet him. Only the suavely elegant John Drew, matinée idol extraordinary, could compete for their attention.

Happier every day that he had been pried out of his studio, Gibson stayed on, wandering through the foreign villages sketching girls of many nations but never wavering in his allegiance to the American girl. His deft drawings of faces and figures at the Fair filled double pages of *Life*. Celebrities in the lobby of the Palmer House. Sketches of Curly the Scout, survivor of the Custer massacre, and the Sioux chief, Rain-in-the-Face, who at first flung his blanket over his head, announced: "Take picture—one dollar," and refused to pose until paid. A pose by Buffalo Bill, followed by an invitation to ride in the famed Deadwood Coach. Seated in it before it began its race around the ring, Gibson heard the classic challenge: "Colonel William F. Cody, will you bring this stage through a country infested by hos-tile Ind-i-ans?" And the resounding reply, "Sir, with God's help I will!"

Famous friends. Parties and popularity. Indelible impressions and a flood of ideas to fill the mental reservoir drawn on so constantly. Such were the Fair's goodly gifts to Gibson. And he was to share munificently in the results of those profound influences which were the Fair's legacy to the nation.

"To mention only one of the many, many effects," wrote Mark Sullivan in *Our Times,* "I think it was the World's Fair, the heightened and more discriminating appreciation of art which it brought, that made possible the vogue that Charles Dana Gibson began to have about 1895. Preceding the nineties, the art that found its way to the walls of the average American homes was a familiar type in

READING THE WILL.

which high vividness of color was the most striking quality. During the later nineties, Charles Dana Gibson's drawings in sheer black-and-white displaced the chromo and achieved an almost universal vogue. Gibson's characters, always clean and fine, composed the models for the manners of a whole generation of Americans, their dress, their pose, their attitude toward life."

III

"Folly loves the martyrdom of fame."

Gibson, illustrating that quotation with a drawing of deluded mortals pursuing the fickle goddess toward the brink of a precipice, believed it no more than did Byron when he penned the line. To Gibson at twenty-seven, fame was a fascinating jade. Her charming company, which he now was beginning to enjoy to the utmost, led, as with other ladies, neither to folly nor to martyrdom if you kept from losing your head.

And Gibson kept his head in the face of blandishments alluring enough to upset the balance of any young man.

His second exhibition proved, like his first, to be a fashionable mecca, and even more successful. Bevies of matinée girls descended upon the show not only to view the art but the artist of whom it came to be said that he out-Sotherned Sothern. Nibbling at boxes of caramels and bonbons (bad for the Gibson Girl figure), holding their heads high like check-reined horses, the young things twittered with ecstatic delight when Gibson appeared. He fled in panic from the mob scene, for there was none of the actor in him. Somebody started a rumor that Gibson had to disguise himself with a set of false whiskers when he walked about town, or whole streets full of women would start striking Gibson attitudes and blocking traffic.

"He's just like the men he draws," one girl confessed after meeting the lion. "He's nice—and he uses slang. I told him I knew two dozen girls who would give their heads to meet him and he grinned and said feelingly, 'You do me proud.' Oh, he wasn't sarcastic. Just sort of patient and resigned."

Gibson preferred to confine the Leap Year idea to his drawings.

It was worth a whole series, with the laugh first on one sex then on the other. The ladies relegated to the back of a theatre box. The gentlemen shooed off to a drawing-room while the ladies lingered around the dinner table to sip their port and smoke (a daring thought, that). The ladies scrambling for refreshments for the gentlemen at a reception. Reluctant men coaxed into the breakers by bold bathing girls. A weeping bridegroom tearing himself away from his parents to depart on a honeymoon with the nonchalant bride. And that hard-hitting picture of the tables turned on man which struck home in many a household—a wife, home late after a gay party, mounting

ONE OF THE ILLUSTRATIONS FOR VERSES
BY ISAAC H. BROMLEY

the stairs unsteadily and stealthily while an anxious husband waited miserably at the top.

At that second exhibition, $3,000 was paid for Gibson originals. Commissions to illustrate stories and novels poured in. In one story Diana stepped down from her perch on the tower of Madison Square Garden to play pranks, a yarn inspired perhaps by the model for the Saint-Gaudens goddess who attended an artists' dinner and anointed bald heads with champagne. Gibson Girls and Men graced another society novel by Mrs. Burton Harrison, *Sweet Bells Out of Tune*. Gibson and Dan Beard made drawings for an amusing screed by Isaac H. Bromley in which the gods, bored by their after-

166

dinner speakers, left Olympus to search for relief on earth and were rewarded with the discovery of Chauncey Depew in his cradle.

> "Enough of this," said Jupiter.
> "Success has crowned our search.
> Let the baby now be christened
> In the Presbyterian Church."

And later when the find had won his spurs as a toastmaster—

> He's been dining and speaking
> For years now a score.
> He has routed the chestnut,
> Evicted the bore.
> No table's without him,
> No dinner complete.
> The fun always waits
> Till he gets on his feet.
>
> Making all men his friends
> Without seeming to try.
> Now he prays with the pious,
> Now drinks with the dry.
> Always sweet as a daisy
> And fresh as the dew,
> No fly ever lighted
> On Chauncey Depew.

For that silver-tongued speaker, Gibson owned immense admiration. Even a Cabinet meeting presided over by the inimitable Depew would be entertaining, thought Gibson—and drew the idea. He himself was far too shy, he was sure, to act as a toastmaster and he refused all invitations to preside at dinners. But Dan Beard began to persuade him otherwise and to train him. It was slow, hard work but it would bear good fruit in 1917.

Far more exciting than illustrating books by others was the publication of a book of one's own. In 1894, Robert H. Russell brought out Gibson's first book, *Drawings by Charles Dana Gibson,* a large folio collecting eighty-four of the artist's pen-and-inks. Good reviews and a large sale blessed it.

"The martyrdom of fame?" What pleasant persecution it was! Yet a man must not become self-satisfied, must not rest on his oars. Pen draftsmanship was the high calling Joseph Pennell termed it. "Unless," Pennell wrote, "you feel that pen drawing is something to be reverenced, something to be studied, something to be believed, something to be wondered at, that you must put all your skill and all your brains and all your technique into your work, you will never become a pen draughtsman. And you should be prouder to illustrate the great magazines of the world . . . thus appealing to millions of readers, than to have your drawings buried in the portfolios of a few score collectors."

Those were lofty standards but worth the striving, fall short though you might. Art, like life, estimated Gibson, was a compromise. Too often you stooped to conquer. He knew that when he was tired or hurried he did "rubber stamp" work. Yet he was forever trying, knowing he could do better, and every now and then justifying his faith by doing it. Good drawings somehow just seemed to happen. Weren't they really done, he wondered, by his subconscious self? He never doubted that they were, but he knew also that that precious inner something never was there to rise to conquer until a man had toiled long and hard to bring it into being.

CHAPTER X

LA VIE PARISIENNE

I

Thousands of Americans sailed for Europe in 1894, returning party calls paid by foreigners on the World's Fair. Gibson, contributing his share to the coffers of appreciative steamship companies, this time made no brief tour and art pilgrimage limited by lack of funds but set up his drawing-board in Paris and stayed almost a year. Before he set foot in his native land again, *Life* and *Harper's* were close to publishing French editions and the Gibson Girl had become a chic Parisienne.

A farewell dinner at the Aldine Club had been tendered Gibson by Gilder, Remington, De Thulstrup, Davis, Arthur Scribner, and Robert Bridges. In England he stopped to pay homage to his two idols, Du Maurier and the transplanted Abbey, the latter at work in his Gloucestershire studio on his splendid Holy Grail murals for the Boston Public Library. Then Gibson settled down in Paris for what was one of the pleasantest epochs of his life.

This third visit found him no longer a student in the ateliers but an artist of standing, his work praised both by his compatriots and by French confreres and shown in the salons. He took a studio at 48 rue Fabert, imposingly decorated with armor and tapestries. His friends—the city seemed full of them—thronged in for a housewarming at which two American girls who were the toasts of the town honored their host by entertaining. Sybyl Sanderson, that seductive *Thais* of the Opera Comique, sang and Loie Fuller gave her celebrated serpentine dance. It was a party Paris long remembered.

MacMonnies and Whistler, who acknowledged a cordial admiration for Gibson drawings, sent the newcomer their favorite models.

IN PARIS.

At the Café Américain.

MacMonnies

Eugenie

IN PARIS.
A CAFÉ ARTIST.

THE AMBASSADEURS'.

Calling to thank the latter, Gibson was gleefully commanded by the great painter and etcher to read through sheafs of newspaper clippings. Whistler, who loved a quarrel next to his art, had filled the press with his resentment at having been caricatured in Du Maurier's novel, *Trilby*. Its character, *Joe Sibley,* said to satirize Whistler, would be deleted from later editions, but the fiery, Whistlerian spirit was still unappeased. Gibson, knowing that Du Maurier had been much hurt by Whistler's letters to clubs asking the expulsion of *Trilby's* author, believed his host had gone too far. The caller suffered uncomfortable moments until he was able to switch the conversation to art.

Numbering many French artists among his friends, Gibson made a determined attempt to learn the language. It was no conspicuous success. Many of his French phrases were declared to have been

© Life Publishing Co.

ARISTIDE BRUANT'S.

Richard Harding Davis .

sent to the morgue where they remained unclaimed; and he was suspected of having inspired this *Life* joke which he illustrated:

> AMERICAN TOURIST: *Vite, garçon! Je suis faim.*
> GARÇON: *Ah! Que Madame est bien déguisée!*

If an interpreter were needed, Gibson could depend on James B. Eustis, the American Ambassador. These two cronies spent merry nights together as men-about-town.

Sometimes they made laudable and profitable efforts to teach Frenchmen to play poker. Sometimes they made calls backstage on Rachel Boyer of the Comédie Française; or the stately Rejane, starring in *Madame Sans-Gêne,* whom Gibson sketched while she enjoyed the originality and abandon of his French; or on Loie Fuller, who lived with her mother in a tiny apartment over the Folies Bergère, quarters so small that the dancer to save room had had the

173

NO RESPECTER OF A WIDOW'S GRIEF.

chairs painted on the walls. The management kept La Fuller close, for the short, plump little woman from Illinois had discovered a combination of light, color, and motion that made her skirt dances under colored spotlights an international hit.

Thus diplomat and artist spent many a jolly evening diplomatically and artistically. Just so, Gibson drew his sociable *Bishop Gullem* combining duty with pleasure in making the rounds of Paris to obtain material for a book.

Paris was even more thoroughly explored by Gibson in company with Richard Harding Davis, who was making a grand tour abroad that year. Note book and sketch book in hand, the comrades with fresh, young eyes scanned the boulevards and the quarters of the city on the Seine in the days when it was emerging with Gallic alacrity from its mourning for the assassinated President Carnot. They wrote of and drew groups in the Jardin de Paris and life at the restaurants among the trees of the Bois de Boulogne, on Mont-

martre, at the Moulin Rouge, and the *cafés chantants*. They watched
the *can-can* danced by damsels who "put their feet very high and
danced with remarkable strength." They chronicled all manner of
French types: midinettes, models, boulevardiers; and tourists and
members of the American colony as well. Soon *About Paris* by
Richard Harding Davis, illustrated by Charles Dana Gibson, began
crossing the Atlantic in installments to enliven the pages of *Harper's
Magazine* and then appear as a book. A fine collaboration and

COPYRIGHT, 1894, BY LIFE PUBLISHING CO.

MADAME RÉJANE.

eminently timely because of American interest in the foreign scene, the serialization and the book were deservedly successful.

Davis in his *About Paris* text, supported by Gibson in *Life,* continued to wage warfare against American heiress-foreign nobleman marriages. The author compiled a nuptial Bradstreet which rated English earls and German counts as better buys than French Napoleonic or Italian Papal Court titles if an American family insisted on speculating with a daughter's happiness. The artist drew a picture advising athletic American girls how to manage bad bargains in titled husbands: square off and knock the rascal across the room.

Then there were days when the sketch book was laid aside and models tripped into the Gibson studio with their Gallic grace. A better linguist than Gibson would have had a struggle making them keep their clothes on. Finally understanding that they were not to pose nude, they cast deprecating glances at their dresses and murmured, *"Mais, si j'avais connu, monsieur."* Thus the popular model, Eugenie, who had posed naked as the babe she bore in her arms for MacMonnies' famous *Bacchante* (a statue installed in New York's Metropolitan Museum after a Boston ban), was drawn fully clothed. Eugenie's piquant features appeared in many of Gibson's Paris pictures and were later transferred into American scenes. *Town Topics* complained that a model priding herself on her figure had been dressed up by Gibson in a sort of "Mother Hubbard."

Suzanne, another Paris model, also was naturalized as a Gibson Girl. It was she who posed for those fine Gibson drawings: *No Respecter of a Widow's Grief* and *A Modern Daniel.* While some critics at home did not approve the introduction of Eugenie and Suzanne into American backgrounds, the French were mightily pleased. M. Gibson, said they, after struggles, *crises,* and transports had created from his French models masterpieces displaying an

POPULAR ILLUSTRATORS AT WORK

C. D. GIBSON

A satire on the Gibson copyists by Rea Irvin

intensity of emotion to which *la Gibson Girl* previously had been a stranger. *"C'était, pour Gibson, la découverte de la vie and des passions humaines."* And Gibson had thought he felt strongly about the American girl!

A CARICATURE OF C. D. G. BY JAMES MONTGOMERY FLAGG

The attainment of a true Parisian flavor was not the only accomplishment to Gibson's credit when he sailed for home. Once more Paris had inspired a remarkable advance in his technique.

"Gibson's experience in Paris," Charles Belmont Davis wrote, "was a most important one for it unquestionably had more effect on his work than any of his later travels. Almost the first of his sketches to reach this country showed the effect of the French school of black-and-white artists. He gradually drew away from his fine line drawing and told his story in a few bold strokes where he would formerly have used a hundred. The change may have been due altogether to an appreciation and to a more intimate knowledge of the French artists and their work, or it is possible that the enthusiasm with which he was received as a master of his art in Paris may have inspired him to strike out in bolder methods."

II

Gibson's progress in technique from, as the eleventh edition of *Encyclopædia Britannica* put it, "exceeding delicacy to a sculpturesque boldness of line without losing its rich texture and without becoming monotonous" was causing imitators no little inconvenience. No sooner had they managed an approximation of one style than Gibson developed another, and one more difficult to follow. An artist friend compared him to a planet whose satellites were flung off into space as it whirled into a new orbit.

For Gibson, like all worthwhile artists, as Albert Sterner affirmed, invented his style to fill his need and so was original. "Gibson became a fine draughtsman, very fine," Sterner added. "His poignant lines passionately flung on to the paper were in their brevity grandly expressive, and his humor subtle and above all *American*. Once when I visited Du Maurier, the celebrated *Punch* man, in London, he was loud in his praises of the master lines of Gibson. At times he (C. D. G.) was capable of great pathos and dramatic statement. His was a style that many imitated but never acquired."

The name of the Gibson copyists was already legion. For them he was inspiration itself, a shining signpost reading, "Art this way." There were, during this decade, few American artists who did not launch themselves on their careers by grasping pens with determi-

H. T. Webster in *The New York World*

nation, gluing their eyes to a Gibson drawing and striving to go and do likewise. They admired his drawing of hands, those tribulations of art. They prized his originals. They sought to capture some of his skill by engaging his models.

AN ORIGINAL GIBSON DRAWING

Copr. 1925 (N. Y. World) Press Pub. Co.

H. T. Webster again in *The New York World*

One member of the Gibson school later recorded his loyalty with the humor which placed him in the front rank of cartoonists. H. T. Webster took a leaf from his own life when in his series, *The Fortunes of Otis Clavering Brown,* he drew the episode: *He reaches*

AT A COMEDY.

the copying-Gibson stage. Webster's first sight of a Gibson drawing in *Life* set him to copying it immediately, copying it twice its size because he had heard that a grand scale was the proper artistic practice in such a case. He would, he decided, rather have a Gibson original than a steam yacht. On coming to New York, he haunted the entrance to the *Life* building in the hope of seeing Gibson plain, for him and for other young artists "the thrill that comes once in a lifetime." He, along with Orson Lowell, James Montgomery Flagg, Ray Crosby, and others who made grateful use of Gibson pictures as their art primer were never reluctant to acknowledge their debt.

Near-Gibsons blossomed forth in every college magazine and year-book. Every boy and girl in the land who yearned to draw responded with efforts which might or might not be subscribed, "With apologies to C. D. Gibson." Mothers knew at whose door to lay the blame for countless ink-stained fingers and floors littered with reams of crumpled paper.

Worship as a pen-and-ink Old Master by earnest young American art before you were thirty years old was sweet incense indeed. Besides its appeal to his own craft, Gibson's work grew steadily more popular with the public. Success smiled its golden smile. Covers and drawings for magazines, book illustrations, exhibition sales, and royalties from his folio published by Russell swelled Gibson's income to two, three, and four thousand dollars a month and higher and higher.

Honest admiration. Popular favor. Money as a measure of success. Through one or all of these motives or desires, artists followed Charles Dana Gibson. Art has made such obeisance since the first novice copied the image limned by his master on the wall of a cave.

Greater and rarer was the compliment which a whole generation paid the Gibson Girl.

IN THE LATIN QUARTER.

CHAPTER XI

THE GIBSON GIRL'S GLORY

I

As a young man, Gibson had dipped his pen in the cosmic urge and tried to draw a girl so alluring that other young men would want to climb into the picture and sit beside her. Anything but aloof, he could nevertheless sense with a certain detachment what a pretty face did to him, and the lines he put on paper served as lightning conductors of the charm he felt to kindred spirits. His genius gloriously materialized the dream girl whom so many young fellows were seeking to express in one way or another. Such was the inspiration for the Gibson Girl and the secret of her phenomenal success.

All the gallant young men *were* eager to climb into the picture with her and, naturally enough, they set out to discover her living image. They urgently asked, to paraphrase the ditty sung to the Gibson Girl of the Florodora Sextette, "Oh, tell me, pretty maiden, are there any girls in life like you?" And if the response was, "Kind sir, there are a few," that was a coy understatement. There were many and their numbers increased every minute.

For the Gibson Girl's fascination for mankind swiftly served as a word to the wise. Feminine intuition could not miss so broad a hint. The girl men loved was on a magazine cover, as Irving Berlin's song put it years later. Obviously she must be brought to life. So the daughters of Eve gazed intently at Gibson drawings and did their best to use them as mirrors. By intense and unanimous efforts they tried to grow as pretty as pictures. They reached into his sketches, as into a wardrobe, and took out more becoming gowns.

THE FLORODORA SEXTETTE SINGING 'TELL ME, PRETTY MAIDEN'

His illustrations were their book of etiquette and the model for their graceful, stately bearing. Mere earthly obstacles never daunted them. Proud heads erect, shoulders back, eyes on the firmament, they descended stairs by the feel, gave conductors dimes instead of nickels, rather than glance down into their purses, and were dragged out of the paths of cable cars by policemen. Being a Gibson Girl, "The Helen of Troy and Cleopatra of her day," as Sinclair Lewis called her, was worth risks.

As Julian Ralph, that star reporter, declared, Gibson was regarded throughout the United States as a combined Worth, McAllister, and *arbiter elegantarium,* with the fair sex looking to him to tell them how to dress, stand, sit, walk, shake hands, enter vehicles or eat. Nor was the oracle only for the socially élite but for girls in every walk of life as well. As early as 1893, Charles Dudley Warner had remarked that an aristocracy of derived rank and inherited privilege was out of the question in the United States; that it "would not wash" because too many had crowded in who had done their own washing. The Gibson Girl, for all her queenly airs and graces, was a truly democratic figure, "a creature not too bright and good for human nature's daily food," a Kiplingesque Colonel's lady willing to acknowledge the relationship of her numerous sisters under the skin.

Little girls everywhere, who relinquished the ambition to be President to little boys and who did not then even hope to be Madam Secretaries in the Cabinet, did determine to be Gibson Girls when they grew up. Many a boarding school miss enshrined in her room a print of *Princess Aline,* Gibson's charming conception of the heroine of Richard Harding Davis's novel. That bright image, even the caustic *Town Topics* admitted, was an ikon for school girls "to gaze at after prayers in the morning and at night before the soft, white sleep of innocence descends." Their worship

Life's Contest of Beauty.

LIFE offers a prize of one hundred dollars to the person who shall correctly select the twenty heads shown above in the order of their beauty.

DIRECTIONS.

Select the face you consider the most beautiful and beneath it place distinctly the figure 1.

Beneath the face you consider second in order of beauty, place the figure 2, and so on through the entire twenty.

When all have been numbered, write your name and address plainly in the margin, tear the page out, and mail it to LIFE's Contest of Beauty, 19 West Thirty-first Street, New York City.

HOW THE PRIZE WILL BE AWARDED.

The contestants themselves will award the prize.

The face which is marked 1 by the greatest number of competitors will be considered the most beautiful. The one marked 2 by the greatest number of competitors will be considered the next most beautiful, and so on to the twentieth.

The prize will be awarded to the person whose page goes furthest down the list in the exact order of selection chosen by the majority.

The same competitor may send in any number of pages.

Under this plan no partiality can be shown, and there is practically no possibility that the prize will be divided. Should this occur, however, LIFE reserves the right to divide it among the successful competitors.

CONDITIONS.

The contest closes at noon on January 14th, 1901. No pages received at LIFE Office after that hour will be considered.

The page will appear in the issues of LIFE dated the 6th, 13th, 20th and 27th of December, 1900.

As soon as possible after the close of the competition, LIFE will send one hundred dollars to the winner, and will print the page showing the order in which the faces were selected by a majority of the competitors, together with the selections of the winner.

Envelopes should contain nothing but the marked pages, and be addressed to LIFE'S CONTEST OF BEAUTY, 19 WEST THIRTY-FIRST STREET, NEW YORK CITY.

was no whit disturbed by Oliver Herford's amusing parody in words and line of *Princess Aline* who "craned her beautiful but rather thin neck over the balcony." They cut Gibson Girls out of magazines and pinned them beside their bureau mirrors, and they begged for Gibson books for Christmas.

That excellent reminiscent series, *The Gay Nineties,* which R. V. Culter drew for *Life* in 1925, included a drawing of two young ladies watching the rather vainglorious passing by of a third. Below were the lines:

THE LAST WORD IN COMPLIMENTS

"What is the matter with Etta Purdy? She hardly speaks to us."
"Oh, she's been that way ever since somebody called her a Gibson Girl."

No aspirant to be a Gibson Girl could complain that directions were lacking. The prolific Gibson pen supplied them generously. It soon appeared that he disliked bangs. Forthwith girls stopped cutting them. "You can always tell," wrote Robert Bridges, "when a girl is taking the Gibson Cure by the way she fixes her hair. I've watched them go through the whole scale from Psyche knots to pompadour, to Bath Buns, to side waves, with a bewitching part in the middle."

Because Gibson drew maidens straight as poplars, girls dared not droop, and the débutante slouch was deferred for a quarter of a century. The modesty and dignity of the Gibson Girl was apparent in every picture. Her copyists perpetuated those attractive qualities until the revolt of the flapper. Although Gibson, as a black-and-white artist, was unable to advise his vast clientèle as to coloring, yet even that he suggested with the name, *Penelope Peachblow,* and with the skillful delicacy of his shading. Otherwise the Gibson Girls in the quick followed their own good judgment which for years left lips and finger nails *au naturel.*

Such were some of the extraordinary consequences of a vision which

THE WEAKER·SEX. VIII.

He goes to the play, but finds it impossible to become interested in the piece

a young man saw *circa* 1890. It was no baseless fantasy. Its fabric was spun from life. Gibson's imagination, glowing with the lovely girls his eyes had looked upon, followed the Gilbertian recipe and, here and there, made bold to

> Take a pair of sparkling eyes,
>   Hidden, ever and anon,
>   In a merciful eclipse—
> Do not heed their mild surprise—
> Having passed the Rubicon,
>   Take a pair of rosy lips;
> Take a figure trimly planned—
>   Such as admiration whets
>   (Be particular in this);
> Take a tender little hand,
>   Fringed with dainty fingerettes,
>   Press it—in parenthesis—
> Ah! Take all these, you lucky man—
> Take and keep them, if you can!

Gibson, lucky man, took and kept them, took and drew them from girls he knew, from his models, from glimpses of fair strangers. For any artist, American girls were glorious material. "They have a way," Charles Dudley Warner wrote in an essay illustrated by Gibson. "They know how to be fascinating, to be agreeable. They unite freedom of manner with modesty of behavior. They are apt to have beauty and if they have not, they know how to make others think they have. Probably the Greek girls in their highest development in the times of Phidias were never so attractive as the American girl of this period; and if we had a Phidias who could put their charms in marble, all the antique galleries would close up and go out of business."

Gibson, putting their charms on paper with such notable success, must be credited with an historic achievement. Until then there had simply been charming girls in America. Now appeared The Ameri-

THE NURSERY.

From *The Seven Ages of Woman*

can Girl, crystallized and typified by Charles Dana Gibson, made a thing of beauty and a joy forever and a worldwide toast.

II

"Mr. Gibson is commendably jealous of his pretty girls," observed Anthony Hope whose *Princess Flavia* was in the gallery of Gibson Girls. "He knows they have much to give and would not have them give it unworthily. He finds for them very handsome young men, fine fellows who worship them as they deserve."

Men were predestined to lose their hearts to counterparts of the Gibson Girl, maidens who had taken such pains to animate the reveries engendered by Gibson drawings and tobacco smoke. Having copied to conquer, having obligingly lived up to what men thought they ought to be, girls proceeded to oblige men to live up to them.

In keeping men up to the mark, the fair sex enjoyed Gibson's heartiest and most valiant support and never lost it unless guilty of extravagance or marrying for titles or money. Through his upbringing and by his own code as he formed it, Gibson was innately chivalrous in his attitude toward women and his drawings faithfully reflected the man. As a young art student, he had studied the works of the Dutch masters and, while admiring them as art, had decided that the rowdy dames portrayed indicated a deplorable lack of respect for the fair sex. That would never be said of his work, he resolved. The women he drew must be loved, honored and—yes, even obeyed.

And they were. The Gibson drawings played a considerable part in a reflorescence of knighthood in this second age of chivalry they depicted. Not since the Middle Ages had there been such vowing of fealty and doing of homage to Queens of Love and Beauty. Gentlemen displayed a new willingness to set forth upon quests, perhaps no more extended than for their lady's long gloves lost under the dining room table, but quests nonetheless. Chargers and palfreys were the new bicycles. The troubadour's lute became a banjo. Warriors helmeted in shocks of hair met in joust and mêlée upon the football gridiron, and at cotillions demoiselles graciously bestowed favors. Romance revived burst into life from between book covers.

Suitors were moved to greater ardor to win a Gibson Girl, husbands waxed more attentive to keep her. Men spruced up generally in emulation of the Gibson Man. They shaved off luxuriant mustaches because Gibson seldom drew them, and women consequently held such upper lip adornments in disesteem. Figures were put on bounds and the "bay window" commenced to disappear as the symbol of middle age and success. Men took time from business not only to give thought to growing latitude, but their longitude also began to concern them. They stood straighter to be taller. A company, sensing the demand, advertised in *Life* its method of adding two or three inches to stature with the slogan: "Every woman admires a tall man."

III

Men wanted to be tall because The Gibson Girl was tall, and what gentleman likes to be towered over by his lady love? Observers in the mid-90's were remarking with astonishment the prevalence of tall girls. While pompadours, picture hats, heels, and the sweeping lines of dresses had something to do with the new altitude, they did not entirely explain it. "It is the fashion for girls to be tall," averred one commentator. "This is much more than saying that tall girls are the fashion. It means not only that the tall girl has come in, but that girls are really becoming tall, because it is the fashion and because there is a demand for that sort of girl."

Opponents of the vogue expressed themselves in no uncertain terms. Some of them deemed Gibson guilty of encouraging the upward tendency. He, they charged, had, like the Alpine youth, borne a banner with the strange device, *"Excelsior."* Mothers of Gibson Girls and Men, snapped these critics, must have been exposed pre-natally to paintings by Rossetti, Burne-Jones, and other æsthetic artists. An editorial writer on the *New York Sun* was inflamed to a diatribe by a personal in the "agony" column setting forth a desire to "meet, woo and wed a woman of the Gibsonian type." The wish was expressed, according to the editor, by a "hunter of giantesses" who was himself probably five feet five inches tall.

"We all know and venerate Mr. Gibson's massive creation," the editorial fulminated, "a cathedral-like lady with an extraordinary reach and Atlantean shoulders. . . . She is the cedar of Lebanon, the Tower of Babel. Architects, interested in the problem of mass and support, have made strange calculations as to the necessary size of her shoes, the pedestals of so heroic a statue. . . . American girls know what to expect of themselves with the Gibson Girl and M. Bartholdi's Liberty before their eyes and do their duty. Were there ever in another age so many tall girls?"

And Mr. Gibson, continued the editor, who evidently liked his ladies little, had composed a giant mate for his goddess, a lofty, beautifully proportioned youth, a composite of Hercules and the beau ideal of a footman, a grandiose and god-like youngster, matchless and mustacheless. But that conception had no like in life, since this was an age of short men. Therefore there was not enough matter and space to Gibsonize both sexes, the editor finished, and the whole situation was to be viewed with alarm.

Good spoofing but the fact remained that the Gibson Girl who was tall without gawkiness, who was willowy without being lean, whose slimness was so graciously alluring, was immensely popular. Even for men who had to look up to her, she "bore her height with a sweet timidity that disarmed fear." Her devotees, summoning the

VACATION TIME

aid of the poets to describe her, avowed "she walked in beauty" and that she was in truth "a daughter of the gods, divinely tall and most divinely fair."

IV

Escorted by coveys of cupids, the Gibson Girl passed through many phases from the wistful appeal of her early days when delicate lines delineated her to the era of her full glory when bold strokes created her imperial but still winsome loveliness. One classifier enumerated seven types of the Gibson Girl: the Beauty, the Athletic Girl, the Flirt, the Sentimental Girl, the Girl with a mind of her own, the Ambitious Girl, and the adaptable and accomplished charmer who was all things to all men and hence a universal favorite.

Sometimes a plain girl slipped into the picture to act as a foil but it had really pained the artist to draw her. He wished all girls could be pretty. Anyway, beauty should be, could be and was the right of the Gibson Girl. In her infinite variety she was maid, wife, and ravishing widow. Always she had passed the age of awkward adolescence and reached the full bloom of womanhood.

Such press notices as she and her creator received when her fame spread at home and abroad! "Mr. Gibson is chiefly beloved by his public for his almost idolatrous realizations of the beautiful American woman of various types, ages, and environments," *Encyclopædia Britannica* decreed. "His works are, however, full of the most subtle character observations and of American men of all walks of life, and foreigners of every type, imparting as much importance to him and to his pages as his 'Gibson Girls' give radiance."

"No artist in this country has done more to typify the American woman and give her graceful charms and supple pose to the public than Charles Dana Gibson," wrote Homer Fort. "His pen has caught the true inspiration and he embodies in one composite picture the vivacity, the independence and hauteur, the condescending amiability, the grace and the catholic spirit of the daughter of this great Republic. You like his women, whether in a magazine or in life and you instantly know she is neither English, French or German. Instinctively you say: 'This is the American woman.'"

"Parents in the United States," remarked a foreign partisan of the Gibson Girl, "are no better than elsewhere, but their Daughters! Divinely tall, brows like Juno, lovely heads poised on throats Aphrodite might envy; mouth exquisitely cut and lovely Italian Renaissance noses; beautiful eyes, half-wistfully hidden by lids but thoughtful and bright with the flash that tells of lurking temper; glossy hair waving into maddening curls in the latest fashion or next; perfectly gowned like a dream of fair women, dreamt by Paquin."

The Gibson Girl was no mere rack for clothes, Robert Bridges maintained. Under her coat she had a pair of shoulders able to drive an oar or put a hunter to a fence. Healthy, brave, independent, well-bred, a flash of mischief lurked in the corners of her intelligent eyes.

THE SEED OF AMBITION.

The "chorus girl's" visit home

She was the ideal girl whom many expected to find some day in flesh and blood. Gibson's large family of girls, Bridges concluded, ranged from the proud and haughty beauty whom only a millionaire, with a superb education in addition to his bank account, would dare propose to, on to the pleasant-faced, black-eyed fascinator who would not mind living in a cheap house in the suburbs if she really loved a man.

Gibson, said H. I. Brock, "drew the girl of the period as his own young eyes saw her—that is to say, as she was, but clothed with a glamour that made her stiff shirt-waist and pompadour crow's nest topped by a hard straw hat, accessories of grace—circumstances of beauty and not of burlesque. (Let any retrospective artist try the trick and see what happens.)"

No wonder Gibson's name was inseparably linked with his Girl. The public, heartily approving the match, refused to allow the pair to be long parted. Just as readers demanded of Conan Doyle the

WHEN A BACHELOR IS ILL

COMPLICATIONS OFTEN ARISE THAT NO AMOUNT OF MEDICINE WILL CURE.

return of *Sherlock Holmes,* Gibson, however frequently he might introduce other characters, always must restore the Gibson Girl to his pages before too extended an absence.

Nor was the artist reluctant to keep on drawing a heroine so faithfully beloved. Through all her career, her adorers gave constant tokens of their affection. Letters of praise in quantities, presaging the "fan mail" of the athlete, the film and the radio star, poured in. At first, Gibson's little sister, Josephine, serving as his secretary as well as a model, busily answered correspondence, scissored and sent the autographs which he dashed off, hundreds to a sheet. But soon it was a good deal more than one small girl could manage and other assistance had to be drafted, especially to handle the flood of applications to name things after the Gibson Girl.

V

In his youth, Gibson had wondered why so many articles in stores were named after *Dolly Varden*. Later, as an inveterate reader of Dickens, he understood the reason for *Dolly's* namesakes and for the christening of *Pickwick* chintzes and cigars, of *Weller* corduroys, and *Boz* cabs. A similar fate awaited a creation of the Gibson pen.

"Why do they call me a Gibson Girl?" a hit song of 1906 would ask. Though ladies who sang it never paused for a reply, it was clear enough why the song had been so titled. A favorite character in art or fiction may share her appeal with anything named after her from music to merchandise, as the enterprising have long been aware.

Inevitably shop windows, counters, and advertisements were filled with Gibson Girl corsets, Gibson Girl shirtwaists, skirts, shoes, hats, pompadours (or rather their "rat" base), and riding stocks. Some manufacturers asked for the right to name their product and paid for it; others simply stole it.

"Gibson Girls love to ride in a Blankmobile," might have been the slogan of one early make of motor car, had the manufacturing company been more diplomatic. It invited Gibson to submit one of his drawings in a competition for use as an advertisement, stating that the drawing, if accepted, would win a cash prize; if rejected, it became the property of the company. Gibson's answer was relished around town. "I am running a competition for automobiles," he wrote the company. "Kindly submit one of yours. If acceptable, it wins an award. If rejected, it becomes my property."

Not only might a lady dress from top to toe in a Gibson Girl ensemble. She might set her dinner table with china and silverware reflecting the Gibson *motif*. "Gibson Picture Plates!" urged an advertisement in *Life*. "Charles Dana Gibson's most famous pictures have been exquisitely burnt into real Doulton porcelain plates. Twenty-four subjects with rich borders in Doulton blue. The minutest details of the original drawings are represented. Fifty cents each."

Once Gibson, with mixed emotions, attended a dinner at which he found himself partaking of soup out of a Gibson picture plate with a Gibson Girl souvenir spoon. A replica of the Gibson Girl on souvenir spoons was inescapable in a day when such commemorative utensils were the rage and there were souvenir spoons for all places and occasions, even—much to the amusement of Manhattanites—of Brooklyn. Otherwise normal persons grew kleptomaniacal when faced with a chance to collect more spoons. Hotels suffered repeated losses. Private homes were not immune. Clubs recognized the situation by placing cash receivers outside their dining rooms so that honest members and guests could pay for spoons abstracted.

Walls and furniture were equally susceptible to the Gibson Girl's captivation. Besides the numerous framed prints of Gibson groups and Gibson Girl heads, a selection of china plaques reproducing Gibson drawings, tastefully decked with a blue border and lover's

GIBSON PILLOW PYROGRAPHY

From a quarter-page advertisement in *Collier's Weekly.*

knot, were a popular parlor embellishment. Wallpaper patterns derived from Gibson pictures were sold as especially suitable for a bachelor's apartment. Gibson had made those drawings as center pages for *Life* and jestingly labelled them designs for wallpaper with never a thought of their practical use as such. The wallpaper makers, however, quickly adopted them. Among these were a pattern of Gibson Girl heads (walls covered with this paper must have kept the bachelors, for whose apartments it was suitable, in a perpetual state of distraction and turmoil) and a frieze of a debonair old gallant buzzing around the honeyed sweetness of flowers whose petals enfolded faces of lovely ladies.

Pyrography, delight of the amateur practitioner of decorative arts and crafts, inscribed Gibsoniana on every wooden and leather surface available throughout the home. Pillow covers, shields, chair backs, table tops, whiskbroom holders, match boxes, umbrella stands, easels, screens—nothing was safe when the pyrography enthusiast swung into action with his benzine burning outfit and its puffer and red-hot metal point. There ensued the reek of burnt leather, the tang of scorched wood and perhaps the yelp of a burned pyrographer. But in spite of hazards and mishaps, the lines of the design traced on the surfaces were followed and the Gibson Girl smiled out from a new background. Sellers of pyrography sets took full advantage of the Gibson vogue. Their conscience clear, since they paid Gibson on a piece-rate basis for the reproduction rights to his pictures, they hitched their wagon to his star and advertised enticingly.

"Pillow covers of burnt leather artistically decorated with Gibson heads," announced one ad. "These covers are decorated with exact reproductions of Mr. Gibson's drawings, every line being carefully drawn by hand, thereby presenting the delicate technique so characteristic of Mr. Gibson's work. Unique in conception, these covers make an attractive addition to the apartment's cozy corner, den or

AN EVENING WITH GIBSON

SKETCHBOOK.

BUENA PARK Aug 29th -95

PROGRAM COVER

library. They may be had in red, fawn, orange, russet, and electric blue. Sent prepaid to the U.S. or Canada for $4."

And again emphasizing the lure: "By contract with *Life,* we have the exclusive right to reproduce Gibson designs for pyrography. Charles Dana Gibson is the most famous living pen-and-ink artist, and his drawings are admirably adapted to pyrography reproduction."

Some, preferring the needle for retracing the Gibson Girl's fair features, embroidered them on silk handkerchiefs. Others strove to

express her blithe charms in music and forthwith appeared waltzes, two-steps, and polkas named in her honor; to dance to such selections young men sought partners nearest like a Gibson Girl. Even more coveted was the opportunity to pose with one's lady love in a Gibson tableau.

These *tableaux vivants* were being performed throughout the length and breadth of the land by the middle-'90's. Fashionable resorts, sewing circles, the altar guilds of churches, and charity bazaars staged them with vast enthusiasm and minute attention to detail. They were particularly favored as "mild Lenten diversion," for innocent Gibson subjects rid the entertainment of the theatre's sinful aura. Receipts rolled in at the door. Down front the local mandolin club tinkled mellifluously. Backstage the actors nervously examined their costumes and struck their attitudes. The audience fluttered through its programs headed "A Night with Gibson" without really needing their aid, since it was completely familiar with Gibson drawings and you could almost always recognize which one the tableau represented. The curtain rose amid sudden silence. There were Jack and Daisy self-consciously enacting the lovers in *Is a Caddy Always*

205

Necessary?, with little Willie fidgeting and grinning as the caddy. Appreciative applause, delighted identification of the actors, and down dropped the curtain to hide the preparation of the next tableau.

In a few years, the Gibson Girl would graduate into the professional theatre, but no real actress portrayed her with greater zest than the pretty amateurs who *lived* her—on stage and off.

VI

From 1890 until the World War, the Gibson Girl held her throne, a long span for a reigning beauty. During those years of grace, she shared her sovereignty for a year or so with one other and one other only—a chit from Paris called *Trilby*.

There was, as has already been mentioned, never any question of the Gibson Girl's supremacy on her native heath over the tall, stately Englishwoman who was the regular Du Maurier girl. But *Trilby* was an irregular Du Maurier girl in more than one sense of the word. Heroine of the novel which Du Maurier, possessed of a precious dual gift, wrote and illustrated with rare charm, *Trilby* proved to be a serious rival of the Gibson Girl. The Irish-Parisienne took the United States by storm, and, against greater odds, duplicated some of the fair American's triumphs.

Never have two rivals for popular favor presented a more startling contrast. They had in common only their good looks and their fascination for men. The Gibson Girl was chastity personified. *Trilby* led a gay, free-and-easy life as an artist's model in The Latin Quarter. She posed for the figure, "in the altogether," as she expressed it. When the Gibson Girl some years later played the lead in a novel by Robert W. Chambers about a model who posed nude, she remained fully clad in the illustrations. While the Gibson Girl was beyond reproach, *Trilby* was, in the euphemistic phrase of the day, a light woman. As her author confessed: "She followed love

"WISTFUL AND SWEET."

Du Maurier's Trilby from "Harper's Magazine"—copyright 1893 by Harper and Brothers

MONDAY MORNING.

for love's sake only, now and then, as she would have followed art if she had been a man—capriciously, desultorily, more in frolicsome spirit of camaraderie than anything else." (That certainly was not the way C. D. Gibson followed art.)

The novel was strong stuff for the '90's, and the Harpers displayed great courage in publishing it in this country. The impact of *Trilby* and her *vie Bohême* on Puritanical-provincial America was terrific. A shocked and horrified reception augmented the popularity which was the book's literary-artistic right.

"How about this *Trilby* business anyway?" demanded one scandalized commentator. "Is the world full of pretty models clad in ballet skirts—when they wear anything? Is it all one mad, joyous mélange of high-brow conversation discreetly peppered with low-brow revelry?" William Dean Howells, who liked heroes and heroines to be born in wedlock and keep true to it, sententiously pronounced: "The trouble with *Trilby* was not that she was what

THE LAST DAY OF SUMMER

she was imagined, but that finally the world could not imaginably act with regard to her as the author feigned. Such as she are to be forgiven, while they sin no more; not exalted and bowed down to by all manner of elect personages."

Of course Du Maurier had not intended *Trilby* to be a moral example and certainly she was none. In spite of that, America forgave her and loved her. For her sake, it grew more broad-minded. After all, she wasn't to blame. She'd been hypnotized by wicked, old *Svengali* to sing and what not.

Like the Gibson Girl, *Trilby* was showered with social and commercial compliments. She inspired sermons, parodies, cartoons, and tableaux ("An Evening with Trilby"). *Life,* citadel of the Gibson Girl, published a *Trilby* examination. Shoes and sausages, bathing suits and cigars were named for her. Her finely-modelled feet— sketched by *Little Billee* on the studio wall—were so famed that "Trilbies" became a synonym for feminine feet through the '90's.

Jewellers made replicas, and ice cream molds in the form of *Trilby's* feet were a favorite confection; the fact that the heroine's feet were not tiny was a matter of gratification to children at dessert time. A dramatization of the novel was a big hit in 1895. In her rich contralto voice, evoked by *Svengali's* passes, *Trilby* had gloriously sung *Au Clair de la Lune* and *Ben Bolt*. At once those songs developed into immensely popular numbers. *Ben Bolt* especially, which Doctor Thomas D. English had composed with little financial return, enjoyed a tremendous revival to the enrichment of the publishing firm. Dana Gibson was soon to hear that mournful ballad sweetly sung by the loveliest Gibson Girl he ever found in real life.

But the invader from France was bound to yield the crown before long to the American. *Trilby* made but one bow. The Gibson Girl curtsied weekly before her host of worshippers. *Trilby* was an intriguing fancy, the Gibson Girl an appealing ideal. Fortunately the maidenhood of the land, after a flurry of wanting to be artist's models *à la Trilby,* continued to follow the Gibson Girl. Their verdict decided the rivalry. The better girl won.

The Gibson Girl easily eclipsed all the other girls whom artists brought forward in her era. She had been long in retirement by the 1930's, so whether she would have been forced to gather her skirts and mount a chair by the apparition of *Mickey Mouse* is a question which never will be decided.

VII

Was there an original Gibson Girl?

Many claimed that proud title. It came to be said that the passenger list of the *Mayflower,* as it lengthened through the years, was a brief document compared to the roll of original Gibson Girls. Members of the original Florodora Sextette, who also multiplied amazingly, were far outnumbered by the army of first models for the Gibson Girl. For years claimants kept bobbing up. As late as 1905, Gibson saw an actress billed in London as "The Original Gibson Girl." He never had drawn her or even met her.

The chief authority, Charles Dana Gibson himself, flatly denied that there was or ever had been an original Gibson Girl. "If I hadn't seen it in the papers," he unassumingly declared, "I should never have known that there was such a thing as a Gibson Girl." Hundreds of girls posed for him, and he always had refused to be limited to any one type.

Be it remembered that the Gibson Girl was originally a composite, not an individual. She was an ideal rather than a portrait, until one night at Delmonico's Gibson discovered the girl who for him would be both.

HIS VACATION OVER.

CHAPTER XII

LOVE STORY, ILLUSTRATED

I

Mrs. Burton Harrison was entertaining a guest in her summer home at Bar Harbor. For his own sake and as the artist who had illustrated two of his hostess's novels quite to her taste, Charles Dana Gibson was a welcome guest.

Through the window they caught a glimpse of a carriage drawing up in the driveway. It brought other welcome callers. Mrs. Harrison swept out to greet friends from her native Virginia. Mrs. Langhorne and her daughter must come in. There was an attractive young New Yorker in the sitting-room who would love to meet Irene. But Mrs. Langhorne, who had a house-full of pretty daughters whom young gentlemen were always wanting to meet, refused with unwonted firmness. She and Irene simply could not stop. They were departing from the Maine resort that night and must leave their cards at so many places. The visitors bowed farewell and departed on the serious business of calling-card distribution. Mrs. Harrison's plan to present her illustrator to just such a beautiful girl as he had drawn for her books was defeated.

Paths which had been about to meet diverged. Perhaps Mrs. Langhorne would have been persuaded to leave her carriage, if Irene had learned whom she was to meet. For the girl from Richmond had attended a finishing school in New York City where the extra-curriculum reading consisted of magazines full of drawings signed "C. D. Gibson," drawings rapturously and romantically scanned. Miss Langhorne's schoolmate, Lizzie Lynch from Flushing, had set the entire school a-twitter the day she announced to an envious group

IRENE LANGHORNE GIBSON

that she had posed for a drawing by a friend from her home town, Dana Gibson.

But what was one man missed in Bar Harbor to a girl who was returning to Richmond to make her début? There were always plenty of men riding out to "Mirador," the Langhorne home. Of Colonel and Mrs. Chiswell Dabney Langhorne's family of eleven, eight had survived past childhood, and four of the girls, Irene, Nancy (the future Lady Astor), Phyllis, and Nora, were beauties. Colonel Langhorne, a civil engineer engaged in railroad construction, hugely enjoyed shepherding daughters and teaching them horsemanship, an accomplishment in which he exacted high proficiency. They were not allowed to stroll with men beyond the limits of the front lawn but they could ride anywhere. He managed his high-spirited girls, did the Colonel, with a judicious mixture of sternness and indulgence.

It took little wheedling to persuade him to organize an excursion when fleets of foreign nations visited Hampton Roads in 1893 in honor of the World's Columbia Exposition. Colonel Langhorne escorted a private car-load of daughters and their friends to the scene of festivities at Old Point Comfort. Though the United States Government had allotted only a small sum for official entertainment of the visitors, Virginia and neighboring States rose unofficially to the occasion with traditional hospitality. Along with the Langhorne contingent, other bevies of pretty girls converged on the port. Southern charm devastated officers of the battleships of England, France, Germany, Russia, Holland, Italy, Spain, the Argentine, and Brazil. Flirtations were carried on in seven languages and sailor cap ribbons of ships of all nations were collected as trophies. Colonel Langhorne's Richmond girls, trim in white dresses and stiff straw sailor hats beneath the brims of which coyly peeked little curls right in the middle of the forehead, boarded vessel after vessel. Irene had captured a Russian admiral, when her hat blew off and was recovered by an officer and handed back to her upside down, with the curl, sewn to the brim, distressingly in evidence.

The year provided another exciting event. Through Richmond the thrilling news spread that Mrs. Langhorne had received a letter from no less a personage than Mr. Ward McAllister, ruler of New York society. Would she permit her daughter Irene to come to the Patriarchs' Ball to lead its grand march with him and its cotillion with Mr. Franklin Bartlett?

Indeed she would. It was as eminently a desirable an invitation as any mother could have wished for her débutante daughter. Since the founding of the Patriarchs' Association in 1873, its annual ball had been New York's most glittering and most exclusive function. Its select list had been sternly defended against all assaults of the covetous, and the fort would be held until 1897 when crumbling of its barricades caused the Patriarchs to abolish themselves rather than open gates wide.

And the invitation was unmistakably a striking compliment to Irene Langhorne. McAllister, his unerring eye for a handsome woman developed since a youth in that exemplary training ground, Savannah, Georgia, was renowned for his regal choice of partners. The old Autocrat of Drawing-Rooms, ever the clever showman, would lead out in the grand march only the fairest of the fair.

Pleased acceptance. Triumphant departure for New York. Frantic shopping. Surprisingly soon the great night. Miss Langhorne, lovely in a gown of white satin and her first non-home-made coiffure, escorted by her father to the stately ballroom at Delmonico's. Her dance card clamored for by good-looking young chaps, including squads of eligible millionaires. The grand march with the imposing Autocrat looking extremely Louis Napoleonic. The cotillion under the skilled and diplomatic direction of Franklin Bartlett. Grand chains, "fans," "baskets," and other figures, and favors—velvet purses, silver boxes, pocket-books and pocket-knives—with every girl counting coups by the number she received. McAllister hovering over it all like a stout patron saint. Lancers, polkas, and more waltzes. Languishing looks, pretty speeches. The supper dance and finally "Home, Sweet Home," greeted with sighs of relief by weary chaperons and waiting maids.

After so memorable an evening, New York was bound to exert a magnetic attraction on Irene Langhorne. She returned a year later for the Horse Show, and that evening a dinner was given for her at Delmonico's. The guest of honor's bright eyes did not miss a group of three young men dining at a table nearer the door. One of them she knew—Robert H. Russell, who had promised her when last they met in Virginia that he would introduce her on her next New York visit to Richard Harding Davis and Charles Dana Gibson. A reminder of that promise would be apropos this very evening, since Russell's companions, recognized by Miss Langhorne from photographs, were the celebrities in question.

Her dinner party over, Miss Langhorne found her way out of the dining room, not by the more obvious avenue but by a rather tortuous passageway which happened to lead past a certain table.

Gibson, who had been seated with his back to the Langhorne party, had been conscious there was a good-looking girl in the room. To a young man sensitive to such presences, sight was secondary, a mere confirmation. Now he heard behind him that seductive rustling and swishing that heralded the approach of femininity in 1894. He was vouchsafed a brief glimpse of a vision—beckoning blue eyes and golden hair under a big, black picture hat. The vision bowed graciously in passing to Mr. Russell. "Ha!" said that man of his word, rising and following the lady to the door. He returned to inform

An Unknown
Irene Tibou

From a photograph by Lallie Charles, London

A LOVE SONG.

his friends that they might come to a tea at his diggings tomorrow and meet her.

There were other pretty girls at the helpful Bobby Russell's tea, but Gibson's eyes were only for the girl from the South. She was more than pretty. She was luminous—like a house, he thought, with the windows all lit up; you could hear sweet music playing and you knew there was a party going on inside.

Gibson determined that he, too, had better give a tea. On the day the guests arrived, a piano stood in one corner of his studio, brought in recently to furnish a drawing, and somebody asked Miss Langhorne to sing. Without demurring, the girl took her place at the keyboard, gazed over the music-rack far into some unknown vista and in a soft, caressing contralto sang Nevin's *Good-night, Beloved*. What a glorious picture she made! Dana Gibson, his eyes drinking in the scene, knew that some day he must draw it. Even the background he would need visualized itself for him behind the girl at the piano—a whole celestial choir of doting cherubim chiming in antiphonally, "Good-night, Beloved."

218

It appeared that Miss Langhorne was attending the Horse Show again next day. So also, it chanced, was Mr. Gibson to make a few sketches. Those sketches and others were neglected until after the young lady left town for the Mardi Gras in New Orleans.

He wrote, sending proofs of some of his drawings. She answered, sending a copy of Thomas Nelson Page's *In Old Virginia*. For quite a while there was no answer, and one can imagine the indifferent tosses of the head with which gaps in the morning's mail were noted. But Gibson had been in Chicago at an exhibition of his drawings. His first letter from New York declared that he had been inspired to visit Old Virginia and might he call while he was in Richmond? He might and did. Irene Langhorne in a dress of mauve taffeta with moss roses at her girdle greeted him, framed by the white columns of "Mirador's" porch. The girl was, so naturally, the center of charming pictures, pictures the artist seemed to remember having dreamed of, pictures into which he would like to climb and sit beside her. Before long he was planning and making other trips to Virginia.

II

Through these months, drawings on romance by the Gibson pen, always abundant, glow with a new fervor. That universally appealing theme ever had been a favorite of his. He had been in love or had thought he was in love before and was rated as a master-hand at depicting symptoms, complications, and results. But now a certain and rather overwhelming conviction was apparent in his work and he could look back at his past drawings with a sympathy that surprised him.

His pages swarmed with cupids. His lovers, gazing deep in each other's eyes, stood oblivious in downpours of rain. Having begun to say a fond farewell in August, they are still at it, covered with snowdrifts, in December. Yes, love was like that.

A Gibson Girl sits at her desk, pen poised, and wonders, "Yes or no?" Again, a demure maiden tells a pleading young man, "I'll be a sister to you," but you feel she may change her mind once she glances at the little dog sitting up and begging as earnestly as his master. And more pictures testify that the Gibson mind at this time is somewhat obsessed with the terrors of asking father.

Gibson, remarked an English critic, was a philosopher who drew his own *Ars Amandi* holding to these tenets—"That nice men are all young and mostly penniless; that middle-aged men are ineligible and have no business whatever to dally with youth and innocence; that elderly bachelors have no claim to connubial happiness, and that it is like their impudence to expect it; that the girls who marry them richly deserve the unhappiness in store—for Mr. Gibson (pure as driven snow in thought and drawing) very properly sees in such a future nothing but misfortune and despair and a sheer waste of beauty, without the compensating 'consolation' which a French artist always allows the lady; that Europeans are fortune-hunters, and what is worse, beauty-snarers; that these fortune-hunters invariably cut a contemptible figure—alike in appearance and banker's balance; that the Comedy of Life is heart-breaking, when it is not farcical. And, saddest of all, that if neglected, 'Love will die' and lie like a crumpled rose-leaf on an altar that will stand between whilom lovers like the very ocean itself."

Yet love can live and last, too. Gibson believed that with all his heart. There is deep feeling in two of his pictures of old age—in *The Last Guest* where, at the party of a gray-haired couple, that last guest is Cupid; and in *An Interrupted Story* where, while aged, life-long lovers wait in each other's arms, Cupid strives to hold the door against Death. How could old age in itself be a tragedy for those who had lived their lives happily together? Gibson mused. Couldn't it be, in spite of inevitable sorrows along the path, the final chapter of an idyll?

Nevertheless, falling in love was a matter not without its hazards and possibilities of dire consequences. Gibson thoughtfully illus-

YES OR NO

trated the proverb, "When poverty comes in at the door, love flies out of the window"—and was paid handsomely for the picture. But there was more food for thought in another drawing he made of a wife and a husband who is beholding the wraith of an old sweetheart. Ran the caption:

"It is only Jim, who happened to marry the wrong girl, and sometimes when she is particularly unendurable, he remembers the other one."

You just could not be too sure. Gibson, journeying down to Richmond again with serious intent, cautiously stopped over en route to see a couple of other girls.

It was all right. He was making no mistake. On to Richmond.

III

The Four Graces was the title which a romantic period, proud of beautiful embodiments of the American Girl, worshipfully bestowed upon Irene Langhorne, May Handy, also of Richmond, Louise Morris of Baltimore, and Lela Harrison of Leesburg, Virginia. Belles in their own towns, these beauties were ardently sought after in the North which still thrilled to the glamor of the South. The stage seemed always to be figuratively set for the Four Graces with moonlight and magnolia blossoms, with the harmonies of spirituals and banjos wafted from the slave quarters.

About the lively Miss Langhorne, flitting between New Orleans and Bar Harbor, was no trace of languor. She was in tune with her times, "that epoch of social metamorphosis when girls were beginning to abandon the rocking-chair and the hotel piazza for the tennis court." She was at once capable and energetic and appealingly feminine. Once in Richmond she had taken the title rôle in "An Evening with Trilby" and sung in that rich contralto of hers of "the masterful Ben Bolt and his over-tender Alice." But it was plain enough that, while she might love devotedly, she would weep with delight at no man's smile nor tremble with fear at his frown. It seems one of destiny's happier manifestations that Irene Langhorne should have taken after the Gibson Girl, not after sweet *Alice* or mesmerized *Trilby*.

The lady had numerous beaux, and Gibson was under no illusions

AS THE DAYS GET SHORTER.

His Horse: "Do you think it's a go?"
Her Horse: "We've been here every day for a month, but then you never can tell."

as to the stiffness of his competition. Also, the fact that an artist was courting Miss Langhorne had somewhat discomfited Richmond. Weren't artists rather rakish fellows and didn't they stage riotous dinners in New York at which four-and-twenty nude models (or thereabouts) popped out of a huge pie on the table? Yet this artist chap seemed well-behaved and Richmond liked him. So did Colonel Langhorne, though he snorted that a "sign-painter" was hanging around Irene, and on Gibson's arrival for this latest visit, quizzically remarked: "That damnyankee down here again?" But the "damn-yankee" was a real man, with a sense of humor. The Colonel roared when, after two of his daughters had appeared with the plackets in the back of their skirts gaping, Gibson remarked: "The Lang-hornes are good soldiers. They never look behind."

The courtship progressed. They went riding together. As Colonel Langhorne conceded, his daughter did bring the horses home in good condition, never overtired. One irresistibly quotes as apposite a Gibson drawing of two horses tied to a rail fence. Below were the lines:

AS THE DAYS GET SHORTER

His Horse: "Do you think it's a go?"
Her Horse: "We've been here every day for a month, but then you never can tell."

It was a go. Gibson had been talking often of a trip to Europe and one day he asked, "Will you go with me?" The lady of his heart answered decisively, "Surely I will."

She invaded her mother's bedroom that night to confide that she really was in love this time. "Pooh-pooh," said Mrs. Langhorne, "I've heard that before."

This time it was true. Gibson bearded the Colonel in his den and offered references. The father, creating the proper suspense, replied that he would do his own investigating. Its favorable outcome was clinched by a splendid send-off for Gibson from Thomas Nelson Page.

The engagement was announced and became a national news event. Here was human interest, a heart throb for every Gibson Girl in the land. Was this Miss Langhorne pretty? She was said to be and as nearly as could be told from line-cuts published in the papers she was. That helped but there was still considerable doubt whether Gibson had not better remain a bachelor. "In the minds of many thousands of impressionable young women," says a sage, "there is a sweet charm in the celibacy of a talented young man." Day dreams could not but be shattered by the word that the creator of the Gibson Girl was to marry. Hell hath no fury like that of women collectively scorned by the elevation and distinction of another woman, a state of affairs familiar to many a matinée idol on marrying.

Gibson Girls in the quick, who were piqued, wondered if the artist were in love with a real girl or only an ideal. Would the chosen lady, they asked, be jealous of the Gibson Girl whom her fiancé had drawn so often and so devotedly?

To that question they had an answer in subsequent Gibson drawings. There, in Irene Langhorne's image without being labelled "Portrait of My Wife," stood the Gibson Girl, lovelier than ever. She could be adored, copied and her like sought in real life as zealously as before. So all was forgiven.

IV

They were married November 7, 1895, at St. Paul's Church, Richmond.

A private car full of friends had come down from New York, and others arrived to augment the throng of local guests. The new Jefferson Hotel was opened two days earlier than scheduled to accommodate the influx. The press copiously chronicled the occasion. "Love Wins from Art," blazoned a headline.

THEIR PRESENCE OF MIND

They had been in their room but a moment when they were startled by a knock

Several hours before the wedding there was a crush around the church door of people eager to see the bride, the bridegroom, and Richard Harding Davis who was an usher. An expensive canopy, specially imported by Colonel Langhorne, was ripped to bits by spectators on the arrival of the bride, radiant in veil and gown (padded at the hips to conceal an unstylish slenderness), and evidently adoring her own wedding as a girl should. "The bride's gown," reported the *Richmond Tribune,* "was of rich ivory satin *en traine,* with high corsage of chiffon and satin sleeves, the shoulders and sleeves being gracefully festooned in Renaissance lace of exquisite pattern. A cluster of orange blossoms adorned the left shoulder. Her tulle veil was fastened by a crescent of diamonds,

© Life Publishing Co.

ON THE WEDDING JOURNEY

THIS IS ABOUT HOW IT SEEMS TO THOSE OBJECTS OF INTEREST, THE BRIDE, AND GROOM.

and her bouquet was lilies of the valley and violets. The bridesmaids wore yellow taffeta with chiffon waists and black Gainsborough hats. They carried bouquets of yellow chrysanthemums." The choir rendered *The Voice that Breathed o'er Eden*. Above the palms, ferns, and chrysanthemums decorating the chancel towered the tall forms of the bridegroom and his brother Langdon in support as best man. Out pealed the Wedding March and the ushers stalked down the aisle: Harry Langhorne, Algernon Craven, James De Kay, T. K. Sykes, Thomas Hastings, John T. Anderson, Lilbrun T. Myers, Thomas McIlwaine, and Davis—each in his best Gibson Man manner. After them floated the bridesmaids: Bessie Martin, Sallie Pemberton, Alys Connelly, Ellen Hobson, May Jones, and Elizabeth Gibson, with Nancy and Phyllis Langhorne as maids of honor. Then the bride on the arm of her father. The minister stepped forward.

Charles Dana Gibson loved beauty and drew it and now he married it. As he led his bride down the aisle, to more than one wedding guest that day must have come the thought: This is one of those idyllic happenings in life-as-it-ought-to-be. Today Fate can use the old fairy tales for its copy-book and write—"And they lived happily ever after."

V

Gibraltar, Spain, Naples, Rome, Florence, Monte Carlo, Paris, and London. The trip abroad Gibson had mentioned, when leading up to an important question, had been no empty lure.

Very properly the eyes of an artist, always on the lookout for ideas to draw, are not blinded by the golden haze of his own honeymoon. How people did stare at a consciously happy young couple! There was a picture in that—the wedding journey as it seems to the bride and groom—eyes everywhere, even in the boiled egg on the breakfast table. And then the drawing of porters bringing a beribboned

SUNDAY MORNING NEAR STANHOPE GATE.

trunk into the hotel room where the blushing bride sits with her hat awry and the groom reads a newspaper with attempted nonchalance. Line: "They had been in their room but a moment when they were startled by a knock."

AT THE NATIONAL SPORTING CLUB.

Marriage with a gentleman wedded to his art demands a sense of balance on both sides. The Gibsons had it and kept it. There was no wifely protest when on the morning after the honeymooners' arrival in London the bridegroom peered out of the hotel window, seized pencil and paper and began to sketch a street scene.

That was the genesis of *London As Seen by Charles Dana Gibson*. Into that book went aspects of the time-mellowed city viewed by the sympathetic and affectionate eyes of an American glad of his British descent. A boy stands wistfully regarding a recruiting sergeant beside a poster: "Able-bodied Men Wanted." A theatre queue waits in the fog. There are pictures of the parks, those show-rooms of people. A toast to the Queen is proposed, with reverence and loyalty clear on the visages of the true Britons raising their glasses. Here sits the bearded Du Maurier and a newer artist friend, the clever and genial Phil May. Among the best of the drawings are scenes of a presentation at Court, for there Gibson's pen was inspired by picturing his leading lady.

United States Ambassador Bayard had invited the Gibsons to be presented at the first drawing-room of the year at Buckingham Palace, and the *London Graphic* had commissioned the artist to make drawings of the occasion, thus combining business with pleasure. After the levée for gentlemen, Gibson remained to sketch in background. Then from a window recess, he drew the presentation of the ladies, while ushers, not at all reluctant to be included in the scene, offered assistance and indicated prominent dowagers. But the central figure was a foregone conclusion—Irene Gibson, the wedding gown doing duty again, ivory shoulders rising from frilly decolletage, plume decking proudly held head, and veil merging gracefully into flowing train as she curtsied to Victoria.

London acclaimed the drawings. On this visit, there was no longer a patriotic chip on Gibson's American shoulder. He met and liked British peers without suspecting them of designs on American heiresses. Said one critic: "In all the crowd of American men of talent who have delighted and fascinated the British people, none has more firmly established himself in favor than Mr. Charles Dana Gibson. . . . His English pictures nearly persuade us that we are almost as clever and charming and beautiful as Americans. We realize that his British 'nobs' are only puppets in a marionette show. He understands and esteems us."

At this time Gibson also drew a series, *People of Dickens,* on order from Editor Edward Bok of the *Ladies' Home Journal,* but to that task his talents were unsuited and other illustrators have better captured the spirit of the great novelist's tales. The critics disapproved.

The Albany Hotel, long an impregnable fastness of bachelors, first surrendered when Gibson brought his bride there for their London sojourn. There Mrs. Gibson, returning some of the hospitality heaped upon them, gave her first dinner party, with John Sargent, Mr. and Mrs. Edwin Austin Abbey, and Henry James the guests. The food ordered ran short, as will happen with a bride's first calculations, and the rest of the winter the guests amused themselves by sending her gifts of provisions. On a visit to Du Maurier, he played Irene Gibson's accompaniment while she sang *Ben Bolt* in her best *Trilby* manner. At one dinner she was seated next to Lord Roberts

AFTER PRESENTATION

whom she thought a delightful old boy and whom she regaled with
a Southerner's view of the Civil War so fervently that he invited
her to a number of military reviews. Then there was another dinner
where her partner, a naval officer who had not caught her name,
inquired as to her husband's profession and was told he was an
artist. "How jolly!" the officer observed. "If only he perseveres, you
know, some day he may have a drawing in *Punch.*"

Anyway, there was *Life,* always eager for Gibson drawings, and
the artist, with his wife, sailed home to fill that magazine's demand.

At the Savoy.

THE EDUCATION OF MR. PIPP.
A TRIP ABROAD IS SUGGESTED BY MRS. PIPP AND THE GIRLS.

CHAPTER XIII

MR. PIPP PASSES

I

There was welcome on *Life's* door-mat for Gibson when he returned from abroad. The prospering weekly had erected its own building at 17 West Thirty-first Street and now it leased the desirable studio apartment on the top floor to its leading artist. On both sides it was the height of convenience. Editor Mitchell kept close at hand the man who, after himself, was the chief factor in *Life's* success; and other magazines, envious of drawings that lifted circulation, must seek out the originator there. Gibson, carrying striking cover drawings and center pages downstairs, must have remembered with a smile that day fourteen years before when in deep discouragement

235

he had toiled up the steps of the old office with that first crude little sketch of a baying mongrel, *The Moon and I.* Why, he had entered art like a poor blind man, hadn't he?—led by a dog.

For the bride, too, the new home was delightful and it was all vastly exciting. Here she was right in the midst of things, with shops and Daly's and Wallack's theatres just around the corner. Also domiciled in the Life Building were some of the bachelor members of the staff who were often in need of a chaperon for parties. Downstairs an entertaining magazine was being brought out every week, a magazine in which her husband was a king pin and in whose pages her own bright countenance was frequently in evidence. Sometimes friends insisted they recognized her twice in the same picture. "That," they said, "is Irene talking to her twin." But it might have been one of the other Langhorne girls who also obliged their brother-in-law by posing. As a conscious and unconscious source of ideas, Mrs. Gibson supplied the theme of many a drawing not likely to have occurred to a bachelor. Only a benedict could have sketched so feelingly *The First Quarrel,* for instance—a couple, backs to each other, pretending to read, with the books upside down—and *After the Quarrel*—a happy pair sitting on the top of the world and gazing up at a rainbow teeming with cupids. Some of Gibson's artist comrades who had expected to see no more of him now that he had "married into the Social Register," found they were mistaken. Irene Gibson's friendliness, charm, and helpfulness were always valuable contributions to her husband's career.

Another free and non-professional model appeared at the studio apartment in 1897, a daughter who was christened Irene Langhorne Gibson. The child was doomed to the common fate of the offspring of artists and authors—supplying parental "copy," but her father waited until she was four weeks old before drafting her to sit for what proved to be a charming sketch. Babs, as they called her, would take the place of Josephine Gibson as the little girl in the paternal pictures. When commandeered, she posed as a filial duty though privately she preferred the funny drawings her mother made for her.

The baby crowded them out of the Life Building into a larger apartment. Gibson, thoughtfully regarding his new responsibilities, resolved that he must not settle down as the staid and static father of a family, with art simply a means of support. His education as an artist was not complete nor did he believe it ever would be. There was a driving force within him that forbade him ever to be satisfied with his work. He could always do better, must always go forward. Art was an essential part of his existence and he must be able to follow when she beckoned, as she did at this moment. Doubleday, McClure was ready to commission Gibson to make a series of drawings in Egypt, a most alluring opportunity. Babs at the age of one year joined her parents in the first of her many trips abroad.

II

Egypt in 1898 was becoming the favorite destination of Americans who had completed the conquest of Europe. For several years thereafter, Exhibit A of the seasoned globe-trotter was always a photograph of self and party, camel- or donkey-mounted, posing with the Sphinx and the Pyramids.

Gibson, setting foot on the soil of antiquity, reflected on the ages Egypt had sat for her likeness. The ancient Egyptian artists must have been very happy, he mused. For them, the great, smooth walls of the temples must have seemed ideal for covering with pictures, pictures which required little accompanying writing, seldom more than Pharaoh's cartouches, and even those made more like a picture than a name. Naturally picture-writing appealed to the

© *The Doubleday McClure Company*

FROM THE TITLE PAGE "SKETCHES IN EGYPT"
BY CHARLES DANA GIBSON

A sketch from
the same book

American illustrator who, like the scribes of Pharaoh, drew most of the stories he had to tell.

The panorama from the porch of Shepheard's Hotel was a command of open sesame to a sketch-book. Europe and Asia passed in review. Trim British soldiers and natives, Baedeker trailers and beggars, donkey drivers and dragomen filled the frame. But Cairo, thought Gibson, was only the foyer of Egypt. Not to go up the Nile was like standing outside a theatre and waiting till the audience comes out to get some idea of the play. Whereupon the Gibsons and

THE WRETCHED HEATHEN.

a group of friends hired a steam *dahabiyah,* comfortable with state-rooms, piano, rugs, and flowering plants on deck, and ascended the storied river. Views of the life along the banks, supplemented by excursions ashore, furnished pictures a-plenty. Yonder, graceful brown maidens danced to weird Oriental pipings and fiddlings, making a merry scene. Gibson drew it as a center page for *Life* and called it *The Miserable Heathen.* At the Assuan cataract, he saw a lamb which seemed to be staring up worshipfully at a colossal stone statue of a ram-headed god. No sooner seen than drawn and titled: *Unrequited Love.*

Numbers of the sketches he made might have come under the general head: The Gibson Girl in Egypt. For he had drawn Irene Gibson, fresh and cool in white dress and straw sailor hat, before the ruined columns of some ancient temple or seated between the graven paws of a mighty beast-divinity. Even there she fitted into the picture naturally, not impertinently—the glory of youth and beauty cleverly contrasted with the grandeur of the centuries. The port-folio had filled with full-sheet drawings and deft vignettes by Christmas Eve when the launch tied up to the bank for celebration.

Lanterns festooned the deck where Mrs. Gibson sat at the piano to play for a slightly homesick singing of *Auld Lang Syne* and then, as a Southerner's reminder to the Nile that there were other noted streams in the world, *'Way Down Upon the Suwanee River.*

Gibson felt an honest pride in his Egyptian sketches, and it was a blow to him when the publishers asked him to write something to go with them. He vainly protested that he was no writer. The publishers insisted. Retiring to Virginia, with toil and travail he strove to oblige. A travel book is a difficult form of literary art, and the struggling author dreaded the criticism of his many writer friends. In the text he produced, here and there Gibson's gift for a phrase, so evident in his conversation, flashed through the otherwise pedestrian prose. It had been an ordeal. Nobody ever persuaded Charles Dana Gibson to write another book. He might draw one, yes. But now he was not even considering it, although, oddly enough, he was on the verge of that very thing.

III

Before going home, the Gibsons had journeyed from the dim past of Egypt to the calm present of Munich. His artist friends often had told Gibson he should make a pilgrimage to the German city as one of Art's capitals. Now he obeyed, taking a studio and faring forth with sketch-book to the haunts of the citizenry from beer gardens to the opera.

It was pleasant to be welcomed and to be made aware that his work was known in Germany. In 1897, *Zeitschrift für Bildende Kunst* had praised the truth of his drawings and his smiling outlook on humanity, its failings and virtues, its loves and its ills; had paid tribute to his gentle humor. Satire, remarked the reviewer, was almost too strong a word for it. "The point is made by insisting

RUDOLPH RASSENDYLL.   PRINCESS FLAVIA.   COLONEL SAPT.   LIEUTENANT BERNENSTEIN.
—Anthony Hope's "Rupert of Hentzau."

enough on the obvious and not troubling the beholder too much with subtlety of thought and observation. And the manner of presentation, the technique, somehow is also so obviously adequate as to satisfy both the average citizen and the artist or connoisseur."

Gibson was not allowed to go sketching, as he loved to, for long. He was shut back up in his studio by a commission from London to illustrate Anthony Hope's novel, *Rupert of Hentzau,* the sequel to *The Prisoner of Zenda.* How lucky to be assigned that romance of ermine, intrigue, and swordplay in a German principality while he was in Munich just in the right atmosphere! The task paid well and *McClure's Magazine* added $1,200 for its use of his pictures serially. He set to work, calling in models for the men characters.

As for *Princess Flavia,* he need not seek far. Irene Gibson assumed her most regal attitude and sat for her. It was these drawings which caused Anthony Hope to pen for Richard Harding Davis a verse conveying the compliments of *Princess Flavia* to Davis's heroine, *Princess Aline:*

> Excepting myself, there never was seen
> A prettier girl than the Princess Aline.

These ladies of fiction had no need to be jealous of each other. They were drawn from the same model.

Although the *Hentzau* drawings were progressing, provision still had to be made for the pages of *Life.* The Gibson brains were cudgelled for ideas. Something about Americans touring abroad might do. There were hordes of them and Gibson as one of them was thoroughly acquainted with all their joys and vicissitudes in foreign lands.

At this juncture, an old German wandered into the studio of the American artist who he had heard was hiring models and apologetically asked to be employed. As an old man "type" he could have been in no more than occasional demand in the Munich art colony. A small, mild, downtrodden fellow, it seemed to be written all over him that a stern Better Half had ordered him out to find work and not come home with any of his excuses. Framed in the doorway, he appeared to be the composite portrait of a thousand hen-pecked husbands.

The kind-hearted Gibson would have hired him even if his features had not worn the appealing expression which was to become so familiar—"a ludicrousness tinged with a vague, elusive pathos, which served only to make those who laughed most heartily love him the better." The old German stepped up on the model stand and forthwith his naturalization papers were taken out on the Gib-

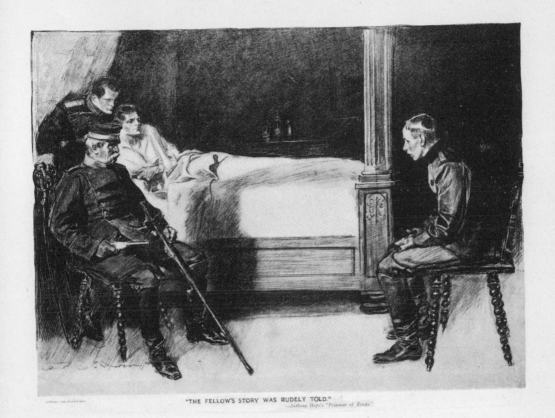

"THE FELLOW'S STORY WAS RUDELY TOLD."
—Anthony Hope's "Prisoner of Zenda."

son drawing-board. He became an American ironmaster and was
endowed with a stout, domineering wife and two beautiful daughters.

Thus entered *Mr. Pipp,* destined for manifold adventures in foreign climes and fame as the best-loved Gibson character after the
Gibson Girl.

In the September 8, 1898, issue of *Life,* readers beheld *Mr. Pipp*
seated in the parlor, with the ladies of his household putting on the
pressure for a trip abroad, a trip which, they were clearly informing
him, would be "a liberal education." Thence *The Education of Mr.
Pipp* proceeded via London, Paris, Rome, Monte Carlo, and the
English provinces.

243

THE FIRST DAY OUT.

EVERY MOMENT OF THE VOYAGE SHOULD BE ENJOYED.

IN PARIS.

HE HAS THE OPPORTUNITY OF ENLARGING HIS HORIZON AND OF DEVELOP-
ING AN INTEREST IN THE REAL PURPOSE OF THE TRIP.

IN THE RUE DE LA PAIX.
BEFORE LEAVING PARIS MR. PIPP, AT THE SUGGESTION OF HIS DAUGHTERS, MAKES
A FEW PURCHASES.

AT MONTE CARLO.
MR. PIPP'S LUCK HAS CHANGED. HE BREAKS THE BANK.

IN THE AMERICAN COLONY.
ON THIS OCCASION MR. PIPP FOLLOWS INSTRUCTIONS HE HAS RECEIVED
AND APPEARS INTERESTED.

Gibson had not intended a series; just a half dozen or so scenes to be played by these new pen-and-ink actors of his. But the audience would not let him drop the curtain. They waited with flattering impatience for the next act in each succeeding number of *Life*. What had happened to the *Pipps* now? They all were eager to know—globetrotters, stay-at-homes who had had to listen to talkative travellers, sympathetic fathers of families, romancers burning to find out whom the Pipp girls would marry.

So *Mr. Pipp's* education turned out to be more liberal than expected. Every phase of it found readers of *Life* who had taken the same course. They felt for *Mr. Pipp,* wretched during a rough crossing, though "every moment of the voyage should be enjoyed." They smiled at his basking in the attention of gentlemen anxious to meet his daughters, and sighed for him dragged to the dressmaker's, his face foreshadowed with the doom of bills. They de-

lighted in every episode: The old boy's night out in Paris; mother
and the girls in voluminous, befrilled nightgowns waiting up for
him; his indisposition on the morning after. *Mrs. Pipp* a prey to
the blandishments of that villain of a courier who makes off with
the jewels in Rome. The rascal sprawling before the bantam rooster,
turning-worm attack of *Mr. Pipp*. His innocent soul-mating with
Lady Viola Fitzmaurice whose son is allowed by the crusader against
heiress-nobleman marriages to win the brunette *Miss Pipp*, though
matters are evened up when the heart of the blonde *Miss Pipp* is
captured by the stalwart *John Willing*, manager of the Pipp Iron
Works. Then the final scene with the announcement: "Although
the education of Mr. Pipp is still incomplete, he has learned that he
has not lived in vain." There sits *Mr. Pipp*, a grandson and granddaughter on either knee and on his face just such an expression of
ineffable benignity and bliss as Charles Dana Gibson would himself
one day display when he regarded his own grandchildren.

When the *Pipp* drawings were brought out in a book, it sold like
a popular novel. De luxe editions cost $25, lesser de luxe $10, and
the regular edition $5. Numerous copies were bought as *bon voyage*
gifts or to be sent to friends abroad. It prompted one of the most
pleasing tributes Gibson ever received. Said a critic in *The Artist*:
"A man must be born with a very unusual combination of qualities
to succeed as a social satirist. He must have strong analytical powers
and the lightest touch in expression, must bubble over with humor
that is always kindly without being a moralist, must detest sham
and vulgarity and must know the society he satirizes well and wisely
enough neither to be out of sympathy with it nor to be infatuated.
His style must be at once witty, serious, pungent and tender. These
are unusual qualities in combination, and they give to the man who,
possessing them, can draw well, deserved popularity and the power
of influencing for good his generation. We believe that they are

A DOUBLE WEDDING.
AT WHICH MR. PIPP MAKES HIS GREATEST SACRIFICE.

traceable with more or less distinctness in this series of *Mr. Pipp*."

Mr. Pipp won a lasting hold on his public. In 1905 his memory was still so green that Augustus Thomas did not hesitate to make a play out of him, its first act laid in the parlor of the *Pipp* home in New York; its second, the lawn of Carony Castle, Herts, England, ancestral seat of *Lady Fitzmaurice;* the third, the courtyard of a small hotel, Paris. The cast included Digby Bell as *Mr. Pipp,* Kate Denin Wilson as *Mrs. Pipp,* Janet Beecher as *Ida Pipp,* the handsome Robert Warwick as *John Willing,* and others who had made or would make their mark on stage and screen. Digby Bell, one of the pioneer American players in the Gilbert and Sullivan operettas, added to his physical suitability a splendid make-up for the star part

A FEW YEARS LATER.

A CHRISTENING OCCURS AND HERE WE LEAVE MR. PIPP WITH THE HONORABLE
VIOLA FITZMAURICE ON ONE KNEE AND MR. HIRAM PIPP WILLING ON THE
OTHER. ALTHOUGH THE EDUCATION OF MR. PIPP IS STILL INCOM-
PLETE, HE HAS LEARNED THAT HE HAS NOT LIVED IN VAIN.

and was *Mr. Pipp* to the life. Thomas, who had skillfully filled in
the Gibson framework, said that none of his plays had been more
fun to write. The comedy ran an entire season in New York, the
next on the road and was subsequently made into a motion picture.

Late in the 1920's Gibson was persuaded against his will to resur-
rect *Mr. Pipp,* to bring him back to *Life* for further education by
flapper granddaughters. But the spell had been broken, both for
the artist and his audience. This faintly sketched little wisp of a
man was not the old, inimitable *Mr. Pipp,* only his ghost, and like
the wraith he was he soon faded away. *Mr. Pipp* belongs to the age
of innocence of American travel in Europe, as a lively relic of which
he is affectionately remembered by his contemporaries.

IV

Before *Mr. Pipp* began his educational journey, the Spanish-American War had run its brief course. Gibson had not enlisted. His wife and his daughter were dependent upon him; he also contributed to the support of his mother and youngest sister, and his son, Langhorne, would be born in 1899. The few war drawings he made were in sympathy with the policy of level-headed *Life* which refused to be stampeded by the martial ardor of the sensational press.

Life pounded away at the embalmed beef scandal. With foresight shared only by an unheeded minority it looked askance at "manifest destiny" and imperialism as exemplified by the annexation of the Philippines. *These Foreign Relations. Do I want to Go in with that Crowd?* was the caption of a Gibson center page cartoon. Miss Columbia as a bathing girl stood hesitant at the edge of an unsavory surf in which the Kaiser, the Czar, and La Belle France were uncomfortably immersed. Again the magazine and its artist espoused the unpopular side when they took up the cudgels for the hard-fighting Regular Army, unhonored and unsung amid loud cheers for the Volunteers.

"Are you one of our heroic 71st?" a citizen in a Gibson cartoon asked a soldier.

"No," came the justly embittered answer. "I ain't no hero. I'm a Regular."

As a finale, Gibson drew sullen little Spain in toreador costume being offered the olive branch by Columbia with the words: "Come, let us forgive and forget."

It was in the service of another and far greater war of his country's that Gibson would use the full power of his pen. Meanwhile he was wielding it with telling effect in a peace-time cause without realizing his partisanship in the struggle. Through the last years of the nineteenth and the first of the twentieth century, scores of his drawings

AFTER THE WAR.

"WELCOME HOME! ARE YOU ONE OF OUR HEROIC 71ST?"

"NO, I AIN'T NO HERO. I'M A REGULAR."

were so many lusty blows in behalf of a social revolution swiftly advancing toward accomplishment. If he had been asked whether he intended his pictures as propaganda, he would have honestly denied it; he was, he would have said, simply illustrating timely and amusing phases of American life. Pressed further, he might have admitted that in some cases his pen was animated by a sense of fair play. Nevertheless and notwithstanding, those drawings directly and indirectly were potent factors in the emancipation of American women.

251

CHAPTER XIV

LADIES FIRST

I

The Goddess of the Wheel, as Gibson and many another artist now drew her, was not the Roman Fortuna. Fortuna, who balanced on but a single wheel and one without a pneumatic tire at that, was out of date. The new deity was a pretty American girl speeding joyously along on a bicycle. On that simple machine she rode like a winged victory, women's rights perched on the handlebars and cramping modes and manners strewn in her track.

For the athletic girl had come into her own, and no longer reserved for men only was the growing cult of sports, which had been promoted by increasing national wealth and resulting leisure and given social standing by British example. Far from a negligible weight in the scales was the advocacy of Gibson, "who did more through his drawings to convince maidens East and West that they wanted to be athletic than any number of health crusades could do," wrote Mildred Adams. "His long-limbed Dianas played tennis and golf, rode horseback (on side saddles), went in swimming, began bicycling out into the country. Every girl wanted to look like them."

The tide could not be stemmed. It was in vain that the etiquette columns of *The Ladies' Home Journal* under the editorship of that soul of propriety, Edward Bok, decreed in the late '90's that it was bad taste for a girl of eighteen to ride out alone with a young man or for a young girl, even for a frolic, to get herself up in any way that would tend to make her look masculine. In spite of such scoldings nobody considered extending Daisy's "bicycle built for two" to accommodate a chaperon, and few duennas could manage scorching and century runs under their own power. Besides, there was that

HER FIRST APPEARANCE IN THIS COSTUME.

SHE THINKS, ON THE WHOLE, SHE FEELS MORE AT HOME IN A BALL DRESS.

advantage in the bicycle era which Culter recalled in his *Gay 'Nineties* series: "A really nice girl in the none-too-safe '90's didn't have to walk home." As for the mannish attire condemned by the *Journal,* severe shirtwaists, Tyrolean and Homburg hats, divided skirts and even bloomers were what the well-dressed woman cyclist would wear and there was no stopping her.

You may read the story in the advertisements, those signs of the times. Cycling costumes are taking space from the evening bonnets and cape wraps. Hosiery is blossoming forth; much more is seen of stockings in this wheeling age, though they continue to be filled by limbs, not legs. Corsets (still decorously pictured unoccupied) are holding their own, hour-glass-shaped still but less armorial. The first shadow of its doom lies on the petticoat, its quantity production fallen off, for what lady likes to pedal against the encumbrance of five or six layers of lingerie beneath her cycling skirt which is heavy, woolen and weighted with lead sewn in the hem to keep it down to high, laced shoe tops and defend modesty? *The Ladies' Home Journal* prints a photograph of a damsel, fully dressed, holding up a union suit before her and looking heartily embarrassed by her pose. Purveyors of cut-glass bowls, zithers, and other objects dear to the feminine heart are yielding all along the line to the enticing ads. in which the bicycle manufacturers cry the merits of their tandems, singles, tires, pumps, brakes, saddles, and lamps. Even the bicycle clip is having its day, not only for men who wore slacks instead of knickers but as an essential employed by all the best boot-blacks who, when ladies climbed up on their high stands for a shine, politely clipped skirts around shoe rims.

A sunburn of feminine complexion, though not sought after, was no longer the tragedy it had been. Parasols were relegated to ladies who drove in victorias and attended garden parties. Fans lost favor to the breeze of the open road, and veils were confined to more formal

PLENTY OF GOOD FISH IN THE SEA.

travel than the bicycle until the automobile voluminously revived them. The trend was shown slightly even by the Florodora Sextette who began to sing and promenade their way across the stage to fame in 1900. Their big hats, pompadours, lavender gowns, and long gloves were in the height of the mode, but their long skirts, five yards around at the bottom, were, on the authority of an earnest student of research in the subject of "unmentionables," lined with ruffles to make the frou-frou sound. There was only an occasional petticoat among the Sextette who chiefly wore lace-trimmed slips and silk or muslin drawers, also scandalously lace-trimmed, as was noted by the audience one night when one of the Florodoras lost hers. She calmly picked it up, tucked it under her arm and went on with the dance.

For years longer there would be yards of skirt to manage, and women would continue to walk pigeon-toed because that allowed them longer steps before shoe tips hit sweeping skirts. They must still waddle when ascending stairs so that knees could assist in lifting the front edge of skirts, also held up at hip or back by a hand reserved to that duty. But a beginning had been made in the "reconciliation of drapery with transit." In wet weather the "Rainy Daisy" skirt swung clear of mud and puddles; it was worth it even though ladies had to organize a club to bolster up their courage to wear that daring garment. On fair days, the bicycle girl with a sigh of relief changed to a skirt short enough to avoid entangling alliances with pedals.

Irene Gibson years afterwards remembered the shock when she donned her first divided skirt for cycling and appeared blushing in that comparatively abbreviated garment. With her husband and a group of friends, she rolled over the asphalt strips, which public demand forced the city to install along the curbs of cobble-paved streets, and sped up and down Riverside Drive with the wheeling throngs. Or risking the perils of horsed trucks and cable cars and

PICTURESQUE AMERICA.
ANYWHERE ALONG THE COAST.

scorning the few wheezing automobiles, they dashed across the bridge to invade furthest Brooklyn with the zest of explorers.

In life and on paper, Gibson Girls were cycling, usually in skirts, since Gibson considered bloomers unbecoming to the female figure and for the most part refused to draw them except for comic purposes. They clearly were having the time of their lives, were these girls, either as adepts or novices. One asks another in *Life,* "Is it any fun getting a man to teach you how to ride a wheel?" And her friend enthusiastically answers, "Fun? Why, I've been taught three times." A Gibson center page drawing suggests the solution of the dilemma of which preachers were complaining when a fair Sunday found their churches scantily attended. The congregation and choir are shown speeding along on bicycles while the minister delivers his sermon perched sitting backward on the rear saddle of a tandem wheel pumped along by the sexton.

Before the day of the bicycle, the American Girl had played stately croquet, a bit of ladylike tennis, had ridden horseback and swum a little, had skated and indulged in the graceful attitudes of archery. Now she advanced, *dea ex machina,* farther and farther into the sphere of athletics, alluringly pictured, aided and abetted by her loyal chronicler, Charles Dana Gibson.

II

The Gibson Girl took up the new game of golf as soon as her creator had tried it. He did not much care for it—it took too much time and was not strenuous enough—but it did furnish a novel and attractive setting. A girl in sailor hat and full skirt, with a club over her shoulder, breezing across the links like a clipper ship under sail, made a picturesque subject. Come to think of it, too, there was some point in the leisureliness of golf if played by a mixed twosome. A man need not go on worrying about keeping his eye on the ball. He could frankly give up that alleged sport, recline against a bunker with his fair opponent and keep his eyes on her. It was at such

GOLF IS NOT THE ONLY GAME ON EARTH.

A LITTLE INCIDENT.
SHOWING THAT EVEN INANIMATE OBJECTS CAN ENTER INTO THE SPIRIT OF THE GAME.

moments, according to the Gibson pen, that the twosome would wonder, "Is a caddy always necessary?"

Right up in the van of the hunt, the Gibson Girl rode to the hounds. High on the box of a four-in-hand, she could tool a coach between "L" pillars and around street excavations when men whips gave up and drove through another street. At the seashore she swam, no longer merely bathed, though she kept struggling to prevent the waves from billowing up her skirt; and when she walked ashore under the gaze of men how pitifully and embarrassingly short that skirt seemed until she got used to it! Secretly the Gibson Girl did not mind the exposure much after all; her artist proved able to draw extremely shapely legs—a light he had hidden under a bushel of petticoats except for a few sketches of ballet girls.

She covered the tennis court with new vim. What if it were a hot game and it was unmaidenly to show the effects of exertion? "Mr. Gibson's beautiful heroines," remarks a commentator, "managed their sporting lives with no more dishevelment than a sparkling eye or a straying tendril." Nor can the artist be accused of falsifying the record. Thus many gifted members of the fair sex still manage in spite of the increased vigor of their athletics.

There was no sport girls wouldn't come to adopt at this rate, thought Gibson, and with a whimsical glance into the future he drew *The Coming Game. Yale vs. Vassar.* A Gibson Girl fullback, football tucked under arm, has broken loose from a lusty scrimmage and is tearing down the gridiron. Her teammates are blocking and interfering for her valiantly—all except for one example of the eternal feminine who has stepped to one side to put up her hair.

III

The battle for women's rights, it might be said, was won on the playing-fields of America. Sports and clothes suitable for them had been the opening gun. If liberty, equality, and fraternity were not yet attained, far more of them had been gained than the most optimistic woman had dreamed possible. That motto of freedom was invisibly engraven on every silver sports trophy cup annexed by maiden or matron.

Before that opener of the road, the bicycle, overlaid the rocking-chair, two other mechanical devices had taken quarterings from the distaff on triumphant womanhood's coat-of-arms: the typewriter and the telephone. The working girls Gibson drew were the governess, the saleswoman, the sempstress, the artist's model, the chorus girl, the housemaid. He had neglected the typist, the stenographer, the telephone operator, those unobtrusive pioneers in the business world. Now, just as it had dawned upon him at the Chicago World's Fair that women had invaded the arts, he perceived that they had stormed commerce and that some bold spirits among them were advancing beyond clerical jobs.

THE COMING GAME.
YALE VERSUS VASSAR.

More and more girls were going to college. The following jest Gibson had illustrated for *Life* in the early days no longer seemed so funny:

> THE GENERAL: Lieutenant Fraser has volunteered to lead the expedition? Why, it is almost certain death! I understood that he was married only about three months ago.
>
> THE COLONEL: He was but his wife believes in the higher education for women, and—
>
> THE GENERAL: Oh, well, let him go then.

For women's colleges could no longer be regarded by the reactionary male as a lay method of taking the veil or as a useful, though not essential preparation for teaching school. Gibson represented sweet girl graduates in cap and gown shyly and uncertainly confronting Old Man World who grinned broadly all across his map and tolerantly nodded his globular head. Actually it was Old Man World who was the more confused by evidence that the girls had acquired something more than a polite accomplishment. They meant to use this higher education of theirs to meet men mentally on equal terms, to break down the ancient male monopolies, to compete in business and the professions.

Such feminine phenomena were rare as yet and highly amusing, to most women as well as to men, particularly if you looked ahead and imagined the length to which ambitious ladies might go. Gibson, gently satiric, developed the comedy of his *In the Days to Come* and *When Our Betters Rule* series. He drew a women's council of war, the participants attired in becoming military tunics and field marshal millinery. Gibson Girls became handsome ambassadors and cabinet ministers. They presided on the bench or filled the pulpit.

Days to come? They were fast arriving in these early years of the twentieth century. When our betters rule? They were doing

STUDIES IN EXPRESSION.

WHEN WOMEN ARE JURORS.

considerable ruling right now, though they still wore the velvet
glove and discreetly directed from behind the scenes. Gibson could
draw his professional women as decoratively and satirically as he
liked and put cupids in his jury box or pumping his church organ.

AN AMBASSADOR'S BALL IN THE DAYS TO COME.

Without his realizing it, his old working coat on the left sleeve of
which he habitually wiped his pen point was the mantle of a prophet.
As with his Leap Year series, he would see every one of these drawings of his come partly or entirely true. By foretelling the future,
however, lightly and sceptically, he helped pave its way.

With Charles Dana Gibson's blessing—and a potent blessing it
was—American women could engage in almost any sport, provided
only that they be graceful about it. Could wear anything they liked
if only it were becoming (which included no species of trousers)
and decently modest. Could enter any honorable profession if they
preserved its and their own dignity. So they could and so they did.
Having gained all those objectives, they could also, as an after-
thought, have the vote if they wanted it. That, too, was only fair,

Gibson acknowledged, though he disliked the violent and vandalistic activities of the early suffragettes and owned misgivings as to the coarsening effect of politics on femininity. He indicated that apprehension when he pictured an especially beautiful Gibson Girl being notified of her election as sheriff. She stands hesitating between the beseeching looks of her dismayed husband and children and the congratulations of the delegation of raffish, dowdy female politicians who have brought her the news. But Gibson lost his doubts when his capable wife later served as a Democratic national committeewoman and worked energetically, if vainly, both in the Al Smith and John W. Davis campaigns. It didn't seem to hurt her.

IV

Let lovely woman stoop to politics if she wished. Perhaps she could elevate them. Certainly they needed the honesty, intelligence, and high-mindedness which always were characteristics of the Gibson Girl. If the day ever came when she lowered her standards and lost her maidenliness and charm—then Gibson would lose his enthusiasm for drawing her.

A campaign badge might find a place in a girl's scrapbook along with invitations, dance cards, concert and theatre programs, valentines, tin foil from bouquets, ribbons from gifts, the wrapping of the box which held her engagement ring, her wedding card and newspaper clippings relating that thrilling event, a railroad map showing the route of the honeymoon, Pullman car slips, hotel menus, and camera views of the children at all ages. But never could such endearing tokens be substituted for by political mementos or those of any other career. Gibson, romantic artist of a frankly romantic era, drew an army of appealing girls led on to victory under the generalship of a small cupid mounted on a pony. That was the keynote of the Gibson platform.

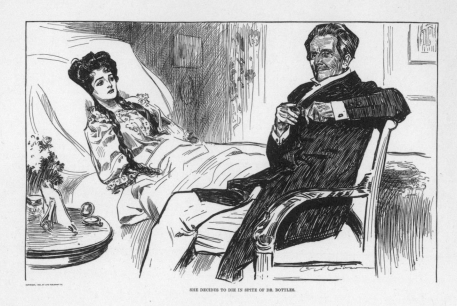

SHE DECIDES TO DIE IN SPITE OF DR. BOTTLES.

During this period appeared Gibson's second most successful character series after *Mr. Pipp: A Widow and Her Friends.* In her grief, *The Widow* contemplates the cloister. She falls ill but decides to die in spite of the doctor, just to be contrary. Bewitching brunette that she is, she finds consolation in her mirror. Exercise in a raven-haunted cemetery does not appeal to her. She emerges from mourning into the world again and widely assorted suitors throng about her—handsome Gibson Men, a persevering fat man, the old doctor, and a callow youth whose wooing of a dangerous widow fills his parents with alarm. Everywhere the suitors follow her. When she adopts a career as a trained nurse, they occupy every bed in her ward. In the hunting field she soars over fences, while her swains come croppers. When she goes to a costume ball as Juliet, every one of the varied crew arrives as Romeo, much to one another's annoyance. She envisions herself as a bride, but that will not do, for she had taken her wedding gown out of the camphor trunk and wept over it. At last, in a clever surprise ending, *The Widow* is seen in the

THE DAY AFTER ARRIVING AT HER JOURNEY'S END.

habit of a nun telling stories to a group of children, while her still faithful suitors, clad in cassock and bereta, sigh disconsolately and admire her from a distance.

V

Gibson, a Warwick behind a drawing-board, had crowned the American girl Queen of Love and Beauty. The times were ripe for her to enthrone herself as uncrowned Queen of the United States and she did not let the moment slip.

He had placed the once-termed weaker sex on a pedestal. They used it as a tier in an ever-rising pyramid.

SHE IS THE SUBJECT OF MORE HOSTILE CRITICISM.

CHAPTER XV

GILT-EDGED ART

I

From 1900 to 1905, Gibson was at the height of his powers as a black-and-white artist, placed in the front rank as a humorist, satirist, and illustrator by authorities at home and abroad. No man ever wore his laurels with more genuine modesty.

He had been elected to the American Institute of Arts and Letters in 1899 (to be elevated to the Academy of that body in 1921 and made a Director in 1932). But when the Society of Illustrators was founded in 1901 by Otto Bacher, Albert Sterner, and Henry Fleming, with W. D. Smedley as its first president, Gibson was not included. It was felt that he was too busy, too successful and perhaps too top-lofty to bother to take part in the Society's defense of the rights of less established artists and its encouragement of novices. That was a most mistaken assumption. Gibson instantly accepted his invitation to join in 1902, serving as president from 1904 to 1907, and from 1909 to 1921, and thereafter as honorary president. For years he took wholehearted part in all its activities. He presided at its brilliant and amusing gatherings at the Hotel Brevoort and the Salmagundi Club. When the Society staged its merry, ribald shows with skits by C. B. Falls, Robert Wildhack, Harry Grant Dart, and others, Gibson invariably occupied a stage box where half the audience delighted in watching him blush all over his bald spot. Gibson himself played a part when the Dutch Treat Club produced for its annual show a movie called "Bohemia, O Bohemia, or Starving for Art." Abandoning his natural dignity with comic effect, he appeared as an artist pleading for his hungry children and trying to sell a drawing to Editor John O'Hara Cosgrave. Gibson also was a congenial member of The Players, that agreeable haunt of the fine arts quartered in the charming old house on Gramercy Park, New York City, presented by Edwin Booth.

His ink bottle was like a horn of plenty. He could afford now to abandon flat-dwelling. After designs by McKim, Meade, & White, he built a handsome, comfortable house on East Seventy-third Street. A year later—in 1903—he was sailing in and out of the harbors of Islesboro on the Maine coast when he sighted the attractive point of Seven Hundred Acre Island. That same summer he bought it and soon began the building of the charming, rambling summer home which would be his refuge in times of stress to come.

Life more than ever wore the look of a Gibson scrapbook. There was much by him on a perennially appealing topic. A Gibson Girl as a flame and a man as the moth. A variation on the ancient theme of two's company, three's a crowd: the surplus man multiplied by the Gibson pen until he actually was a crowd. Kissing in the conservatory, that splendid sanctuary of romance soon doomed to disappear in a more cramped age, with no better substitute than a stairway. Couples riding in *Love's Express;* its engine is strenuously fired by cupids but its right of way runs over a rickety trestle and there are dark tunnels ahead. Gibson Girls in society and sports. *Easter Morning from a Susceptible Person's Point of View:* a panorama of pretty worshippers crowned by the imposing millinery of 1901. (*Life* averred that current hats had "delirium trimmings.") A satiric glimpse of a fashionable funeral. *Some of the Caretaker's Relations:* revelry in a town house whose owners are away for the summer. A gaudy chorus girl visiting her parents back on the farm. A series on *Mr. Tagg,* a snob, a minor and uninspired Gibson effort. The automobile made its appearance as a Gibson accessory with a drawing of collided runabouts driven by a girl and a man; with lovelorn looks they gaze across the wreckage at each other; title:

All Broken Up. But there was tragedy, too, in the new vehicle as
W. H. Walker had shown in his powerful cartoon called *Must We
Take the Law in Our Own Hands?* A woman lies limp beside a
smashed horse and buggy, the driver of which has struggled to his
feet with a rifle and shot the hit-and-run motorist fleeing down
the road.

LOVE'S EXPRESS.

There was never too much Gibson in *Life,* for wise editor Mitchell
kept a balance. During these years, the magazine's pages were
enhanced by such excellent series as Will Crawford's *Historic Bits*
and C. Allan Gilbert's *Reflections in a Mirror,* the love story of a
belle of the Revolution. Both of those series won praise from Gibson.

A good sportsman, he could take a joke on himself and even bear
the acid test of parody. Oliver Herford in 1907 drew for *Life* his
clever Gibson take-off: *The Astonishing Tale of a Pen and Ink Puppet, or The Genteel Art of Illustrating.* Here were stiff, wooden,
jointed Gibson Girls and Gibson-Davis Men, each figure part

AS HE APPROACHED, SHE TOSSED THE FLUTTERING
PAPER INTO THE SEA

"I am so tired of hearing they never lost a life on this line," she cried wearily

BISHOP VAN BRUT WAS A TREMENDOUS FAVORITE
AMONG THE LADIES OF HIS SET

From Oliver Herford's *The Astonishing Tale of a Pen and Ink Puppet*

marionette and part Noah's Ark. Dressed in evening clothes on all occasions, they took part in a series of ridiculous adventures. The accompanying lines hit off the puns to which *Life* was sometimes prone, as for instance:

"You are charmingly arch," said he.

"It is in the family," she replied airily. "My grandfather was an archbishop."

And *Bertie* saves Angelina's *Life*—when it blows overboard.

The famed Herford wit could be, and frequently was, biting. Gibson, however, took the travesty in good part and was highly amused by it.

Not only were fore pages of *Life* sprinkled with pictures by and material about Gibson but "the back of the book" was spotted with Gibsonian advertisements. It was at this period that the ads. recommended leather pillows to be burned with pyrography designs after Gibson, Gibson china plates, and the books collecting his drawings: *A Widow and Her Friends, The Weaker Sex, The Social Ladder, Everyday People, Americans.*

Nor was he neglected by the promotion department. Offers of Gibson calendars and of signed proofs of Gibson drawings with every subscription beckoned the new reader. The lure of the contest was dangled regularly. "What is a good title for this Gibson picture?" *Life* asked, and there were responses in plenty since $500 was the prize for the best answer. Then the crafty periodical ran a page adorned with the heads of twenty types of Gibson Girls, soliciting votes for favorites, the heads to be numbered in the order of preference and the winner to be the contestant who made the majority choice of Number One and so on down through the twenty. A maiden from a small Pennsylvania town won the $100 prize.

What with one attraction and another, subscriptions rolled in, followed by their inevitable and pleasing sequel, advertisements.

THE TRAGEDIAN AND HIS LANDLADY

Gold crammed the coffers of *Life*. Other magazines, enviously observing effect and delving back into cause, clearly perceived the prominent contribution to the latter by Charles Dana Gibson.

II

P. F. Collier, the Old Rough-and-Ready of the publishing world, was among those magazine geniuses who rose to power and wealth through the '90's—a group including Cyrus H. K. Curtis, who masked his might behind a mild manner and a set of snow-white whiskers; S. S. McClure, an eccentric, supercharged human dynamo, and the relentless Frank A. Munsey, the Merger. Pat Collier, who made his start by publishing Bibles and other books in the public domain and adding the name of nearly every purchaser to the subscription list of his weekly, passed on the torch into the uncalloused but even more able hands of his son, Robert. Although the education of that scion of a shirtsleeves generation had included such inconsequentials as when properly to present a lady with violets and the apt quotation of Swinburne and Verlaine, his inheritance of practicality remained undiluted. It was he who engineered the promotion of that considerable success, Dr. Eliot's Five-foot Shelf of Classics, and he fanned the spark of enterprise which was characteristic of *Collier's*.

It did not matter greatly that Bob Collier, when he became head of the firm after his father's death, strenuously pursued a career as a *bon-vivant,* spending much of his winters gadding about in society and Europe and his summers on his princely Adirondack estate. Like Curtis, McClure, and Munsey, he had surrounded himself with a talented staff in all departments. Between conferences with their chief in the mountains where they would be sent out fishing only to be upset when Robert the Magnificent playfully darted around them in his speed-boat, his editors and advertising managers carried on with his helpful, if occasional, direction. *Collier's,* altered from an amorphous review to a popular weekly, staged such splendid crusades as its fight for a pure food and drug law, and its pages were magnetized by the work of foremost writers and artists of the day.

Beautifully illustrated though the magazine was by such lights as Maxfield Parrish, Remington, Frost, Pyle, and Smedley, a valuable addition was indicated. Collier and his staff, shrewdly observing *Life's* well-being, determined on action. The word went forth to get Gibson—to pay him as high as $800 or $900 a drawing if necessary—to sign him up exclusively.

The price was dazzling, but the proposition instantly struck a snag. The loyal Gibson refused to desert *Life* and John Ames Mitchell who had launched him on his career and whose friendship and counsel had meant so much to him through nearly a score of years. Forsake all others Gibson might, but not *Life*. Since he could not be swerved from that resolution, *Collier's* decided to take the next best course and share the coveted artist with the humorous weekly.

Through the grapevine of the publishing world the news spread that Gibson was about to sign a contract. From Philadelphia opposition manifested itself. Edward Bok of *The Ladies' Home Journal* objected.

Among other astute editorial qualities of the Dutch immigrant who had risen to the command of one of the most influential and profitable magazines in the United States was frugality. Bok once had bought a Gibson Girl head for a song at one of the artist's exhibitions and used it for a *Journal* cover; similarly he had picked up cheaply at a second serial right price an illustration from *The Social Ladder*. However, when the bargain counter was empty he had paid as high as $500 apiece for Gibson drawings. Now here was *Collier's* proposing to hoist that considerable sum several hundred dollars and shut out competition. Intimations issued from Philadelphia that the New York weekly's alleged offer was, if true, downright extravagance and arrant publicity ballyhoo in the opinion of an editor who had purchased an original Gibson for as low as $80.

Publicity value was far from being discounted by Bob Collier and his acute business manager, Condé Nast. It is said they were prompted by the Bok strictures to raise the contemplated Gibson rate to an even $1,000 per drawing. Better yet, why not contract for one hundred drawings at one hundred thousand dollars? There

LOST

was a round, resounding sum that ought to hold Philadelphia and the rest of the country, not to mention foreign parts. Lest "misleading comments" create any doubt about it, *Collier's* took considerable newspaper space to broadcast Gibson's acceptance as follows:

> P. F. Collier & Son.
> Dear Sirs:
> I hereby accept your offer of $100,000 for one hundred double-page cartoons to be delivered to you during the next four years. And I agree to draw only for "Collier's Weekly" and "Life."
> Sincerely yours,
> C. D. GIBSON

This was recorded as the largest amount ever paid an illustrator for such a commission. So great an expenditure was made possible by advertising revenue, for the magazine advertiser, as Mark Sullivan declared, had taken over the rôle once played by the Medici and the noble patrons of English literature. Authors and artists with Big Names (or their makings)—readers—circulation—advertising—profits, profits which supplied motive power to continue the golden cycle's revolution. That wheel of fortune could not fail, granted editors able to keep it pivoted on fickle, sometimes unaccountable and unpredictable, public taste.

In the light of that essential, was the huge investment in Gibsons justified? At first there was some doubt about it. Gibson society drawings proved too rich and delicate fare for many an old-time *Collier's* subscriber. Cancellations and returns from the American News Company, ominous signs, came in. But soon new orders more than compensated, and many of these new readers, coming from a higher income class, represented the purchasing power which is dear to the hearts of advertisers. On that score alone, Gibson was worth all he was being paid.

HIS FORTUNE.
"YOU ARE GOING ON A LONG, LONG JOURNEY."

Out blossomed *Collier's* on October 15, 1904, with a special Gibson Number, an extraordinary featuring seldom given a contributor by any magazine. From start to finish, it fairly teemed with Gibson, and a less balanced man might easily have suffered a severe attack of megalomania when he glanced through this table of contents:

Cover Design. (A Gibson Girl head in pastel.)

Frontispiece. "Dangerous." (A Gibson Girl in the vast hat and menacing hatpins of the day.)

Notable Gibson Drawings for *Collier's*. (Excerpts of eight favorite Gibson Girls.)

A Letter from Mr. Gibson. (Advice to young artists on pen-and-ink drawing, illustrated by a photograph of the author at work in his studio.)

Charles Dana Gibson. An Appreciation by Robert Bridges.

The Flat-Dwellers and *Brothers and Sisters*. (Two social satire drawings by Gibson.)

His Fortune. You Are Going on a Long Journey. (This splendid double-page is one of Gibson's most memorable pictures. A benign

THE STORY OF AN EMPTY SLEEVE.

old gentleman gazes unafraid across a table at the appealing little cherub who is glancing up at him from an array of fortune-telling cards foretelling death.)

A Dialogue of Disarmament. Verses by Wallace Irwin, illustrated by Gibson.

A Disturber of the Peace. (Another Gibson Girl.)

Sandwiched in between successive Gibsons were articles on graft, the Russo-Japanese War, and the launching of the battleship *Connecticut,* along with a story, and some miscellany. Nobody noticed them particularly. It was the Gibson drawings which sold the issue so prodigiously at ten cents a copy. And many availed themselves of the offer of proofs of pictures in the number ("suitable for framing") at fifty cents each.

A year later *Collier's* repeated with a second Gibson Number. Again there were a Gibson cover and frontispiece, with ten more of his drawings and a glowing tribute by Robert W. Chambers; also that notable double-page, *The Story of an Empty Sleeve,* in which a lad, posed by Lang Gibson, hangs with grave and fascinated absorption upon a Civil War veteran's tale of his battles.

GOING TO WORK.

DEDICATED TO THE EMPLOYERS OF CHILDREN.

The format of *Collier's,* larger than *Life's,* gave Gibson greater scope. Although his originals would take reduction excellently, they now needed less, and his bold, sweeping, confident lines were more noteworthy than ever—a technique which displayed mastery of his medium. Once Phil May, the English artist whose style embodied the same elimination of non-essentials, was asked by a fussy art editor to finish up a drawing. "When I can leave out half the lines I now use," May replied, "I shall want six times the money!"

With George Wharton Edwards, art editor of *Collier's,* and his assistant, Frank De Sales Casey, Gibson worked in complete harmony. They always could depend on him to send in his drawings on time; the high-priced star refrained from becoming temperamental. The only occasion on which he rose in wrath was when an engraver presumed to cut out some of the whites in a drawing of his. Gibson, tipped off by Casey, arrived and raised thunder until copy was followed exactly. All the staff grew fond of the unassuming artist. Young Wallace Irwin, looking up to him with a cub's adulation, would later bring Gibson into his renowned *Japanese Schoolboy* series. Relating an incident in the 1914 American invasion of Mexico when Richard Harding Davis was captured by the Mexicans and in danger of being shot at sunrise as a spy, Irwin made his ingenuous Oriental quote one of the other imprisoned correspondents thus: "It was deliciously easy for Hon. Dick to obtain own mistaken and injust arrest so we can suffer in prison and thusly become International Issue. International Issues are worth 25c a word . . . And to be shot at sunrise are more luck than we could deserve! Think of the picture it would make! If Gibson was only with us."

On *Collier's,* Gibson was entirely his own idea man. Love continued to be a theme. A girl and a man at chess (*His Move*) or at bridge where they failed to keep their minds on the game to the irritation of their old and crabbed partners. *A Castle in the Air—*

A CASTLE IN THE AIR.

THESE YOUNG GIRLS WHO MARRY OLD MILLIONAIRES SHOULD STOP DREAMING.

age married to youth. Also there were many keen studies of types: fellow passengers on street car or ferryboat; at the matinee; the baseball bleechers—*Two Out and the Bases Full; Lost,* which showed a heterogeneous crowd comforting a frightened child. And some of the drawings had the force of moving sociological documents, such as *The Army of Work,* a street scene of a morning throng on its way to office and factory, with a thin, wistful little girl in the foreground. That picture helped to forward the long, hard fight against child labor.

Gibson and Conan Doyle's *Sherlock Holmes* (forever visualized by Frederick Dorr Steele's illustrations and William Gillette's stage impersonation) were rated as *Collier's* greatest circulation makers. Constantly exploiting Gibson's work, the magazine extracted its money's worth.

Gibson was in full swing as a *Collier's* artist when some field work was suggested by Editor Norman Hapgood whose editorials and choice of timely, vital issues had so definitely raised the prestige of the magazine. Its gospel might be further spread and its title as "The National Weekly" better secured if a tour of the country were undertaken by its editor. And lest that praiseworthy effort escape the notice of the customers, it might be well to take along the celebrated Mr. Gibson.

In spite of his dislike for publicity, Gibson dutifully agreed to go. Hapgood found him pleasant, companionable and cheerful though eager to have it all over with and return home. Public interest had not been overestimated. Going about with Gibson was, as Mitchell once remarked, like travelling with a circus. People, learning the artist's identity, which Hapgood was at no pains to conceal, flocked about the lion. There was more to it than gazing upon a celebrity and telling him which of his drawings you liked best, for the man was a witty conversationalist and an entertaining speaker at clubs

SERIOUS BUSINESS

A young lawyer arguing his first important case

THE GREATEST GAME IN THE WORLD—HIS MOVE

and chambers of commerce. He was fair game for innumerable
interviewers and photographers. Everywhere vast enthusiasm
greeted him, led but by no means monopolized by human copies
of the Gibson Girl.

Such was Fame. The artist knew that gracious goddess well by
this time. Hadn't he sketched her himself in black-and-white? But
now he realized overwhelmingly that, so portrayed, she could no
longer entrance him. She lacked color.

COPYRIGHT, 1904, BY COLLIER'S WEEKLY, NEW YORK.   "TWO STRIKES AND THE BASES FULL."

CHAPTER XVI

A RAINBOW FADES

I

A Study in Black and White could have been the title of Charles Dana Gibson's life story from the silhouettes of his childhood on through his heyday as a pen draftsman until 1905 when he made an extraordinary decision.

No other choice than pen-and-ink had been open in the '80's to a young artist ambitious to make his way in the field of illustration. But now American Art was spiritedly showing its colors. Color printing was advancing steadily toward that remarkable proficiency it would attain in the 1930's. American canvases and murals were no longer without honor in their own country. One by one, Gibson had watched his colleagues, Abbey, Frost, Remington, Parrish, Smedley, abandoning ink for oils.

"I don't paint because I have no time for it. I can't afford it," Gibson had declared. But he could afford it now, and of course he had wanted to paint for years. There never was a penman who did not yearn sooner or later for the palette. If it were only a new medium that was desired, Gibson might have taken up etching; in fact, he once bought the paraphernalia but went no further. His craving was for color, the color of life. Critics had stated that his black-and-whites possessed the quality of suggesting color. That was not enough; he must depict it. Work he had done in pastels spurred him on. It remained to be discovered whether Joseph Pennell, who was not given to light verdicts, was right when he affirmed that Gibson could be a colorist.

The question mark loomed large. Gibson's occasional use of the brush for half-tones had been criticized as confused. Painting meant

CHARLES DANA GIBSON AT THE HEIGHT OF HIS CAREER

—not starting all over again, for he could build on solid foundations of fine draftsmanship and composition—but setting himself back to an amateur status at the height of his career as a pen-and-ink artist. There was no guaranty of success. With his eyes fully open to the risks but without hesitation, once his mind was made up, Gibson announced his decision.

What a tremendous stir it caused! Such is the penalty of celebrity. Upon the discomfited artist descended a cascade of solicitude and well-intentioned advice the burden of which was: Don't. Even casual acquaintances presumed to discuss with him his hopes and ambitions. He did not resent it—his own drawings had plunged him into this goldfish bowl—but it bothered him by placing mental hazards in his course. Financially-minded friends figured up Gibson's losses for him. Here he was, tossing away a cool $65,000 a year at least: $25,000 from *Collier's*, $20,000 from *Life*, and $20,000 in book royalties at the rate they had been coming in. Gibson let heads be shaken and tongues cluck pityingly over his rash action. Maybe it was foolish and reckless. What these people failed to understand was that money and applause were not his immediate goals now. All he wanted was to go off and, as he expressed it, "have his kittens alone."

Those who knew the man best appreciated that his determination was natural and characteristic. He believed that in pen-and-ink he had reached, by no means the summit, but his limit of achievement. Progress was a primary requirement of his being, and color was the logical line of endeavor. Coasting along on the crest of his pen's popularity would bring him only eventual unhappiness and frustration.

The income from his large earnings was quite sufficient to keep his family in comfort for the rest of their lives under normal circumstances; his savings had been carefully invested not according to

JUST A SKETCH ABOUT NOTHING IN PARTICULAR

LEAP YEAR

He: YOU NEVER COMPLIMENT ME ANY MORE ON MY APPEARANCE.
She: OH, CHARMING! CHARMING! CHARMING!

an artist's vagaries but by the counsel of Wall Street friends who should know whereof they spoke. Nor, with such a backlog, need he ever be reduced to the struggles and flatteries of portrait painting as had been the lot of Great-grandfather "Guillaume" Lovett. It would never be advertised that Charlot D. Gibson, of Rue 73me est, New York, "practiced his art with speed and fidelity and hoped for the honor of orders."

So Gibson took his radical, almost unparalleled step and departed amid fanfares and flourishes. His magazines announced their anticipation of his forthcoming work in oils. Richard Harding Davis said of his friend: "He need not worry about the future, for he can always go back to his past." In an appreciation in *Collier's*, Robert W. Chambers wrote of "the firm admixture of humility and pride with which he [Gibson] leaves behind what for most men would have been a satisfying success, and starts, when nearly 40, on an absolutely unknown road. . . . Wherever he goes, whatever he purposes, let him remember that we do not forget him nor forget what he has done for us. Let him remember that we wish him well, that we believe in him, that we will be unchanged when, in his own time, he returns to his people."

Last chance for Gibson Calendars, advertised *Life*. Most heart-warming of all was that periodical's send-off of its favorite artist: a double-page composite in the issue of November 30, 1905, arranged by Victor S. Perard. Under the title, *Au Revoir, Gibson,* a throng of Gibson characters crowd the dock to wish their creator Godspeed. How many and varied they were! Few readers had realized that before. There were *Mr. Pipp* and *The Widow,* dowagers and house-maids, peers and chorus girls, types from every walk of life, cherubs and children, and everywhere Gibson Girls, blonde and brunette, all beautiful and all dissolved in tears.

It was only a fantasy, just a page of paper. Yet there was some-

AU REVOIR, GIBSON!

thing affecting in that tribute and the affection it expressed. Friends and all whom Gibson drawings had given joy for years need only scan that page, need not themselves wave farewell from the real dock, to feel the pangs of parting.

As the liner steamed toward Europe, at Gibson's side was that pearl without price, a wife with faith in him, and a daughter and son of whom he could also be proud. A year in Spain, a year in France, a year in Italy stretched before them. The prow of the steamship seemed pointed through the arch of a brilliant, beckoning rainbow. Yonder lay color and high adventure.

II

So often the public's memory is short. An idol passes and is swiftly forgotten. But Gibson had made too deep an impress on his times for his to be a case of out of sight, out of mind. His work had attained the stature of an American tradition. Months after the echoes of his send-off had died away and his drawings which magazines had "in the barrel" had been printed, his name was on more lips than ever. People were singing it now.

For the Gibson Girl was firmly refusing a lace cap and a chair by the fireside. Old? Nonsense! She was in her prime. While her creator was absent in Europe considering her coloring, she quietly bought a make-up box of her own, studied dramatics and went on the stage.

She long had had experience in *tableaux vivants*. In 1901, Marguerite Merrington had written for her *The Gibson Play,* a two-act comedy based on *A Widow and Her Friends,* and it had been performed by amateurs. She became a professional in 1905 with the performance of Thomas's *Mr. Pipp.* Now, gayer than ever, she left comedy for musical comedy and revues. As if to show her sire that she was as much at home abroad as he was, she opened in London.

WAITING FOR TABLES.

The Belle of Mayfair by H. E. Brookfield and Cosmo Hamilton was produced in 1906 and immediately took the town by storm. Edna May was the star, but another actress sang the song which turned out to be the hit of the show. It was Camille Clifford, a Swedish-American girl, tall, slim and golden-blonde, who advanced to the footlights, followed by a chorus as débutantes, and coquettishly and tunefully asked (in the words of Leslie Stiles and to music by Leslie Stuart) why she was called a Gibson Girl.

> I walked one day along Broadway (ran the first verse)
>   When I was in New York.
> A friend of mine said, "My, you're fine.
>   You've got the Gibson walk.
> You have the pose and Gibson nose
>   And quite the Gibson leer.
> You've surely heard of the man called Gibson."
> GIRLS: You mean the fellow called Dana Gibson.
> SOLO: What he meant was not quite clear
>   Until I landed over here.

295

Chorus

Why do they call me a Gibson Girl,
Gibson Girl, Gibson Girl?
What is the matter with Mister Ibsen?
Why Dana Gibson!
Wear a blank expression and a monumental curl
And walk around with a bend in your back,
Then they call you a Gibson Girl.

II

Just walk round town, look up and down,
    The girls affect a style
As they pass by with dreamy eye
    Or a bored and languid smile.
They look as if they'd had a tiff
    With Hicks or Beerbohm Tree.
They do their best, for they've seen pictures,
    The pictures by the man called Gibson . . . *etc.*

False rhymes and inanities never affect the success of a song possessing the unidentifiable germ of popularity as this song did. In this case, no damage was done even by dragging in the name of a Scandinavian dramatist because the lyric writer was stumped for a rhyme with "Gibson," nor by references, esoteric outside of England, to a couple of British actor-managers. Cleverly staged and capably sung, the song "went over."

Miss Clifford's "blank expression" and "bored and languid smile" as called for in the script were nevertheless charming. She was encored again and again. It had not been intended of course to give her the hit number; that the song became so was one of those unpredictable happenings of the theatre. Now it was too late to do anything about it. Naturally Edna May was piqued when a minor character stole the show, and she retired in high dudgeon from the cast. Miss Clifford, who had further consolidated her position on the stage by marrying the soldier scion of a noble British family, sang her triumphant way through the season.

TRAGIC MOMENTS

ACCEPTING THE MAN YOU DON'T WANT

The startling fact that his name had been set to music broke upon Gibson when he reached London. A billboard advised him in large letters that Camille Clifford was "The Original Gibson Girl." That was news to him as similar claims had been on other occasions. He never had seen or heard of her before. Years later the lady called on him in New York and begged him to make a sketch of her in her album. He obliged and she became an authentic Gibson Girl at last.

Now he inquisitively bought a seat for *The Belle of Mayfair,* stipulating that he be given an inconspicuous one. For once at Daly's Theatre in New York he had been surprised by the appearance of a Gibson Girl sketch and, since he had seen friends of his in the audience, he rose and unobtrusively left. Those friends might think, he feared, that he had come to see himself and his characters applauded. At the show in London, noticing no one he knew, he stayed through the performance and gave ear to Miss Clifford's alleged wonder as to why she was called a Gibson Girl.

It was long before he heard the last of that song. Crossing the Channel, he dropped in at the Jardin de Paris to behold a whole chorus tunefully expressing the same perplexity. *"Pourquoi m'appelle-t-on une fille Gibson?"* they demanded. All over the city the *midinettes* echoed the question. If anybody knew the answer, it was the French models who once had posed for Gibson, Eugenie and Suzanne.

Valeska Surratt sang the song in the New York production of *The Belle of Mayfair* and made it as much of a sensation as it had been in London. To top off the number, the Gibson Girl chorus posed tableaux of several of the artist's best-known pictures to tumultuous applause. Said a review: "The posings which followed the celebrated Gibson pictures were admirable, and the chorus work puts to shame any other chorus effect in New York."

Other legitimate shows and vaudeville sketches hurried out with

VALESKA SURRATT

THE STOUT GENTLEMAN HOPED HE HAD FOUND A SECLUDED SPOT FOR THE HONEYMOON.

Gibson numbers. In *The Tenderfoot,* Richard Carle perpetrated a song in which the Gibson Girl was described as "sylph-like, spiritu-elle, graceful as a gazelle." The first Ziegfeld *Follies* blossomed out with an elaborate act glorifying the Gibson Girl on the beach, at sea, and as *The Widow* who was "waiting for another Gibson Man." The song hit of the revue was *The Gibson Bathing Girl,* winsomely sung by Annabelle Whitford. To music by Alfred Solman, she sang these lyrics of Paul West—far cleverer than their predecessors:

I

I am one of the queens
Of the best magazines,
Long by Charles Dana Gibson made famous.
We have shown you the charms
Of our shoulders and arms,
And we really don't think you can blame us;
But we hated to hide
Other beauties beside,
And we fumed at the artist's omission.
So one day we rose
In revolt at long clothes,
And presented this tearful petition:

Chorus

Mister Gibson, Mister Gibson!
Why can't we take a swim?
Paint us, please, with dimpled knees,
And plenty of rounded limb.
Mister Gibson, Mister Gibson,
Just give your brush a whirl!
And they'll say on the beach, "There's a peach,
A peach of a Gibson Bathing Girl!"

II

There are mermaids, they say,
Swimming round in the bay,
And the rocks by the sea they look grand on,
But we Gibson girls smile,
We can beat them a mile,
For they haven't a leg they can stand on.
As we stroll by the shore,
Loud the breakers may roar,
But the brokers roar more to get to us,
And they gaze at us long,
And we murmur the song
That we sang to the artist who drew us.

Chorus

Mister Gibson, Mister Gibson . . . etc.

Bathing costumes were responding to such urgings, skirts and sleeves growing shorter, and some daring damsels were whispering to each other that stockings were a bother in swimming. Peek-a-boo shirtwaists were the mode. Evening gowns were beginning to cling a bit, and scandalized observers muttered against such "sculptural indiscretions." Many an old-fashioned husband, called upon to hook up the back of his wife's dress, was more shocked than relieved to find how fast that chore was shrinking.

But the song of those sirens, the Gibson bathing girls, fell on deaf ears so far as Mister Gibson was concerned. It would take a crash that shook the United States to distract him.

III

His whole endeavor was concentrated on his painting. From Spain where he worshipped at the shrine of Velasquez, he moved on to Paris and became a student once more. It was slow, hard work, yet Gibson was content since he had not expected it to be otherwise.

Although one of his portraits was hung in a salon, he did not esteem it highly. Most of his canvases he threw away. Americans who saw his work, fellow-artists and critics, declared that it lacked distinction nor would he himself have quarrelled with that verdict. Albert Sterner was one of a few who believed that Gibson's paintings were underrated. Anyway, there was plenty of time and he was determined that eventually he would succeed.

Then Fate snatched the palette out of his hands.

Over the cables came dismaying news. In Wall Street, the messenger boys were scurrying about more frantically than young Dana Gibson ever had in his day there. If he were now to re-draw his picture, *Some Ticker Faces,* he would limn far more distraught looks on the countenances of the brokers and customers staring at the sinking figures on the tape. The Panic of 1907 had the country in its grip.

Life finally was able to print a cartoon showing President Theodore Roosevelt unveiling a statue of J. P. Morgan as the saviour of his country, with both bulls and bears cheering. But before the flood was dammed, terrific damage had been done.

A large part of Gibson's savings were wiped out with the failure of the Knickerbocker Trust Company. He could not reproach himself with improvidence or carelessness, for he had sought the most competent advice he knew on his finances. Fortunately he had enough money left and there would be sufficient salvage so that this debacle need not mean poverty or hardship for himself and his family.

What it did mean was the end of a cherished, brightly colored dream. He must give up his painting, with study abroad. Never would he sacrifice the advantages he planned for his children to his own ambition. He must go home and take up his pen again.

When his steamer sailed westward, the rainbow had vanished from the horizon and cloudy skies were a dull, dispiriting gray.

SOME TICKER FACES.

CHAPTER XVII

BLACK-AND-WHITE RENAISSANCE

I

Back in the United States, Gibson watched the summer sun glisten on calm waters lapping the shores of islands off the Maine coast. In his sailboat, rounding the point where his home stood, he struggled with the readjustment of his life. Financial worries to which he had so long been a stranger pressed upon him.

"Another trick at the wheel," he told himself, seeing the duty that lay ahead, with no alternative. He did not brood over it—that was foreign to his nature—but he could not throw off the burden of his crushing disappointment. He firmly believed that he was through in his early forties. He might, he probably could, earn his way with his pen again, yet he would lack that vital impulse: a sense of progress.

Landing at his dock, he was told that Mr. William C. Gibson had arrived from New York to see him. In "Pop" Gibson, the host greeted an old friend for whom, as art editor of *Puck,* he had drawn years ago. Now art editor of *Cosmopolitan Magazine,* "Pop" Gibson came bearing an invitation back into the world of black-and-white, a commission to illustrate the serialization of *The Common Law,* a novel by Robert W. Chambers.

That assignment did not appeal to the artist, nor would any have attracted him in his present frame of mind. But it was pleasing to be sought after, to learn that he had not been forgotten. Above all, he could not afford to refuse an offer which paid $900 an installment, with the serial scheduled to run for eight months.

"Pop" Gibson carried back an acceptance of the project he had originated. The *Cosmopolitan* recently had been bought by William Randolph Hearst, whose eagle eye for a promising property had not

"I KNOW PERFECTLY WELL THAT THIS ISN'T RIGHT"

From *The Common Law* by Robert W. Chambers

failed him. He lavishly supplied the sinews and the magazine announced as a slogan: "The very best at any price," pointing as proof to its acquisition of Gibson and Chambers whom it termed the highest-paid illustrator and the highest-paid novelist. Under the editorship of Perriton Maxwell, the *Cosmopolitan* was beginning to flourish like the green bay tree. The editor was bagging readers with such sure-fire material as the stories of Jack London, Arthur B. Reeve, David Graham Phillips, and George Randolph Chester, in-

DRAWN BY CHARLES DANA GIBSON

This was the man—across there on a step-ladder. And he was evidently not yet thirty; and his name was Neville, and his friends called him Kelly

© *Cosmopolitan Magazine*

From *The Common Law* by Robert W. Chambers

CHARLES DANA GIBSON AND ROBERT W. CHAMBERS DISCUSSING THE ILLUSTRATIONS FOR "THE TURNING POINT"

Gibson's miniature preliminary layouts can be seen on the cardboard

ventor of that fat, jolly, popular rogue, *Get-Rich-Quick Wallingford;* also with numerous, large-scale illustrations by Harrison Fisher, James Montgomery Flagg, and Howard Chandler Christy.

As loudly as *Collier's,* the *Cosmopolitan* trumpeted for its new, costly talent. *The Common Law,* it vaingloriously stated, was "probably the most compelling piece of fiction since *Uncle Tom's Cabin* and *Trilby."* It was a "palpitating serial, superbly and profusely illustrated by Charles Dana Gibson, creator of the 'Gibson Girl' and foremost of American illustrators. . . . Scarcely an American home but contains a reproduction of this artist's work."

While *The Common Law* was far from being the masterpiece it was asserted to be (critics considered it much inferior to Chambers' preceding historical novels), it fulfilled the rosiest hopes for its reception. This story of the beautiful, refined *Valerie West,* artist's model through force of circumstances, and the handsome, chivalrous artist, *"Kelly" Neville,* was the sex-thriller of the day. It would have caused scarcely a ripple in 1936, but it shocked and titillated the readers of 1910-11 to the core. Would *Valerie* ("a new *Trilby"*) forego her innate modesty and pose in the altogether? Good Heavens, yes! After considerable soul-conflict, she would and did. In view of the fact that *Neville's* aristocratic family so strongly opposed a mesalliance, would this fair heroine give herself to the hero "in the simple bonds of love without the form of marriage"? Readers were on tenterhooks to find out. The magazine, taking gleeful note of the storm of discussion aroused, remarked that "there is a vast difference, it should be remembered, between intention and execution." And the over-scandalized were soothed with the information that "concluding installments would bring home a strongly moral lesson."

Gibson and Chambers, who had worked at neighboring drawing-boards at the Art Students' League in 1883, collaborated closely.

The artist ruled a yard square sheet into forty-eight oblongs, six by eight inches, in correspondence to the eight installments of the serial. Consulting marked paragraphs in the proof, he filled in the oblongs with rough sketches after close study of the characters and situations. Thus he obtained a comprehensive view of the whole work and achieved the economy of finishing several pictures without recalling a model again and again. The best models in New York were employed, said the magazine, and "for each one chosen, a dozen eagerly apply at the red-painted door of the artist's studio overlooking Central Park."

It was a splendid job of illustration. You can scan the bold, sure pen-strokes and never suspect that Gibson's heart was not in his work; that the zest with which he had illustrated Davis's *Gallegher* and *Princess Aline,* for instance, was absent. *Valerie* upheld the Gibson Girl tradition. Gibson even managed to make tolerable an ugly mode of the day, the hobble skirt and inverted dishpan hat— that costume which, said *Life,* frightened children and forced men to reassure: "Don't cry, Tommy, it's only a woman."

But readers searched in vain for an illustration of the scene where the embarrassed *Valerie* poses in the nude. Gibson, not a little disturbed by the fact that the story had been called sexy, left that episode to the text and skated around it with great circumspection. There was no hint of such appeal in his drawings. There never had been and there never would be.

The Common Law began in the November, 1910, issue. In December and February, Gibson contributed pastel portraits of the heroine for the cover, with his name in large letters beneath. For his friend, Chambers, he did his best and gave value received to the magazine. Its circulation started its rise from 200,000 to top the million mark. "The Chambers-Gibson combination is unquestionably the biggest hit of the decade in the magazine world. It is im-

Collier's

THE NATIONAL WEEKLY

VOL XLVI NO 6   DRAWN BY CHARLES DANA GIBSON   COPYRIGHT 1910 BY P. F. COLLIER & SON   OCTOBER 29 1910

A "COLLIER'S" COVER OF 1910

mensely popular with *Cosmopolitan* readers," the magazine reported. Appearing as a book ("Dedicated to Charles Dana Gibson, a friend of many years"), Chambers' novel sold heavily. Many of the Gibson illustrations were reproduced, taking reduction well to the book's smaller format. Book publishers in these years were still embellishing their novels with pictures and happily had not yet resorted to the economy of omitting all art work except on the dust jackets.

311

Maxwell secured Gibson's signature to a three-year contract and when it expired desired to extend it three years. More Chambers-Gibson collaborations followed in quick succession: *The Turning Point* (book title, *Japonette*); *The Streets of Ascalon, The Story of a Woman's Sacrifice for the Love of a Man; The Business of Life, A Modern-Day Story of Love, Life, and Passion.* Gibson next illustrated Rex Beach's *The Auction Block, A Story of Stage Life and a Young Girl's Sacrifice.* The formula was too successful to be abandoned. Gibson drew a succession of harassed heroines named Diana, Cynthia, Sylvia, and so on, drew them in their dilemmas rather wearily but drew them beautifully.

II

Gibson's drawings were in demand also by *Good Housekeeping, McCall's* and *Hearst's International,* now edited by Norman Hapgood. The Luxembourg Museum wrote to purchase a Gibson pen-and-ink to hang in its collection, and the artist selected one of his best, *The Champion.* Along a street swings a prizefighter, obviously James J. Jeffries, his gorilla bulk adorned by frock coat and top hat; he towers above a surrounding crowd of small boys who hurry to keep pace, gazing up at him in transports of hero-worship.

And Gibson had thought that nobody wanted his work any more! Most cheering of all was the fact that Mitchell and *Life* were as cordially receptive as ever.

Life in its Thirtieth Birthday Number, January, 1913, looked back on its career. Those years, it observed, had "found New York four or five stories high and they have left it largely in the clouds. They have found its shopping district below Twenty-third Street and they have shoved it up the hill and along two miles of Fifth Avenue."

THE CHAMPION.

Frederick enjoys the Flower Show in Our Village

They had brought the telephone, the electric light, the trolley car, typewriter, cash register, bicycle, subway, graphophone, camera, motion pictures, aeroplane, and automobile, with business offices full of girls; beef raised from fifteen cents a pound to twenty-eight, and cooks from $16 a month to $35. Yet though *Life* had advanced with the times, it was happy to revive a feature of its glorious past. Once more its cover was emblazoned with a Gibson Girl; she was lending a pretty ear to a cupid's tale beginning, "Once upon a time, thirty years ago." A center page by C. J. Budd, entitled *Some Old Friends,* showed Gibson standing at an easel, palette and brushes in hand and his well-loved characters emerging from the shadows of the background. Though the picture must have revived the bitterness of Gibson's disappointment, he could not help but feel the warmth of his welcome back.

314

Mobilizing for the Summer Campaign

Our Uncharted Coast
VERY DANGEROUS

These days the Gibson Girl wore her hair wound about her brow in becoming coronet braids. Sometimes she rested her head from a Merry Widow hat, perch for one or more birds, with a trim toque. She wore skirts with paniers or with layers which gave a pagoda or ear-of-corn effect, and they were shorter. For one reason, she was driving an automobile more often, now that self-starters spared her from attempting to crank, and her skirt must be kept clear of the pedals. Never before had she been such an enthusiastic devotee of Terpsichore. She could not wait for formal balls but dashed out to tea dances in restaurants, to country club parties or turned on the graphophone at home. The beau, used to sinking somnolently back on the sofa, was routed out of it, made to roll back the rug, wind up

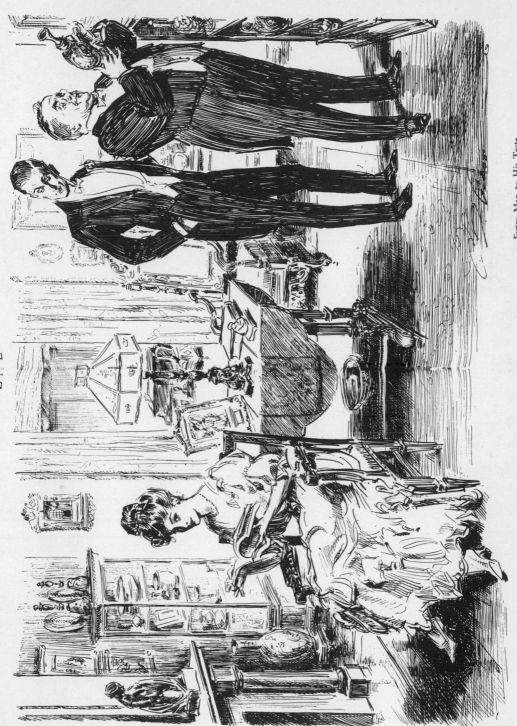

Every Man to His Taste

the machine, change the needle and dance strenuously. Everywhere the Gibson Girl, sub-deb or grandmother, was cutting queer capers, hopping about in turkey trots to the lively rhythms of ragtime, gliding through a waist-bending exercise named the maxixe, slinking along in a tango, or indulging in queer, zoological antics called the lame duck, the bunny hug, the grizzly bear, and the camel walk. When she sat out—which was rarely and only as a concession to fatigued gentlemen—she might cross her legs, in spite of the reproofs of great-grandmothers, but she was not yet ready to join her partner in a cigarette.

She fell in love as usual. She moved in society, although that institution in the old, exclusive sense had died with Mrs. William Astor in 1908. In ever-increasing numbers she went in for athletics, the professions, and business. Eying the escapades and martyrdoms of the English suffragettes, she sometimes was induced to copy them or, more often, to forward the cause with parades. She was not encouraged in such demonstrations by her creator. "In a mass of women, you lose entirely the irresistible appeal of the individual," Gibson remarked. "They are rather terrifying *en masse*. You don't get the usual feeling but a chilly sensation and you think you ought to see a doctor," he added with a grin. "Architecturally women don't fit into a parade. They lack the swing of soldiers, and the careful selection a stage manager uses in picking a chorus is impossible."

And yet when the fateful month of August, 1914, had come and gone, the Gibson Girl suddenly and surprisingly turned into the most militant lady in the land. She donned liberty cap and graceful, flowing robes and became a lovely, determined, warlike Miss Columbia. One hand held aloft the flaming torch of freedom and civilization, the other fingered the sword hilt at her side. "It's a long, long way to Tipperary," she sang, "but my heart's right there."

CHAPTER XVIII

PEN AND SWORD

I

Once during regatta week at Kiel, Mrs. Gibson, Senior, was visiting friends aboard their yacht. A small boat of the Imperial German Navy came smartly alongside and an officer boarded with an invitation. Wilhelm II, Emperor of Germany, requested the presence of Mrs. Gibson on the *Hohenzollern*. His Majesty desired to meet the mother of Charles Dana Gibson whose drawings he long had admired and a set of whose books graced the shelves of his private library.

It was a gratifying compliment, but the day now approached when its donor would deeply regret it. For Gibson, his pen point leveled like a bayonet, was in the forefront of the World War cartoonists' charge against the "All-Highest."

As early as 1896, *Life* had taken a dislike to the Kaiser because of his arrogant conceit and overweening ambition. Gibson had cartooned him in the Spanish-American War and on other occasions but mildly only since he was reluctant to indulge in personalities, even as symbols. For the artist, as for millions of others, it was the German invasion of Belgium that unbalanced the scales of neutrality. The sinking of the *Lusitania* cast down the gage of mortal combat.

"Humor is the only way in the world to kill war, hatred, envy, spite, and ignorance," Gibson had said. "If the Germans only had more sense of humor, they might have thought 'Der Tag' funny instead of taking it altogether too seriously."

That statement held merit as psychology, but now it was too late for humor. *Der Tag* had dawned with an assault of the strong on the weak. Poison gas, unrestricted submarine warfare—one alienat-

·LIFE·

© Life Publishing Co.

HOW LONG WILL SHE STAND IT?

NOT YET, BUT SOON

© Life Publishing Co.

· LIFE ·

"I KNOW YOU. WE MET IN 1776, 1812 AND 1861"

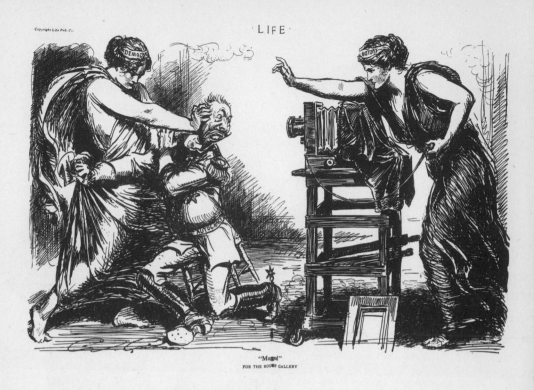

"Mugged"
FOR THE ROGUES GALLERY

ing, desperate German expedient followed another. The chivalrous Gibson rose in righteous wrath. For him, humor was literally and figuratively out of the picture now. He only knew he hated the Kaiser and all he stood for. That America was in honor bound to march to the rescue of civilization. That she would face a day of reckoning if Germany won.

No cartoonist ever drew a grander Uncle Sam than Gibson's—tall, stalwart, and muscular in his starry coat and striped breeches, a figure of homely, Lincolnesque dignity. The only trouble with the old gentleman these days of 1916 and early 1917 was his lack of decision. How could he hesitate? The Gibson cover on the *Lusitania* number of *Life* showed Columbia pointing to the sinking liner while she spoke earnestly into the ear of Uncle Sam whose face was darkening with anger. *Not So Deaf as He Used to Be,* declared the caption. Again she offered him a musical score in a drawing en-

· L I F E ·

His Mother: HERE HE IS, SIR

titled: *Has He Forgotten How to Sing It? My Country 'Tis of Thee*. In a third picture, she was giving him an eye examination and asking him to read the last line which was: "Preparation." For, as another cartoon declared, Uncle Sam had been unable to perceive that he was carrying water to his burning house in two very leaky pails labeled "Army" and "Navy." At times, Gibson left the symbolic Uncle Sam and directly chided Woodrow Wilson for keeping us out of war, but his cartoons of the President always were respectful.

Uncle Sam's fair counsellor and companion in these war drawings is most often Columbia; sometimes Civilization, Peace or Democracy. The noblest types of Gibson Girl, their mien is martial, yet seldom unfeminine; they are never Valkyrie. Their emotions toward Germany, represented as a buxom Brunhilde, are sisterly, since they have no doubt that she has been deluded and enslaved by her rulers. The Kaiser, the Crown Prince, Hindenburg, Ludendorff, and the Junker class—theirs was the guilt.

When he drew those worthies, Gibson's customarily gentle pen dripped with venom. Sentiment gave way to savage satire. Sternly he marched the German war lords across his drawing-board at the pen's point. Ludendorff, cold and ruthless. Hindenburg, heavy-featured and gross. The thin, cruel hauteur of the Crown Prince. The Kaiser, hollow-eyed, despicable with cringing bravado, his hands bloody, the mark of Cain upon his forehead. A more damning caricature never has been drawn.

"Not yet but soon," mutters the Gibson Uncle Sam, whittling a club and glaring at Wilhelm and his apprehensive scion in Death's Head Hussar shako. Again the Kaiser is a false lover pledging his worthless word of honor to Civilization. At a ball, he dances with grisly Death while beautiful Peace is a wallflower. Civilization thrusts the All-Highest into a garbage can. Democracy with a smashing right to the jaw knocks him into an open grave. As Old

CONGRATULATIONS OF PRUSSIAN SPORTSMEN

DECORATIONS

Man Autocracy, he wakes disillusioned from a pipe dream in an opium den. He finds himself in a cell with Death as his jailer. At last, caught red-handed, the culprit is about to be hanged by Uncle Sam to the nearest tree.

With a thrill of exultation, evident in every line he drew, Gibson greeted his country's declaration of war. Liberty, head held high now, bore her torch like a banner. Columbia waded into the Atlantic towing the American fleet and led her khaki-clad legions into battle.

Life welcomed the stirring Gibson pictures with open pages. Nothing could have been more acceptable to Editor Mitchell, friend of France since his student days and pro-Ally from the start. Readers awoke to a development in the Gibson they knew so well. The man had become a great cartoonist. This war had moved him as politics never had been able to do. The scorn, the elation, the passionate conviction which make a great cartoonist now were his. Color for a time was forgotten in the power which surged genii-like from his ink bottle. Never had he drawn with such vigor and verve. His soldiers fixed bayonets and leapt into action. Columbia's robe swept back outlining her beautifully molded body as she rushed forward toward victory.

Gibson was doing his part—and no small one—as a private in the ranks of the artists. But soon after the United States' entry into the war it was determined that he could no longer be allowed to serve in the ranks. He was promoted to command.

II

American artists, admiringly scanning the cartoons and effective posters of the Allies and Central Powers, saw their opportunity. War songs and fiery speeches were echoing and presses were whirring through a nation which had at last taken up the gauntlet. Art, too, must do its part.

THE GIRL HE LEFT BEHIND HIM

Gibson was one of a group of artists who met in a studio and pledged themselves to contribute their utmost toward winning the war. Out of the Society of Illustrators as a nucleus, the Vigilantes were organized. Gibson, because of his long tenure as President of the Society and the respect and esteem in which he was so widely held, was nominated for leadership.

His retiring disposition instinctively shrank from the prominence. Well aware of the jealousies which would be aroused and the feelings which would be bruised in such an aggregation of artistic temperaments, he longed to refuse this command with every fibre of his being. But what, he asked himself, did the stress and strain on his emotions amount to at a time when so many young men were ready to give their lives for their country? His colleagues insisted. Gibson, knowing that he could count upon the patriotism and loyalty of the majority, accepted. He faced one of the most difficult tasks of his career, a task in which he was forced to cope with everything from revolt in the ranks to difficulties raised by the Administration.

He named steady, dependable Frank De S. Casey as his adjutant. One noted artist, unfriendly to him, he placed on his staff for the same reason that Lincoln took Stanton into his Cabinet. Such belligerent spirits as Jack Sheridan, C. B. Falls, and James Montgomery Flagg were ready to lead any assaults that might be necessary. Thus organized, the Vigilantes offered their services to the Government without compensation.

It was not enough for the artists to volunteer. The Government was preoccupied with a cartoon contest it had launched and a committee of judges had been called to Washington to select from a landslide of 2,500 drawings. That copious response, cramming storerooms, betokened immense and earnest effort but produced little of value. The contest, Gibson objected, had resulted only in waste and in heartaches of the unsuccessful. He maintained that this job must

© *Life Publishing Co.*   MEN WANTED

be one of organization, control, and direction which would speedily bring forth the best endeavors of trained artists in the fields where they were acknowledged masters.

Even after the energetic George Creel, as chairman of the Committee of Public Information, asked Gibson to form and head under it a Division of Pictorial Publicity, little progress was made at first. Trouble started at one of the early dinner meetings of the artists. From the outset they had emphasized that they expected no pay for the work they would do for the Government; that was their gift to their country, their gladly given share in the war effort. Nevertheless, Secretary William G. McAdoo of the Treasury, under which the

Committee of Public Information was organized, was playing safe. A Treasury agent rose at the dinner and read a long contract specifying that the Government was without obligation for posters supplied. Offended artists began pitching pennies in the back of the room and then walking out of the meeting. From one corner came the scornful observation, "McAdoo about nothing."

Quelling the riot, Gibson assured the agent of the artists' sincerity. Unfortunately the affair was featured in the papers. On receipt of a sarcastic letter from Mr. McAdoo, Gibson went to Washington and found the Secretary's desk so full of clippings on the dinner incident that for a moment he thought the war was being waged with the artists, not the Germans. With all the tact he possessed he smoothed down the matter.

That the artists meant what they promised was proved at a subsequent dinner when a Philadelphian took the floor to declare that work not paid for was of little value and that there should be a Government fund to pay for posters and thus put the project on the sound business basis that produces worthy works of art. Montie Flagg rose in the heavy silence to reply briefly and conclusively.

"The only answer to the gentleman from Philadelphia," he snorted, "is ———!" and with that short, succinct, derisive word he ended the argument.

Again there were signs of insubordination at a meeting when a member made the charge that a bunch of New York artists were monopolizing the glory. Gibson quietly asked all from the other sections to stand up. Only the critic proved to have been born in New York. The fact was, of course, that artists from all parts of the country were concentrated in New York because it was the publishing capital. Throughout the war, Gibson refrained from confining himself to New York but held meetings in Chicago, Philadelphia, and other cities. He paid his own travelling expenses as did

© Life Publishing Co.   PARTNERS

the trusty Casey until the Government made an allowance to cover the latter's modest expenses in running the Division's office.

After several months of official obstacle-racing and red tape unwinding, a few posters were accepted and displayed. They made a tremendous hit. Rush orders overwhelmed the Division. Casey journeyed weekly to Washington with a 75-pound load of drawings and returned with a list of the needs of the various departments. These commissions Gibson assigned to the artists best fitted to execute them. Pens and brushes were plied busily in a hundred studios. Wallace Morgan, Harvey Dunn, Ernest Peixotto, George Harding, Harry Townsend, J. André Smith, W. S. Aylward, and Walter Jack Duncan were commissioned captains and sent to France to make sketches at the front.

Thus opened up the bombardment of posters which was called "The Battle of the Fences." For it painters, sculptors, designers, illustrators, and cartoonists—all the battalions of art—were mobilized.

It was one of those strenuous efforts behind the lines which modern warfare demands of a nation. Recruiting, speeding of munitions supply, Liberty Loans, conservation of food and other resources—on all these fronts the Division of Pictorial Publicity made drives with results of which it could justly be proud. All of the drawings used were effective. The best of them rang like a trumpet blast in the call to arms, capturing the martial glamor of battle-bound infantry, of a cavalry charge, of artillery galloping into action.

They stirred the pulse of the nation, did those war posters. Wallace Irwin, looking back on their achievement, commemorated it with one of those pieces of occasional verse he wrote so aptly.

THOUGHTS INSPIRED BY A WAR-TIME BILLBOARD

I stand by a fence on a peaceable street
   And gaze on the posters in colors of flame,
Historical documents, sheet upon sheet,
   Of our share in the war ere the armistice came.

And I think of Art as a Lady-at-Arms;
   She's a studio character most people say,
With a feminine trick of displaying her charms
   In a manner to puzzle the ignorant lay.

But now as I study that row upon row
   Of wind-blown engravings I feel satisfaction
Deep down in my star-spangled heart, for I know
   How Art put on khaki and went into action.

There are posters for drives—now triumphantly o'er—
   I look with a smile reminiscently fond,
As mobilized Fishers and Christys implore
   In a feminine voice, "Win the War—Buy a Bond!"

There's a Jonas Lie shipbuilder, fit for a frame:
  Wallie Morg's "Feed a Fighter" lurks deep in his trench;
There's Blashfield's Columbia setting her name
  In classical draperies, trimmed by the French.

Charles Livingston Bull in marine composition
  Exhorts us to Hooverize (portrait of bass).
Jack Sheridan tells us the Food's Ammunition—
  We've all tackled war biscuits under that class.

See the winged Polish warrior that Benda has wrought!
  Is he private or captain? I cannot tell which,
For printed below is the patriot thought
  Which Poles pronounce "Sladami Ojcow Naszych."

There's the Christy Girl wishing that she was a boy,
  There's Leyendecker coaling for Garfield in jeans,
There's the Montie Flagg Guy with an air of fierce joy
  Inviting the public to Tell the Marines.

And the noble Six Thousand—they count up to that—
  Are marshalled before me in battered review.
They have uttered a thought that is All in One Hat
  In infinite shadings of red, white and blue.

And if brave Uncle Sam—Dana Gibson, please bow—
  Has called for our labors as never before,
Let him stand in salute in acknowledgment now
  Of the fighters that trooped from the studio door.

III

This war was on a grand scale and the Division of Pictorial Publicity met its challenge by erecting huge canvases, 90 x 25 feet, in front of the New York Public Library and working there before great crowds to promote the Liberty Loan drives. From outlines previously blocked in they painted figures representing the branches of the Service and the various Allies, a most effective publicity device. Charley Falls made himself assignment editor for this enterprise, taking some of the weight from the shoulders of the embarrassed and grateful Gibson. Falls gave the Army to N. C. Wyeth, the Navy to Henry Reuterdahl, and the major countries to major artists. Deaf to protests, he relegated other, none-too-pleased painters to such smaller lands as Czecho-Slovakia and Liberia. To Gibson he assigned the United States.

It was the dinner meeting every Thursday night at Keene's Chop House and later the Salmagundi Club that fired the enthusiasm of the artists and inspired their best efforts. Almost always the programs were excellent. Foreign officers, returned Americans, and civilians prominent in war work spoke. No "stuffed shirt" dared face that frankly critical crew of artists for long. Gibson presided as toastmaster, shaking in his boots as he always did, until he forced himself up on his feet. His simple eloquence, the fervor of his feeling, his genius for saying the right thing never failed to stir the emotions of the assemblage of several hundred, many of whom came chiefly to hear him. His wit sparkled, and in making a point or introducing a speaker he was never reminded of a stale story about Pat and Mike. His ready tact handled every uneasy situation. When that tall, commanding presence rose at the center of the speaker's table, the very attitude of the audience paid him tribute. With the rugged nobility of his features, he seemed cast in the image of a Roman Soldier-Cæsar, laurel wreath slipped down from bald and massive brow to become a stand-up collar, toga changed into a suit of sober blue.

He gave unsparingly of his time and energy. His evenings and much of his days were spent on the affairs of the Division and his contributions of posters to the cause. He also managed to make many drawings for *Life*. It is interesting to trace through them the American attitude toward the new Russia, first seen as a babe fondled by

CHARLES DANA GIBSON AT WORK UPON A WAR POSTER,
1918, IN FRONT OF THE NEW YORK PUBLIC LIBRARY,
FIFTH AVENUE

Liberty; then as a child stabbed by the dagger of Bolshevism; finally as a howling cat at which Uncle Sam is throwing bricks.

Profiteers and slackers were excoriated by the Gibson pen. Soldiers, farmerettes, and housewives were encouraged in their patriotism. One of the finest of the Gibson war pictures is the drawing: *"Here He Is, Sir,"* in which a mother is offering Uncle Sam her sturdy young son. Lang Gibson, who posed for the boy in the picture, followed its action. As soon as he was old enough, he left Yale to enlist in the navy and served on a destroyer through the latter months of the war.

· LIFE ·

"THEY ARE COMING!"

© *Life Publishing Co.*

IV

November 11, 1918, and victory. At a celebration dinner the artists of the Division of Pictorial Publicity gave Gibson a bust of himself executed by James L. Fraser. Another gift he prized highly was a handsome, leather-bound volume containing reproductions of war posters drawn under his chairmanship and dedicated to him by his friends and associates "in recognition of his services to the nation through the arts in the Great War."

France made him a chevalier of the Legion of Honor and Belgium an officer of the Crown. Clemenceau expressed his thanks when, on a post-war visit to the United States, he stayed at the Gibson home. Regaled with his cherished onion soup, "The Tiger" expanded and imparted the information that a Gibson drawing, *Reading the Will,* hung on a wall of his Paris residence.

What strong proof Gibson had given like great artists before him, of *The Power of the Cartoon*! In an article under that title written for *The Mentor* he had said of the cartoon:

"With it Hogarth scourged and corrected many of the abuses of his age. With it the half-insane Gillray kept England in a fever of heat of hatred against Napoleon. With it Philipon, with the famous 'Pear,' drove Louis Philippe from the French throne. With it Tenniel brought down the full flood of the British Lion's vengeance upon the Bengal Tiger at the time of the Sepoy Rebellion. With it Leech made the whole world shudder when the Russian Czar died in 1855. With it Nast drew tens of thousands of volunteers to the flag and won President Lincoln's commendation of his pictures as 'the best recruiting sergeant on the side of the Union.' With it, after Ledau, Daumier solidified the French Republic by painting the extent of the disaster which the Empire had brought. With it Du Maurier laughed the esthetes of London into oblivion. Its power undiminished, it has served to mold the events of history within the memory of the present generation. Old is the saying that the pen is mightier than the sword. But in the nineteenth century the pencil was a swaying force—as it is in the present day."

Gibson did not abruptly drop the war on its cessation. He might (though he did not) have parodied one of his own famous drawings, *The Bachelor's Supper,* a favorite of the Kaiser's, and shown that fallen monarch haunted by the ghosts of the might-have-been. But the artist preferred to represent such after-the-war aspects as the pretty girl with radiant face reading a letter and announcing, "He's Coming Back!" Or *The Girl Who Didn't Wait* which shows a returned soldier staggered by the sight of his sweetheart married to a

ANNO DOMINI

Drawn by C. D. G. for *The Times's* Neediest Cases

fat stay-at-home. Or the wistful look on the face of the ex-Red Cross nurse reduced in peacetime to caring for a mere civilian.

Fini la guerre. "The War to End War" was over. But for Gibson there loomed ahead a conflict of his own that would try his soul.

LIFE

© *Life Publishing Co.*   IN THE RANKS

CHAPTER XIX

ARTIST INTO EDITOR

I

John Ames Mitchell, editor of *Life,* had died June 29, 1918, hopeful of victory for the Allies and happy that the two countries he loved best, the United States and France, were fighting side by side. Into the fray he had flung the whole might of the magazine he had founded and raised to such eminent success. Now the chair of a great editor stood vacant. *Life's* symbolic cupid wept for "The General" and all the staff mourned with him, experiencing a deep sense of their loss. The severity of that loss was not realized then nor during the early months of peace when few looked far ahead. It was enough that the war was ended and that the world could heal its battle scars and hopefully strive on toward a brighter destiny.

Mitchell himself may have felt no misgivings for the day when the editor's pencil would drop from his hand, for he had nominated no successor. He left *Life* vigorous and prosperous. Andrew Miller, the highly capable business manager who had been with the magazine from the outset, continued in his department. The efficient and devoted staff carried on. Gibson, drawing exclusively for *Life* again, in addition took over its art editorship.

Gibson's reputation, revived by his war cartoons, stood as high as ever. His drawings hung in the Tate Galleries, London, as well as in the Luxembourg of Paris, and also formed part of the permanent exhibition of galleries in Munich, Canada, and Australia. In 1935, the artist would respond to a request of long standing and present a selection of his drawings to the Cabinet of American Illustration of the Library of Congress. Its chief of the Division of Fine Arts, Dr. Leicester B. Holland, praised Gibson's work "not only for the amount of his production, but for the marked individuality and high artistic quality of it," and declared that the Cabinet without a good representation of Gibsons would be almost *Hamlet* with the Prince of Denmark left out.

Since the dark days of the Panic of 1907, Gibson had made a remarkable financial recovery. The stimulus of war days still throbbed through his pen, though it would have required no seer to foretell that that force would spend itself sooner or later as the ambition to paint returned. Before that could happen, however, an event took place which diverted the course of his life into a new and tortuous channel.

Miller survived Mitchell only a year and a half. Came then the ominous, shattering news which many a magazine and newspaper staff has heard with dismay. *Life* was placed on the market by the Mitchell estate—for sale to the highest bidder. It was not alone the loss of their jobs in the clean sweeping of a new broom that the staff dreaded. Such veterans as Martin, Masson, Metcalfe, Lucinda Flynn, Henry Richter, and contributors of long standing cherished a sentimental fondness for the paper to which they had given their best years. They could not bear the thought of its passing into unfeeling, alien hands. To them *Life's* cupid was a beloved child who, a court suddenly had ruled, was to be adopted by any man who offered the most money.

Of course there would be bidders for such a fine property. The firm of Doubleday, Page, for one, was known to be ready to bid and bid high. Alarums and excursions, flurries and factions filled *Life's* office. Outsiders must be repelled and *Life* saved for its own people. Inevitably all turned to the one man behind whom they could unite —Charles Dana Gibson. The staff backed him to head its syndicate to buy the magazine. Other friends added their urging and he agreed.

There were critical moments at that sale. An attorney for Double-

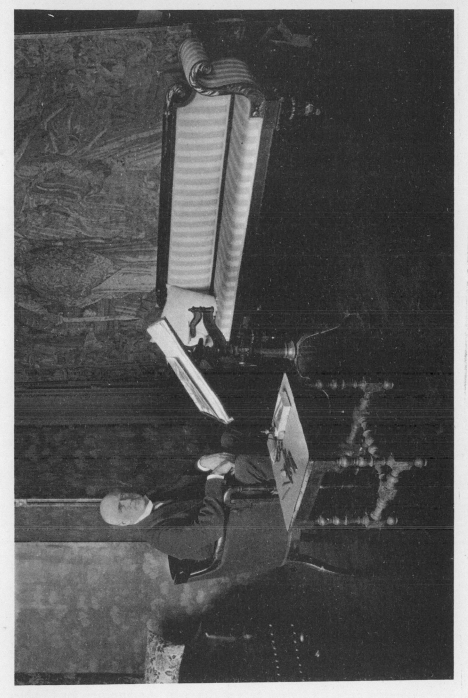

CHARLES DANA GIBSON IN HIS 57TH STREET STUDIO

HIS NEW FATHER

day, Page bid strongly. His every offer was topped by Gibson. At last the attorney put the price up to $1,000 a share. "One thousand and one dollars," Gibson called. His rival hesitated, having reached the limit authorized by his instructions. He asked permission to wire Frank Doubleday at Palm Beach but the *Life* contingent, insisting that the sale must be consummated at once, managed to push it through at the last figure bid by Gibson.

Charles Dana Gibson was the owner of *Life,* vested with the controlling interest by virtue of his own large contribution to the purchase fund. What a happy, suitable culmination it seemed! Here was another telling of the ever-thrilling American success story. The youth who had climbed the stairs of the old office in 1885 with a batch of crude drawings had in 1920 become editor-in-chief. To many, *Life* would not be *Life* without Gibson. He *was Life,* they said, but that was not true, for Gibson and the others who made *Life* always had served under the quiet, sterling command of "The General."

Gibson's elation and excitement at owning *Life* were tempered as he left the sale in a cab with one of the editors whose conversation foreshadowed trouble among the staff. It was, thought Gibson ruefully, a bit like a bicker starting between newlyweds right after they left the church. But he brushed forebodings aside. Hadn't he been able to handle the hundreds of temperamental artists in the Division of Pictorial Publicity? *Life,* common enterprise of a band loyal to its great traditions, would swing along.

II

And in truth a number of banner years lay ahead for *Life*. Its pictures were deft and pointed, its prose and verse witty and sparkling. People kept talking about it. "Have you seen such-and-such a thing in the latest number of *Life?*" they would ask.

Such old-timers as Oliver Herford, Reginald Birch, and T. S. Sullivant, master of the grotesque in man or beast, were joined by bright, new talent. Percy Crosby's *Skippy,* Robert L. Dickey's dogs, Webster's cartoons, and R. V. Culter's *Gay Nineties* series made readers eager for the next issue. Thousands were content to be guided by the rhymed book reviews by Arthur Guiterman, play reports by Robert C. Benchley (successor to Metcalfe), and motion picture critiques by Robert E. Sherwood; all these both informed and entertained. Issues burlesquing other magazines were highly popular; to them Marc Connolly and George Kaufman, who were establishing their reputation as foremost American dramatists, contributed. Smiles or snarls of satisfaction greeted Dorothy Parker's *Hymns of Hate.* Anton Otto Fischer told stories of the sea in double-page drawings. *Life's* high standard in pretty girls was maintained by Coles Phillips, McClelland Barclay, and John La Gatta. Phillips used a clever device of merging dress colors with background and he had a flair for drawing silk stockings and filling them to the king's taste; his covers meant big sales, as did J. C. Leyendeker's. Gluyas Williams chafed the foibles and failings of the human race, and John Held, Jr., concentrated on its now most ubiquitous member—that giddy young thing, the flapper.

III

Now the flapper reigned. Petite girls, thin girls, hoydenish girls, who would have had a terrible time trying to look Gibsonian, won their day in the sun in the compensating swing of the cycle of fashion. None of them sang *Why Do They Call Me a Gibson Girl?*, for they never had heard of that ancient lay. They hummed only the latest jazz ditty as they danced with cheek against partner's. They were familiarly squired by sleek-haired, baggy-trousered young men of the world who were never as bored as they wished to appear—youths clad in dinner coats or enveloped by day in overcoats for which raccoons perished by the thousand. No observer could doubt that the boys and girls were enjoying themselves to the utmost, kicking up their heels in the Charleston and other antics ranging from innocent merriment to hip flasks, petting parties, and gate-crashing.

The flapper Held pictured was a caricature but close to the original and capturing the youthful *joie de vivre,* the pertness, and the friskiness which were as appealing in the flapper as in any other young creature. Gay assurance lurked behind the baby-doll stare the artist gave her. The flapper was well aware that she was queening it now and that the Gibson Girl was definitely dated. *Life* clinched the point when it printed a picture of a modern Held flapper side by side with an old-fashioned Gibson Girl.

Yet if Gibson, meeting *Life's* demands, were to continue illustrating the contemporary scene, he must draw flappers. He did, but

1896   1926

Thirty Years of "Progress"!

it came hard. When Held drew the girl of the period, it was youth drawing youth. When Gibson's pen outlined her, there was apparent more than a trace of the wonder, the incomprehension, and the dismay of the older generation beholding a rather alarming phenomenon.

The Gibson flapper was denounced as "a pathetically insolent and slimsy person," immature or super-sophisticated, graceless and vaguely drawn. She was a portrait, true enough, but not altogether typical. Only once did the artist portray the flapper at her best—a picture of a comely maiden sprawled in an armchair listening to the radio.

Few can wonder at Gibson's lack of sympathy. The female form divine had been planed down to a boyish silhouette. Graceful carriage had become a slouch or a swagger. A pen adept at pompadours and coronet braids was reduced to bobs and shingles, "a most unkindest cut" which destroyed the charming knot or tendril of soft tresses at the nape of the neck. Skirts could not flow when they were abruptly dammed at the knee line. Love, the tender passion, was being all mixed up with an urge frankly called sex appeal or "S.A." for short. Some of Gibson's contemporaries unsparingly condemned the excesses of the post-war reaction. "The injunction to 'be good, sweet maid, and let who will be clever,' " wrote Arthur Train in the foreword to his novel, *High Winds,* "ceased to appeal to a younger generation fully aware that if one could be clever it was unnecessary to be good; and who regarded with derision, if not with pity, fathers and mothers, who must needs be virtuous when virtue was no longer a reward."

Gibson himself preferred to keep to gentle satire. He drew a grandfather turning from granddaughter puffing a cigarette to regard wistfully grandmother's portrait. He revived *Mr. Pipp* and tried to make the old gentleman keep up with the younger generation; *Mr.*

A personal friend of John L. Sullivan.

Some Gibson flappers

Pipp did not really seem to enjoy being modern. Gibson's most successful essay in that direction was the all-too-briefly carried on series: *Aunt Jane from the Country*. There was first-rate comedy in *Aunt Jane's* visits to her city nieces and nephews and her innocent efforts to promote their good times. Once she offered "to play a good, lively two-step so you children can dance." And again she urged: "If you children want to go anywheres evenings while I'm here, don't hesitate about asking me to chaperon."

Curiously it was ladies of the theatre who kept the Gibson Girl in print during these years—not the ingenues, who embraced flapperdom with delight, but the leading ladies. Many of them, despite the modernity of their lines and situations, retained the gracious charm of yore. Gibson drew a long series of portraits of them, brightening the pages of *Life* and enhancing the annals of the stage. The drawings were accompanied by sparkling praise in verse by George Chappell and others. Such lovely ladies as Lynn Fontanne, Elsie Ferguson, and Ina Claire were beautifully portrayed by the artist, and Miss Claire may well have spoken for them all when she said that any woman was flattered to be drawn by Charles Dana Gibson.

Except for that all-star revival, the Gibson Girl resigned herself to retirement as the mother of flappers and stepped gracefully into history.

It was as history she reappeared in *Life* in 1925 and then she was not drawn by Gibson.

IV

R. V. Culter's entertaining series, *The Gay Nineties* (coining that phrase), began running in that year. For the first time on a grand scale, Gibson found his own pictures being used for reference, a

· LIFE ·

Aunt Jane (from the country): If you children want to go anywhere evenings while I'm here, don't hesitate about asking me to chaperon you.

practice many an artist, reproducing the period, thereafter would follow. He could not but regard it with confused reactions. Certainly it was complimentary but it did carry the effect of filing a man away in the past. Gibson's appreciation and quizzical sensations at being classified as a research item both may be read between the lines of the illuminating introduction he contributed when Culter's series was published as a book in 1927.

"In the spring of 1925," wrote Gibson, "Richard Culter came into the *Life* office with three drawings of scenes and people in the Eighteen-nineties. He submitted them to Robert Sherwood, the editor of *Life,* Frank Casey, the art editor, and myself in the hope that they might develop into a series under the general heading, The Gay Nineties.

"We liked Mr. Culter's drawings enormously—I can't imagine anyone would fail to appreciate the perfection of his draughtsmanship or the complete truthfulness of his subjects. But we frankly doubted that the Gay Nineties would appeal to a wide circle of our readers.

"Nevertheless, we published the three drawings—and have continued the series in *Life* ever since. It proved to be one of those rare features—so eagerly sought by all harassed editors, and so infrequently found—which are characterized in the jargon of our trade as sure-fire.

"Doddering, decrepit veterans who have lived to the ripe old age of 35 enjoy Mr. Culter's drawings because they reflect, so honestly, the costumes and customs of their dear, dead youth. Children who have been born in this century relish 'The Gay Nineties' because of their archeological interest—much as children of my generation were fascinated by reminiscences of the Civil War.

"Mr. Culter has the ability to reflect life in terms of humor, and he has succeeded in reproducing the Gay Nineties as really gay.

LIFE·

"BETWEEN ME AN' YOU, UNCLE JASPER, DON'T YOU GET AWFUL TIRED OF DOIN' WHAT YOU'RE TOLD?
DON'T BE SCARED TO ANSWER. I WON'T GIVE YOU AWAY TO AUNT JANE"

Look through the pages of this book and study the people that Mr. Culter has drawn; even though you survey them from the eminence of 1927—even though you laugh heartily at their ludicrous attire, their ridiculous headdresses—you will come to conclude that they must have had a thoroughly good time.

"Which, if memory has not utterly failed me, they did."

It was vaguely disturbing to relics of the '90's that the whole series was based on the humor of contrast. For instance, Culter drew authentically the styles of the '90's, but he sometimes put them, just as authentically, on women and men they did not become. That Gibson never had done. Though drawn without malice, the series at times registered its effect by holding up to ridicule clothes and customs of a bygone day which remained a golden age for the generation which had lived it. Gibson and his contemporaries were perfectly sincere in their appreciation of *The Gay Nineties*. They laughed at it, yet in their laughter was a note of nostalgic fondness and yearning sentiment. In the mirth of some of the younger generation was a rather discomfiting tone of mockery at the carryings-on of the funny old folks who were still on the map and trying to run things.

No matter. *The Gay Nineties* helped *Life* continue to succeed, and *Life* was beginning to need such spurs to circulation.

V

The Big Three of the humorous weeklies had fallen upon evil days. *Puck* had expired in 1918; its Ariel was a pallid ghost at the masthead of a Hearst newspaper Sunday supplement. *Judge* had entered on a decline and *Life* was slipping, though not yet perceptibly. Diagnosing the ailments of the Big Three, Alexander King wrote in *Vanity Fair*: "They became arrogant, conservative, and stuffy, and losing complete sight of their prime functions as humorous weeklies, they standardized their material until it lost all contact with the turbulent life and reality about them." That severe indictment was less true of *Life,* yet it, too, was guilty. The comic magazines were victims of the post-war flux in which change and innovation were so often necessities of survival. It was the brilliant Harold Ross, founder and editor of *The New Yorker,* who caught the tide and far outdistanced his rivals with the journalistic slant which readers were demanding. Gone were the leisurely, contemplative days. First-rate reporting and up-to-the-minute comment, not only for newspapers but in magazines, was the essential thing. That *The New Yorker* developed, plus a sophisticated tone, welcomed by a world which had sloughed off so many of its illusions. The journalistic quality was a feature of the two other outstanding magazine successes of the period—of *Time,* of course, and of *Fortune.*

Could Mitchell have sensed the trend of the times? Perhaps. He was a great editor. Gibson was not. In fact, he was unfortunately lacking in most of the rather rare abilities which make for editorial genius. He was not long in discovering it, clear-sighted as he was toward his own deficiencies, and he planned to lean on the strong staff of *Life.* Having answered an emergency call, entirely unprompted on his part, he had optimistically and wholeheartedly buckled down to the task. But this was no war crisis, with the flame of patriotism burning white to drive the power plant. Then he led an army. Now he commanded a body which owned some of the aspects of a soviet. To put it another way, *Life* changed from an absolute monarchy to a democracy governed by a president, vexed by an unruly cabinet and congress. There had been and there still were discordant elements in the staff. Masson and Metcalfe had long been at odds; they attended the weekly editorial luncheons without speaking to each other. The autocratic Mitchell, ruling with a rod of iron, had sternly suppressed temperament and demanded harmony.

Gibson summoned from the ivory tower of his studio into the hurly-burly of the *Life* office, proved to be no autocrat of the editorial table. He could not bring himself to extend the strict command he imposed upon himself to others. To rule by the respect and loyalty he inspired was not enough. His kindliness, at once a fault and a virtue, led to indecision. He was continually hampered, as Sherwood expressed it, by an almost passionate desire to shrink from trouble of any kind and to avoid hurting anyone's feelings. The situation called—and called in vain—for a hardboiled boss.

As an editor, he was reluctant to attack anybody or anything. They used to insist on *Life,* "We need a good hate," but Gibson could trump up none now that the Kaiser was safely cooped up in Holland. In his direction of the magazine, Gibson made other mistakes. He replaced Rea Irwin, who went to *The New Yorker,* with Frank Casey, as art editor; Casey's talent was better suited to *Collier's* than to a humorous magazine. Gibson turned down Peter Arno whose early drawings contributed to the success of *The New Yorker;* Arno's themes were apt to be rowdy but so nowadays was the taste of many readers. At other times, Gibson listened too readily to advice and allowed too much divided authority.

Life's removal from 17 West Thirty-first Street to a new office, a floor of 598 Madison Avenue, seemed to dispel the atmosphere of the good old days. And yet the magazine's tradition was a dead weight, hanging around the neck of its symbolic cupid like the *Ancient Mariner's* albatross. Reprints from files, under the heading *"Life's* Family Album," sometimes pointed an unfortunate contrast.

Valiant strivings for improvement never ceased. One short-lived

Life dynasty followed another. Masson, Martin, Louis Evan Shipman, Sherwood, and Norman Anthony succeeded each other in the editorial chair. None of them evolved a policy with the vital spark that would carry *Life* through, although each contributed something of value, and the magazine, though its income steadily dwindled, kept on the profit side of the ledger until the Depression.

"Double, double toil and trouble." In 1925, the widow of Andrew Miller brought a suit charging Gibson with extravagance in management and asking a receivership for *Life*. The suit, called without basis, was dropped, but constant difficulties continued. Gibson was unable to drive those two sometimes balky horses, the editorial and advertising departments, in double-harness with Mitchell's skill. He could justly complain that his staff did not always give him complete support but was diverted by outside interests. Twinkling Tom Masson, able editor and copious fount of ideas though he was, was somewhat distracted by his voluminous writing for other publications. Shipman mistakenly tried to make *Life* a second *Punch*. The long and lanky Bob Sherwood, who came closest to making the magazine click, was seduced by his new-found ability as a playwright, an ability which was to turn in such hits as *The Road to Rome, Reunion in Vienna,* and *The Petrified Forest*. When Langhorne Gibson joined the staff, Gibson cherished a hope, not originally held when he bought the magazine, that his son might carry on *Life* after him. But Lang was not an editor or a humorous writer (he would later find his *métier* as a naval historian) and his assignment to the business office did not appeal to him. He much preferred fox-hunting.

Gibson's own work showed the strain of his mental distress. Through the '20's he produced few drawings of note other than those on the Lindbergh flight and the death of Woodrow Wilson. The editorial board kept calling for more Gibson. Surely those drawings which had been the glory of *Life's* past would exert their spell again. But the spell was broken. The artist was worn by the cares of editorship, weary of the pen, and his work showed it. A once-abundant reservoir of ideas had run dry. Again the brush was beckoning, yet the few covers Gibson painted for *Life* were amateurish and no encouragement to his ambition.

From 1927 into 1929, Gibson was drawing again for the *Cosmopolitan*. Ray Long, its editor, was buying big names as usual and spreading striking art work across his pages. Gibson was paid the highest prices of his career for his pen-and-ink double pages— $1,750 and then $2,000 for each drawing. Some of these cartoons sounded a timely note such as *On the Road to Hollywood,* picturing a procession of movie-struck women of widely varying ages and looks. Others held the human appeal of the Gibson of yore. For instance, *Expert Advice on Their First Quarrel* in which an elderly couple are smoothing things over for newlyweds who have fallen out. Or *The Jack of Hearts Missing*—a young man playing solitaire while a neglected pretty girl languishes. And the one where the artist, that doting grandfather, warned himself—*The Man Who Talks About His Grandchildren.*

Although Gibson's skill flashed out from time to time in these drawings, many of them betrayed his vanished enthusiasm for pen-and-ink. When Long and Sidney Heideman, the art editor, deemed it wise to discontinue the series after two years, they suggested that Gibson shift to illustration. The artist refused. He always had been more the cartoonist than the illustrator, he declared, and rather than revert to the latter rôle, he would be glad to cancel the contract. The editors accepted to Gibson's relief. Frankly he acknowledged to himself that he had made the *Cosmopolitan* drawings for the money they brought him; that he was not proud of them. He was through with that part of his life. In prolonging it, he saw himself as an old singer vainly reaching for the high notes or an

"OUR BOY"

old actor still trying to play *Romeo*. Without self-pity, without sighing for past glories, he told himself that he had outstayed his welcome.

When the book, forming his latest collection of drawings, sold poorly, he went to the Scribner office and generously tore up the contract, the royalties provisions of which were high in accordance with former successes.

DEATH OF PRESIDENT WILSON

VI

Nineteen-twenty-nine and another panic. There is an eerily prophetic glimpse of that resounding crash in Mitchell's fantasy, *The Last American,* published in 1889. The author, visualizing the future, relates a visit by Persian explorers to the shores of America, relapsed into a wilderness after an era of destruction and desolation in which Americans had turned from history to chronicles of crime and allowed commercial honor to become a jest. The Persians land on Manhattan and discover an interesting ruin, identified as the New York Stock Exchange, and among the crumbling marble columns of Washington they slay the last "Mehrikan" and his family.

While Gibson again suffered heavy financial losses forcing him to live on a reduced scale, they did not wipe out the competence he had set aside. He could still smile, though wryly, at a coincidence of this crash with that of 1907. "You can always tell when a panic is coming," he remarked, "by when I start to paint."

For *Life,* as for countless other enterprises, the depression was a disastrous blow. Gibson, discouraged, almost sickened by difficulties and arguments, came less and less frequently to the office. He was convinced that he was more of a hindrance than a help to *Life* and that he could do no better than leave it to the devices of the board. For some years past, he had carried on only because of loyalty to the magazine which had given him his start and to his friends on the staff whose hearts and futures, he knew, were bound up in it.

At last he surrendered. In 1932, he sold his entire interest to Clair Maxwell and Henry Richter who made *Life* into a monthly and commenced a gallant fight to restore its former prestige.

Plenty of brains and talent had tried to stave off the decline of *Life.* It may be fair to assume that nothing could have saved it from a downward swing in that cycle which is the common lot of magazines.

It was bitter—but not surprising—that a man who had swayed the thought and tastes of a nation as an artist should have failed to repeat his achievement as an editor. Few realized the cost of that failure to a sensitive soul, to an unselfish spirit always deeply concerned with the hopes and fears of others affected by his actions.

Gibson shouldered his share of the blame and more than his share. Then he ceased to torture himself with vain regrets. In his mind he drew a curtain before those years.

CHAPTER XX

RAINBOW OVER MAINE

I

On the rocky point which Seven Hunderd Acre Island thrusts into the waters of Islesboro, Maine, rise the gray stone, vine-clad tower and walls of a tiny chapel. When first it meets the sight of one who approaches, cruising through the island channels, it is easy to imagine that Norsemen built it or that it was magically transplanted from the coast of Norman England. Centuries seem to have passed over it, though it was erected only in 1925. Dominating the point, the chapel somehow sacrifices neither illusion nor harmony as one's glance includes the summer home which crowns the green hill behind it. Viewed from the porch of the house, the chapel merges naturally into a prospect of azure seas and wooded isles.

Stones carven with inscriptions are set in the interior walls, but none bears a legend which a visitor, conversant with the circumstances of the building, more than half expects—a richly medieval legend which might read:

> C. D. GIBSON FECIT
> PRO PACE SUAE ANIMAE

For Gibson did build the chapel for the peace of his soul. In the Middle Ages, a builder would have proclaimed it frankly. It went without public acknowledgment in the case of this modern builder, always reticent about his religion or his personal code save for a rare reference to the Golden Rule. Nevertheless the chapel was indeed a votive offering, made in the days when trials and tribulation began to press heavily. Messengers with ill tidings from *Life* had found Gibson at work on the chapel and other buildings.

THE CHAPEL

There was only partial sanctuary for him in Maine during his summer vacations. He did not expect to escape entirely from the treadmill in which he had been caught. Yet as his despondency grew and he became more certain of his inability to save the situation at *Life,* he lengthened out his weeks in Maine. Since it was not enough for him simply to absent himself from the scene of problems and wrangles, he sought solace in the work of his hands like many another man.

That boyhood fascination with which he had watched and helped carpenters and masons returned, and Gibson proved that he was more than handy with tools—he was a true artificer. He was his own architect, making scale models and following them accurately. In design and actual construction, the dozen or so varied buildings, which lend such charm to his point acres on the Maine island, were fairly his own. He employed helpers only in the collections of stones from the shore and the delivery of other raw materials, in the mortar mixing, and in heavy lifting operations.

It was the sight of his daughter in her girlhood sweeping a brick walk in the garden that started Gibson on one of his earliest buildings. He looked up from a book to watch Babs toiling away reluctantly and ineptly at her task. Rather than scold her, her father decided to give her some incentive for learning domestic duties. So he purchased Ensign Island, a short sail from his point, and there erected for Babs and Lang a stone house with a large living room, and a completely equipped kitchen. In running a home of one's own, sweeping, cooking, and keeping house came much easier. On Ensign Island took place many a jolly picnic, house party, and dance to the light of lanterns and bonfires.

Another early building was a conical stone tool house, with shingled roof and mullioned window, situated in the corner of the flower garden designed and cared for by Mrs. Gibson. During the 1920's when hard work with hammer and saw and trowel gave him such comfort, Gibson built a child's house for his granddaughter, Nancy Langhorne Post. It is a delightful miniature with casement windows, corner cupboards, fireplace, chimney closets, and a steep-sloping roof; all its furniture is in scale: kitchen range, chairs, tables, hook rugs, color prints, and even the surrounding garden. Several other small buildings and a farmer's house followed.

Between buildings, Gibson busied himself with stone walls and docks. The octagonal pump house, containing artesian well, pump, pressure-tank, and electrical power plant, was one of the most difficult pieces of construction he undertook.

In his building of the chapel, it was not only design but cleverly chosen materials and quaint irregularities in the setting of stones and the use of old bricks which gave that edifice its effect of great age. Inscriptions within announce: its dedication to Mrs. Gibson; that

C. D. G. AT WORK UPON A PLAYHOUSE FOR HIS
GRANDDAUGHTER

"Charles Dana Gibson II landed here June 21, 1929"; that "Onward, Christian Soldiers" was first sung here by Nancy Langhorne Post and George B. Post III (while their grandmother played the organ). The chapel's panelled tower room is reserved and furnished as a retreat—and one gratefully resorted to at times—for that grandmother.

II

So it had never been solely for his own peace of mind that Gibson had set his hand to the builder's craft. That he was building for those he loved deeply was the greater part of his contentment.

He had lost his elder brother Langdon in 1919 and his mother in 1923. Now the mantle of the patriarch set well upon his natural dignity, and his Maine acres wore the aspect of an ancestral seat. With his devoted and understanding wife by his side, he looked forward with intense eagerness to the summer gatherings of the clan. Lang Gibson, who had married Marian Taylor, would sail up to the dock, with his wife and their two sons, Charles Dana II and Harry. Babs, whose marriage to George B. Post II (grandson of the architect who had apprenticed young Dana Gibson to Saint-Gaudens) had ended in divorce, arrived with the children of that marriage: Nancy Langhorne Post and George B. Post III. Later she was married to John J. Emery in the island chapel. Three daughters born of that marriage, Rene, Lela, and Melissa, added to the welcome contingent of grandchildren demanding the addition of wings to the main house and special play houses as well. Divorce also terminated Lang Gibson's marriage; he subsequently married Parthenia Ross.

Gibson made an ideal grandfather, considerate of the prior rights of parents and careful never to demand too much of or to intrude on his grandchildren. He was content to watch them play or, when they asked it, to sail with them or work for or with them in the carpenter shop.

It was his family and his building that had carried Gibson through his trying years. The load lifted from him when he sold out his *Life* holdings revived an old yearning, an unfulfilled dream. Brush and palette in hand, he faced an easel again in his Maine and New York studios, faced it at the age of sixty-five with the same undaunted determination he had displayed at thirty-eight.

WHEN GRANDPA THINKS OF HIS MOTHER

III

Syracuse University had conferred a degree as Doctor of Fine Arts upon Gibson in 1931. A year before, two of his paintings, *The Family* and *Speaking of Prohibition,* had won favorable comment when shown in exhibitions. Not until 1932 did he begin to give all his time to painting. Then it was as if the flood-gates had been opened and a long-pent torrent joyously rushed forth.

Gibson painted hard and fast—with all his heart in it. He experimented constantly and discarded a great deal, but at last he began to see the light of progress and what a radiant effulgence it was! As always he painted where his interest lay—people and scenes of the life about him. Sturdy old Maine sea captains and other local folk. Racing sloops. The Gibson grandchildren playing on the green lawns and in the bright flower gardens of Seven Hundred Acre Island or working in its carpenter shop or going boating from its docks; even though they were the most restless of models, nothing inspired him more. In the New York studio, old man "types" and girl models sat. Analyzing pictures of the latter, H. I. Brock, writing in *The New York Times Magazine,* saw a third stage in the evolution of the Gibson Girl, "An uneasy creature, exotically hand-painted and precociously self-sophisticated . . . the Nineteen Thirties model needing color in the reproduction . . . woman emancipated, triumphant, adrift and dismayed, but, above all, avid for experiments and expedients, such as we find her—superficially, at least—today." But others will prefer to discard a theory of evolution for fundamentalism in this case and enshrine in their memories the Gibson Girl who held sovereign sway before the World War.

The Academy of Arts and Letters, holding an annual one-man show of work by one of its members, invited Gibson to exhibit during the 1934-35 season. Hesitating, feeling unworthy, yet never lacking the courage to stand a test, the artist accepted. A striking

THE QUEEN

array of more than eighty paintings covered the walls of the large exhibition hall when Gibson had finished superintending the hanging. By a happy thought, it had been decided also to show a selection of his pen-and-inks, and two smaller outer rooms were filled with drawings. They began chronologically with the cartoon, *Time,* published in *Life* in 1888, and ran on through Paris, London, and Egypt sketches, *Mr. Pipp,* Gibson Girls in black-and-white and water colors, and the boldly limned double-pages for *Collier's.* They formed, did those drawings and paintings, a brilliant panorama of a fine artist's endeavor for four and a half decades—a writing on the wall that told a story of splendid achievement.

Gibson, giving his overjoyed wife a pre-view of the exhibition, took quiet pleasure in her pride. Whatever adverse comments might be made on his oils, he could not be robbed of the serenity their painting had given him nor of his determination to continue with color until he mastered it.

But the critics, like the crowds who came to the exhibition, were impressed. Edward Alden Jewell wrote in part in *The New York Times:*

"One approaches this exhibition prepared to renew one's acquaintance with the famous 'Gibson Girl' of yesteryear and with other celebrated creations of this adventurous pen. They are, indeed, all there, bringing the long-ago most vividly back to us. However, few are likely to be prepared for the spectacle provided by nearly a hundred paintings, a large part of them produced within the last two or three years, by an artist who recently passed his sixty-seventh birthday.

"Never before, so far as I know, has Charles Dana Gibson held a painting show. We do not all associate his name with canvas and brush. The surprise thus afforded is considerable; but it becomes enhanced as, crossing the threshold of so amazing a demonstration of inextinguishable youth, one goes about the gallery, impelled, step

From a painting by C. D. G. photographed by The American Academy of Arts and Letters

MRS. GIBSON READING IN A CORNER OF THE LIVING
ROOM AT DARK HARBOR

by step, to recognition of a talent audacious in its attack, absolutely undaunted by any painting problem that might present itself, and technically equipped to carry many an exploit through with real distinction.

"Make no mistake about it. Charles Dana Gibson is a painter. He proves it again and again in a way the visitor is not likely soon to forget. This is scarcely the gesture of a first-rate black-and-white artist who tentatively tries his hand in another medium, just as a lark, or to see if he can manage a surprise come-back. This is really painting. The exuberance, the blithe letting go, is persuasively reinforced by an intelligent, though not infallible, knowledge of craft. The technique preferred, and for the most part employed, is one that makes heavy inroads upon the paint dealer's supply of material. It is an impasto technique. Pigment lathers the canvas with what often looks like prodigal abandon. But there is method in this loading; an impetuous procedure that as a rule justifies itself and leaves the subject robustly articulate."

Another veteran critic, Royal Cortissoz of *The New York Herald Tribune,* while more critical of the technique of his old friend, Dana Gibson, also reviewed the paintings favorably. He said in part:

"The result is an animated type of canvas, vivid, sharp in its effects of light and color, and, as was to be expected of Mr. Gibson, full of the interest that lies in human character sympathetically observed. He may be careless about the delicate modulations of form and tone, but he knows perfectly well how to construct a head and how to give it meaning. Witness such a portrait as that of the old man in 'Violin for Sale,' or, indeed, the heads and faces in a dozen other studies here. They are so richly vitalized that one can't help wishing that Mr. Gibson were a little less impatient of the niceties of his art. Especially as he can develop them with a fastidious touch when he cares to do so. There is an instance in 'Babs,' a portrait of a girl with a

From a painting by C. D. G. photographed by The American Academy of Arts and Letters

"BABS"

Gibson's daughter Irene: Mrs. J. J. Emery

The Cloud-Shifters

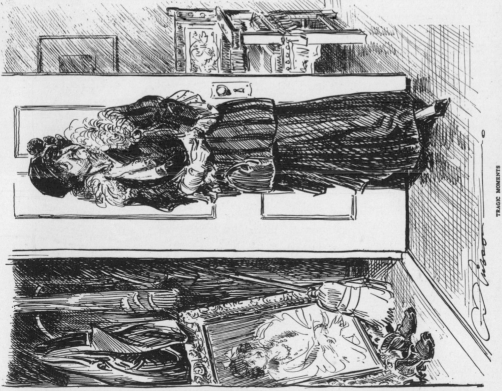

TRAGIC MOMENTS

WHEN YOUR RICH AUNT ARRIVES UNEXPECTEDLY AND FINDS YOU HAVEN'T HUNG THE PORTRAIT SHE SENT YOU AT CHRISTMAS

Advice to Radio Beginners
Do not become discouraged at static trouble. It may not be static at all, but merely trouble in the receiving set.

dog in her lap, quite the best of all the exhibits in color. It is suavely and thoughtfully handled, the features well drawn, the brush work attentive to every nuance, the whole affair one of charm and of skill. The same tender care that was lavished upon this portrait would have bettered numbers of the others. It would have been apposite, also, but in the open air studies anything would have been out of place save just the brisk, direct manner in which the artist has executed them. In the boating scene observed from amidst trees in the foreground, the picture called 'Uncle Lang Wins,' the very sparkle and movement of the subject are captured. There are many sketches like this one in the show and they include some of Mr. Gibson's most beguiling impressions.

"In the hall and in the smaller rooms he has assembled a quantity of his work as a pen draughtsman, beginning with a cartoon drawn for *Life* as far back as 1888. This work has long been famous, and the reason is plain. It is fresh and strong and individualized, delightful to see again, so full is it of life and humor and that new, confident touch which marks a pictorial satirist out from amongst his fellows. Mr. Gibson's line has force and certainty. Beside it the line of

LANGHORNE AND IRENE WITH THEIR FATHER
IN PARIS IN 1907

At 22 Square du Bois, Avenue Bois de Boulogne

Du Maurier, for example, his nearest analogue, looks positively feeble. He knows exactly what he wants to do with it and from under his pen Mr. Pipp and the rest spring into a lasting reality. There is nothing here of the headlong improvisatore visible in the paintings, but, in his place, an authoritative craftsman using his black and white with enkindling vivacity and point. How distinctive a Gibson drawing is and how well it wears!"

IV

The paintings, as the *Times* said in a later article, revealed a talent "vigorous, forthright and underivative;" they represented work which at its best was "spirited, adventurous and, on the craft side, adroit."

It is the province of the biographer, not the art critic's, to offer his conception of the spiritual significance of those paintings to the man whose hand wrought them. They are, as these pages have sought to express, a dream come true, a high adventure undertaken after cruel disappointments, the promise of a rainbow fulfilled at last. The many who know and love Charles Dana Gibson can wish him no happier a destiny.

He is painting as these lines are written, painting every day as he means to paint all his life. He would say that he is wielding his brush for his own satisfaction, though it is as true as it always has been that he will never be satisfied with his work but continually strive onward.

Back of this bright present, stands the record of his magnificent past when his drawings flew to the four corners of the earth. When his satire smote the snob and the hypocrite. When his pen brought beauty and pleasure and tenderness to millions. When a testament of his times was imperishably set down by a gallant and great-hearted gentleman.

From a painting by C. D. G. photographed by The American Academy of Arts and Letters

THE LONG DOCK AT SEVEN HUNDRED ACRE ISLAND, DARK HARBOR

Granddaughter Irene watching the launching of her brother's boat

From a painting by C. D. G. photographed by The American Academy of Arts and Letters

STUDY OF "OLD TIM"

ACKNOWLEDGMENTS

The vast indebtedness of this biographer to his subject for unfailing aid and friendship has been stated in the foreword. I am also most grateful for the help of Mrs. Gibson, Langhorne Gibson, Mrs. Daniel R. Knowlton (Josephine Gibson), and Mrs. John J. Emery.

In many instances the mention of a name in the text testifies to a living source of welcome material. May those kind people understand the references as tokens of my gratitude.

Since the story of Charles Dana Gibson is also, largely, the story of *Life,* I owe particular thanks to Clair Maxwell and Henry Richter, proprietors of that magazine, for their generous permission to quote from drawings and text. Similarly, I wish to thank *Collier's, Cosmopolitan,* and other magazines and newspapers from the files of which I have quoted, as acknowledged in text and bibliography.

For advice and assistance in revision, I am deeply indebted to Royal Cortissoz, the noted art critic of *The New York Herald Tribune,* and to Charles Hanson Towne and John T. Winterich, two of the ablest editors I have known as a free-lance writer.

Again I am most appreciative of the encouragement and understanding of Maxwell E. Perkins, editor of Charles Scribner's Sons, and of the hearty co-operation of the publisher's art director, Joseph Hawley Chapin, in the pleasant but considerable task of choosing the illustrations for this volume from a wealth of material. There, too, I had Mr. Gibson's help and his permission to make use of any of his work we desired.

The New York Public Library, which possesses an excellent Gibson collection, extended to me the courtesy of its facilities. So also did the Library of Congress, the New York Society Library, the "morgue" of *The New York Herald Tribune,* and other libraries.

Behind many an author in the making of a book stands a sturdy ally— his wife. Content with anonymity though she is and with the author's personal and inadequate expression of gratitude, she should in simple justice receive homage in print. Which is hereby devotedly given to Mildred Adams Downey for unsparing criticism, tireless typing, and all manner of efficient first-aid in this, as in every other book I have written.

FAIRFAX DOWNEY
New York City, 1936.

THE GIBSON GIRL'S DAUGHTER

First published and copyrighted by *Arts and Decoration*

BIBLIOGRAPHY

BOOKS BY C. D. GIBSON

Gibson, Charles Dana, *Drawings*. New York; 1894.
——*Pictures of People*. New York; 1896.
——*London as Seen by Charles Dana Gibson*. New York; 1897.
——*Sketches and Cartoons*. New York and London; 1898.
——*Sketches of Egypt*. New York; 1899.
——*The Education of Mr. Pipp*. New York; 1899.
——*Americans*. New York; 1900.
——*A Widow and Her Friends*. New York; 1901.
——*The Social Ladder*. New York; 1902.
——*The Weaker Sex*. New York; 1903.
——*Eighty Drawings*. New York and London; 1903.
——*Everyday People*. New York; 1904.
——*Our Neighbors*. New York; 1905.
——*The Gibson Book* (2 Vols.). New York; 1906.
——*Other People*. New York; 1911.
——*New Cartoons*. New York; 1916.
—— Article in *Scribner's,* November, 1928. *A. B. Frost, A Personal Tribute.*
——*People of Dickens* in *Ladies' Home Journal.*
——*Some Family Records.*

BOOKS ILLUSTRATED BY C. D. GIBSON

Bangs, John Kendrick, *The Booming of Acre Hill*. New York; 1900.
Bromley, Isaac H., *Our Chauncey*. Illustrated by Daniel Carter Beard and Charles Dana Gibson. New York; 1891.
Chambers, Robert W., *The Common Law*. New York; 1912.
——*Japonette*. New York; 1912. (*The Turning Point.*)
——*The Streets of Ascalon*. New York; 1912.
Davis, Richard Harding, *Gallegher and Other Stories*. New York; 1891.
——*About Paris*. New York; 1895.
——*The Princess Aline*. New York; 1895.
——*The King's Jackal*. New York; 1898.
——*Her First Appearance*. Illustrated by C. D. Gibson and E. M. Ashe. New York; 1901.
——*Soldiers of Fortune*. New York; 1906.
Goodloe, Abbe Carter, *College Girls*. New York; 1906.

Harrison, Mrs. Burton (Constance Cary), *The Anglomaniacs*. New York; 1890.

——*Sweet Bells Out of Tune*. New York; 1893.

Hope, Anthony, *The Prisoner of Zenda*. New York; 1898.

——*Rupert of Hentzau*. New York; 1906.

Magruder, Julia, *The Princess Sonia*. New York, 1895.

——*The Violet*. New York and London; 1896.

Mitchell, John Ames, *That First Affair and Other Sketches*. Illustrated by C. D. Gibson and Others. New York; 1896.

Stockton, Frank R., *The "Merry-Chanter."* New York; 1890.

GENERAL

Art Students' League, *Report No. 1 for 1885-86*.

Bancroft, Huber Howe, *The Book of the Fair—Chicago and San Francisco;* 1893.

Black, Alexander, *Modern Daughters*. New York; 1899.

Brock, H. J., Article in *New York Times Magazine,* May 6, 1934.

Brown, Henry Collins, *In the Golden Nineties*. Hastings-on-Hudson, New York; 1928.

Bullock, J. M., "Charles Dana Gibson" in *The Studio,* London; Vol. 8, 1896.

Century Magazine, Files.

Chambers, Robert W., Article on Charles Dana Gibson in *Collier's,* Oct. 21, 1905.

Chappell, George S., *Shoal Water*. New York; 1933.

Chicago World's Columbian Exposition. 1893.

Collier, P. F. and Son, *Charles Dana Gibson, A Study of the Man and Some Recent Examples of His Best Work*. New York; 1905.

Columbia School of Journalism Library.

Coon, Spencer H., "Gibson's American Girl." *Metropolitan Magazine,* Dec., 1896.

Cortissoz, Royal, *American Artists*. New York and London; 1923.

Cosmopolitan Magazine, Files. 1910–1914.

Creel, George, *How We Advertised America*. New York; 1920.

Criterion, The, Dec., 1897. "An Estimate of Charles Dana Gibson."

Culter, R. F., *The Gay Nineties*.

Cutting, Juliana, Articles in *Saturday Evening Post,* April 1, and May 6, 1933.

Davis, Charles Belmont, Article on Gibson in *The Critic,* Jan., 1899.

Davis, Richard Harding, Article, "The Original and Type of the American Girl." *Quarterly Illustrator,* Dec., 1895.

Du Maurier, George, *English Society.* New York; 1897.

——*Social Pictorial Satire.* New York and London; 1898.

Dunne, Finley Peter, *Mr. Dooley in Peace and War.* New York; 1898.

Figaro, La Gibson Girl—Paris. Jan., 1923.

Ford, James L., *The Literary Shop and Other Tales.* New York; 1894.

Gilder, J. B. and J. L., *Trilbyana.* New York; 1895.

Harper's Magazine, Files.

Harper's Weekly, Files.

Harrison, Mrs. Burton (Constance Cary), *Recollections Grave and Gay.* New York; 1911.

Herford, Oliver, *The Astonishing Tale of a Pen-and-Ink Puppet, or The Genteel Art of Illustrating.* New York; 1907.

Herrick, Christine Terhune, "The Gibson Boy." *St. Nicholas,* Feb., 1896.

Hope, Anthony, "Mr. C. D. Gibson on Love and Life." *McClure's,* Sept., 1897.

Holliday, Robert Cortes, *Unmentionables; from Figleaves to Scanties.* New York; 1933.

Howe, Winifred E., *A History of the Metropolitan Museum of Art.* New York; 1913.

Isham, Samuel and Cortissoz, Royal, *The History of American Painting.* New York; 1927.

Johnson, Robert Underwood, *Remembered Yesterdays.* Boston; 1933.

Ladies' Home Journal, The, Files. 1890-1900.

Life. New York; 1883-1932.

London Graphic, The, Files.

Lucas, E. V., *Edwin Austin Abbey* (2 Vols.). London and New York; 1921.

Martin, E. S., "John Ames Mitchell," in *Harvard Graduates' Magazine,* Sept., 1918.

Maxwell, Perriton, "Charles Dana Gibson, Man and Artist," in *Arts and Decoration,* May, 1922.

McCardell, Ray L., in *New York Morning Telegraph,* Sept. 19, 1920.

McVickar, Harry Whitney, *Society, The Greatest Show on Earth.* New York; 1892.

Mitchell, John Ames, "Contemporary American Caricature," in *Scribner's Magazine,* Dec., 1889.

Mitchell, John Ames, *The Summer School of Philosophy at Mount Desert.* New York; 1881.

Morton, Frederick W., "Charles Dana Gibson, Illustrator," in *Brush and Pencil*, Feb., 1901.

New York Advertiser, Files.

New York American, Files.

New York Public Library. Theatre Section Files, Gibson Scrap Books.

New York Sun, Files.

New York Tribune, and *Herald Tribune*, Files.

New York World, Files.

Pennell, Elizabeth Robins, *The Life and Letters of Joseph Pennell* (2 Vols.). Boston, 1929.

Pennell, Joseph, *Pen Drawing and Pen Draughtsmen*. New York and London; 1920.

Potter, Cora Urquhart, *My Recitations*. 1886.

Pulitzer, Ralph, *New York Society on Parade*. New York; 1910.

Reid, J. A., "Charles Dana Gibson," in *The Art Journal*. London; 1900.

Rogers, W. A., *A World Worth While*. New York and London; 1922.

Roof, Katherine Metcalf, *The Life and Art of William Merritt Chase*. New York; 1917.

Saint-Gaudens, Augustus and Homer, *The Reminiscences of Augustus Saint-Gaudens*. New York; 1913.

Scribner's Magazine, Files.

Smith, F. Hopkinson, *American Illustrators*. New York; 1892.

Spielmann, Milt, "Charles Dana Gibson, Apostle of American Beauty and Humor," in *The Magazine of Art*. London; 1903.

Sullivan, Mark, *Our Times*, Vols. I-V. New York; 1926-33.

Thompson, Vance, Article on Gibson in *Buffalo Times*, Aug. 26, 1894.

Thorpe, James, *Phil May, Master-Draughtsman and Humorist*. London; 1932.

Tid-bits. 1884-1890 (Name changed to *Time* 1889).

Tidy, Gordon, *A Little About Leech*. London; 1931.

Town Topics, Files.

Train, Arthur, *High Winds*. 1927.

——*Puritan's Progress*. New York; 1931.

Walton, William, *World's Columbian Exposition; Art and Architecture*. Philadelphia; 1893.

Weitenkampf, F., *American Graphic Art*. New York; 1912.

Wood, T. Martin, *George Du Maurier*. London; 1913.

Zeitschrift für Bildende Kunst, 1897. Leipzig, Germany.

INDEX